Graham Bartlett was a Sussex police officer for thirty years. In 1989 he was posted to Brighton and Hove, becoming a detective the following year. Quite uniquely, he served the city through every rank, rising to become a homicide senior investigating officer and Detective Superintendent for Public Protection as well as a strategic firearms and public order commander. He then achieved his life's ambition, as Chief Superintendent, to become the city's Police Commander – or, as Peter James jokingly called him – the 'Sheriff of Brighton', a job he held and loved for four years. He pioneered Operation Reduction, the enduring approach to slashing drugs deaths and reducing crime as well as cutting disorder at protests by adopting methods developed by one of the world's foremost crowd psychologists. He lives in Sussex.

Visit his website at www.southdownsleadership.com
Or follow him on Twitter @GrahamBSDLM
Or Facebook www.facebook.com/sdlmservices

Peter James is a UK number one bestselling author, best known for writing crime and thriller novels, and the creator of the much-loved Detective Superintendent Roy Grace series. Globally, his books have been translated into thirty-seven languages. Synonymous with plot-twisting page-turners, Peter has garnered an army of loyal fans throughout his storytelling career – which has also included stints writing for TV and producing films. He has won over forty awards for his work, including the WHSmith Best Crime Author of All Time Award, the Crime Writers' Association Diamond Dagger and a BAFTA nomination for *The Merchant of Venice*, starring Al Pacino and Jeremy Irons, for which he was an Executive Producer. Many of Peter's novels have been adapted for film, TV and stage.

Visit his website at www.peterjames.com
Or follow him on Twitter @peterjamesuk
Or Facebook: facebook.com/peterjames.roygrace
Or YouTube: www.peterjames.com/YouTube
Or Instagram: Instagram.com/peterjamesuk

This is Peter and Graham's second non-fiction collaboration, following the *Sunday Times* top ten bestseller *Death Comes Knocking*.

Graham Bartlett *with* Peter James

BABES IN THE WOOD

TWO GIRLS MURDERED.
A GUILTY MAN WALKS FREE.
CAN THE POLICE GET JUSTICE?

PAN BOOKS

First published 2020 by Pan Books
an imprint of Pan Macmillan
The Smithson, 6 Briset Street, London EC1M 5NR
EU representative: Macmillan Publishers Ireland Limited,
Mallard Lodge, Lansdowne Village, Dublin 4
Associated companies throughout the world
www.panmacmillan.com

ISBN 978-1-5290-2556-9

5 7 9 8 6 4

A CIP catalogue record for this book is available from the British Library.

Maps by Martin Lubikowski, ML Design, London
Contains OS data © Crown copyright and database right (2019)

Typeset in Utopia by Jouve (UK), Milton Keynes
Printed and bound by CPI Group (UK) Ltd, Croydon, CR0 4YY

MIX
Paper from
responsible sources
FSC® C116313
FSC
www.fsc.org

Visit **www.panmacmillan.com** to read more about all our books
and to buy them. You will also find features, author interviews and
news of any author events, and you can sign up for e-newsletters
so that you're always first to hear about our new releases.

For Nicola and Karen – rest in peace

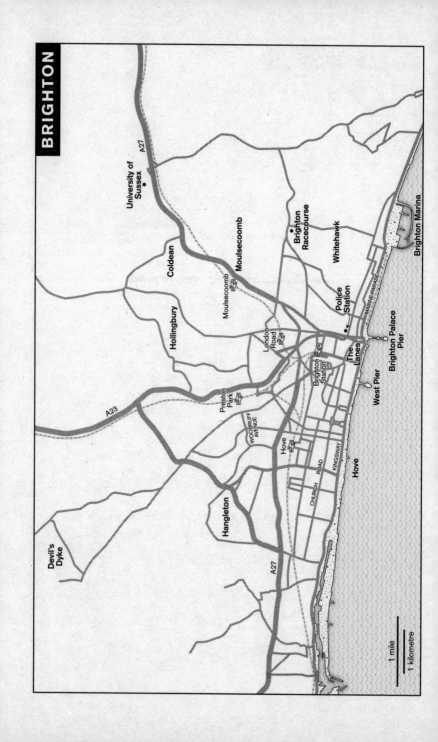

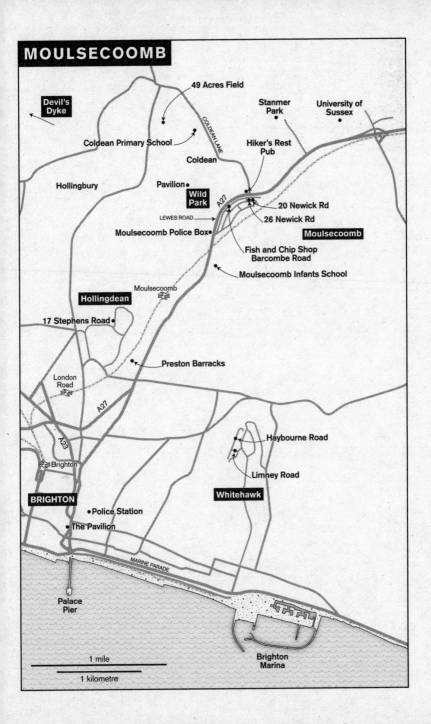

We feel this is an important story to be told, because it shows how one of the nastiest and slipperiest child-killers in UK criminal history so very nearly escaped justice.

PROLOGUE

On the evening of 9 October 1986, as the worldwide smash hit musical *Phantom of the Opera* opened in London, two nine-year-old girls full of excitement, with their lives ahead of them, were about to encounter someone infinitely more terrifying than the blockbuster's haunting namesake.

Thousands of children, like them, would have been clutching at the few remaining light evenings of the year, making up for the washout of a summer they had just endured.

It should have been a day that they would never need to remember, melding into similar laughter-filled times that would have defined their carefree childhood. Instead they innocently stumbled upon a real-life monster, someone they knew and should have been able to trust. Someone whose depravity and utter evil could never have been imagined, let alone predicted.

Crossing one road too many trapped them in his clutches and what happened next would shatter two families, a community and a police force forever. It would take a third of a century for the truth of those few heinous minutes to be exposed.

Justice delayed is always justice denied.

PART ONE

PART ONE

1

On the northern fringe of Brighton sits a council estate that has lurked under a murderously dark shadow for a generation. The very mention of Moulsecoomb evokes conflicting reactions depending on how you view the world.

If you are sucked in by cheap sound bites and feed off scandal-ridden rumours, you may think of it as a dumping ground for Brighton and Hove's low life; a cauldron of depravation and malevolence into which no outsider dare venture.

If, on the other hand, you can look beyond the provocative headlines and tired brickwork, you will appreciate it as a place that is certainly neglected but is home to a warm and caring community of 9,000, where kids play in the street and everyone looks out for each other.

Its labyrinth of small, tatty semis, crammed higgledy-piggledy along its narrow streets, line one side of the main Brighton to Lewes trunk road. Originally it was built to house returning war heroes in an attractive environment.

Despite the council's lacklustre efforts to spruce up the two and a half square miles of rabbit warren, arguably to fuel the mid-1990s 'Right to Buy' market, the shoddy gardens and perfunctory street lighting gives the estate a dingy feel that its cheek-by-jowl design only accentuates.

Although at the time I was posted to Gatwick Airport, prior to joining the CID in 1990 and the start of my climb to every rank in the city, Moulsecoomb was my patch. In the dedicated response car, my partner PC Dave Leeney and I would constantly be called upon to quell warring families or arrest career criminals. Rarely were we thanked for our efforts and the prospect of returning to find our police car jacked up on bricks, with the wheels missing, was very real.

Like every other officer charged with keeping the estate safe, I saw through this animosity to appreciate a proud and cohesive community where families remained for generations.

The local nature reserve, Wild Park, served Moulsecoomb well. It spills down from the Iron Age site of Hollingbury Hill Fort to the foot of the estate. Its dense woodland and vast grassland provide the perfect relief from the cramped conditions just across the busy road.

Despite its beauty and the affection the locals have for it, nowadays it is synonymous with the horror that unfolded on a single day in October 1986.

I remember it well. My role at the time was to patrol Gatwick Airport's sole terminal building, a Smith and Wesson .357 revolver stuffed in my trouser pocket. It was the most tedious detail I endured in all my thirty years' service.

I had been posted there in 1985 from Bognor Regis, at the end of my two-year probationary period. Sussex Police had a frustrating policy of waiting until its single officers had been certified as efficient and effective before sending them to Gatwick; a place where millions passed through, but few lingered long enough to commit a crime. Standing watching perfectly ordinary people embark and disembark from certain Irish and Israeli flights and then hot-footing it to security to seize cans of Mace from American tourists who did not know our laws was not why I joined the police. Terrorism, while an underlying threat, had not reached today's levels, so airport policing was more about catching low-level criminals and reassuring the public than being the combat-ready warriors we see today.

The proliferation of single officers made for a great social life though. Most of us lived at the majestic Slaugham Manor, a former country house hotel converted into police accommodation. Its en-suite bedrooms, restaurant (well, canteen), two bars, gym and swimming pool not only made up for the tedious day job but also served as a great party venue, to which we would invite scores of airline and airport staff.

When news broke of the dark events occurring in Moulse-coomb, I was transfixed and desperate to join the hordes of cops drafted in, but I was soon to be disappointed. Apparently my eighteen rounds of ammunition and I were too critical to national security for me to be released. I grumpily resigned myself to watch the events from afar.

At Slaugham Manor, we all held our breath as the details began to emerge.

2

Best friends Nicola Fellows and Karen Hadaway popped out to play before tea late one early October afternoon.

Nicola, a happy, cheeky and plucky dark-haired cherub of a girl, was the apple of her father's eye. She made friends easily and was well-liked at school and in her neighbourhood. The precocious exuberance the outside world saw belied the cuddly home-loving girl she really was though. She knew her own mind, and the boundaries. Her mother, Susan, recalled that after rows Nicola would pack her little bag and storm off, saying she was running away. Moments later she would return. When asked what had happened to her plans, she would solemnly remind her parents that she could not go very far, as she was not allowed to cross the road alone.

Barrie Fellows, Nicola's dad, had a tough-guy image which hid the soft-hearted devotion of a family man who lived for his children. An in-your-face Londoner, he moved to Brighton in the 1960s where his brash ways were not everyone's cup of tea. His rugged good looks and stocky frame were well known around the estate and he enjoyed his standing as one of the go-to fixers. None of this could prevent his life being ripped apart that day, when he was just thirty-seven.

He and Susan had been married for sixteen years and they lived with Nicola, her brother Jonathan and Susan's mother in Newick Road, a run of houses that sits back from the main Lewes Road but just in view of Wild Park. Susan was meeker than Barrie and loved nothing more than being surrounded by her family, of all generations.

Both speak fondly of Nicola's steadfast ambition to become a nurse. Hers was often the first face Barrie saw when he came round from an epileptic fit. When Susan was in hospital, she remembers Nicola grilling the nurses on all that their job entailed, cheekily trying their hats on for size. Susan hoped that one day Nicola would go to university, but worried about the cost.

In my uniform days responding to 999 calls, I was often called to Newick Road. One of the city's most prolific car thieves lived there and he never served tea and biscuits when we came knocking. Aside from him, the road seemed to have more wanted criminals and domestic incidents than any other in Brighton. But I was never dispatched to the Fellows or Hadaway households..

Barrie's close friend was Dougie Judd, a much younger man, who shared Barrie's passion for Citizens Band – or CB – radio, the social media of the day. CB radio 'hams' would spend hours at home or in their cars parked in remote locations, willowy aerials swaying from their roofs, chatting inanely to total strangers under pseudonyms, or 'handles', that gave no clue as to their real identity. One of Judd's handles was 'Pain Killer' and Fellows went by the name of 'Basil Brush'. Looking back, it is strange to think how we regarded this new-fangled communication craze as such a threat to our operations. It was unthinkable that people could now organize themselves without land-line telephones and chats in the pub. Life was so much simpler then.

Dougie had fallen out with his mother, not uncommon for a twenty-one-year-old living at home, prompting him to beg a room from Barrie. When he moved in, a year before the girls went missing, the already-cramped three-bedroomed household became even more congested. Nicola was forced to double up with her grandmother, freeing the downstairs room for Dougie.

His and Barrie's close friendship would soon come under the spotlight and would vex the police throughout the next thirty years.

*

Karen, like Nicola, was absolutely cherished by her parents. She had a beautiful, beaming smile and fair hair and freckles. She shared a love for life and adventure – providing it was within the rules. By their own admission, her mother and father slightly over-protected her. They drummed in to her time and time again the hidden dangers lurking on the streets around them, warning her never to go off with strangers. She flourished and, as far as her parents were aware, never broke their rules.

Michelle and Lee Hadaway's early married life saw them forever moving around Brighton through a string of poor council and other social houses and flats. It was not until Karen was born in 1977 that they finally settled in Moulsecoomb.

By October 1986, the Hadaways' house, like the Fellows', was bursting at the seams. Not only were there the parents and three children, but Michelle's recently widowed mother had also moved in and Michelle was pregnant with her fourth child. Aside from the diminishing floor space, this suited the Hadaways to a tee, especially Karen, who was particularly attached to her siblings. This kind of overcrowding was commonplace in these tiny three- and four-bedroom houses, but in those days families were close and liked to stay close, even if that meant turning every spare corner into a sleeping space.

Lee and Michelle lived for their children. Lee's job as a builders' labourer took him away from home so much that, in 1985, he quit. With three children and one on the way, that made life a struggle. He was forced to take casual work where he could find it – but only if that meant not leaving his family for too long. He made great efforts to set up a window-cleaning round and would sometimes act as driver's mate to Dougie Judd's brother, Stephen. It was this job that led him to be miles away and helpless on the day his and Michelle's quiet life changed forever.

3

Karen and Nicola went to separate primary schools; Karen to Coldean and Nicola to Moulsecoomb, both just a stone's throw from their estate. After school on 9 October 1986, Karen and three friends had been so busy horsing around that she missed her usual bus. She eventually arrived home later than normal, just after 4 p.m. Nicola was late home too, having walked the short distance home after choir practice. As soon as she got indoors, she went upstairs to change.

Not long after, Nicola answered a knock on the door. A twenty-year-old local man, Russell Bishop, dressed in a pale sweatshirt with a white diagonal stripe, was standing there with two teenage girls: his girlfriend, Marion Stevenson, and her pal, Tracey Cox.

You could pass Bishop in a crowd. His five foot five, ten-and-a-half-stone frame gave him an air of weakness, and his drab, limp, straight fair hair did little to counter that. A caterpillar effort of a moustache aged him a little but his bearing still revealed him as an insignificant post-teenager. When he asked if Dougie Judd was in, Nicola was curt beyond her years. She, much like the rest of North Brighton, knew and disapproved of Bishop's infidelity towards his common-law wife, Jenny Johnson. Marion was his bit on the side who followed him everywhere. Nicola snapped that Judd was not at home then slammed the door in his face, shouting 'slag' after them. Karen's mother, Michelle, by coincidence, was at the Fellows' house when Bishop called and she heard the exchange from the kitchen. She was another who disliked Bishop and had forbidden Karen from spending time with him.

When Karen got home, her growing excitement about the following day's school disco was evident. Almost at once, she took herself off to a nearby sweetshop, returning around twenty minutes later. When she left she was still wearing her school uniform: a green long-sleeved sweatshirt, a T-shirt, a kilt-type skirt, white knickers and school shoes.

By the time Karen came in from the shop that afternoon, Michelle noticed she had discarded her school jacket and had changed her school shoes for pink trainers. Karen then announced she was going outside to play. Michelle called after her, telling her not to be long as she had just put a chicken pie in the oven for tea.

At 5 p.m, Karen, her sister Lindsey, Nicola and some other children were playing in and around the front gardens of Newick Road. It was that sort of place, a playground where kids could safely mess about, wind up the grown-ups and just be kids. Every now and then, Susan looked out of her window and could see Nicola playing. By now the girl was wearing red shoes, a brown and white chequered skirt and a pink and brown V–neck sweatshirt, but no socks or coat.

A short while later, Karen and Nicola broke off from the rest of the group and ran, laughing and joking, towards Barcombe Road, which runs parallel to Newick Road opposite Wild Park. Karen rarely missed her tea, but the draw of hanging out with her friend proved too strong. At various times over the next hour or so they were seen playing around the area, as kids do. They did not have a care in the world, although they probably knew they would be in trouble for staying out longer than they should but, when you are young, the world is an exciting place and grown-ups soon get over their grumpy moods.

At 5.15 p.m., park constable PC Roy Dadswell saw them swinging on a tree in Wild Park. He stopped to warn them to come down as they might get hurt. He was with Albert Barnes, an elderly gent who was just passing through. The four of them chatted for a few moments, the girls giving them each a parting gift of a leaf which they playfully tucked in the men's pockets. Mr Barnes left the park soon after and did not return that night.

About an hour later, a neighbour spotted the girls unwrapping a bag of chips outside the Barcombe Road fish shop, yards from both their homes and just across the Lewes Road from Wild Park.

Ten minutes later, another neighbour saw the girls back over by Wild Park, both holding what looked like chip bags. Nicola waved at the lady as they knew each other. This story ties in with a motorist who later told police that he saw two girls heading in that direction from near the chip shop around 6.30 p.m.

About the same time fourteen-year-old Michelle Tippett saw the girls in Barcombe Road. Nicola told her they were going back over to Wild Park. The older girl told them they should tell their mothers where they were going because they would get worried but the girls seemed too excited. She heard Nicola repeatedly urge Karen: 'Come on, let's go over the park.' If only they had heeded the advice.

4

Lee Hadaway, Karen's father, should not have been out of town that day. Stephen Judd's employers had specifically forbidden him from using anyone to assist him on his deliveries. However, he was not one for rules and Lee needed the money – so what Stephen's bosses did not know would not hurt them.

By the time they reached their destination, some 200 miles away, at 10.15 p.m. the night before the girls disappeared, Stephen had to stop driving almost immediately as he was dangerously close to exceeding his permitted driving hours. This was one rule he had to obey as his tachograph – the device that records a driver's hours – would not lie, thereby jeopardizing his heavy goods vehicle licence and his job. Having called it a day, they bedded down in the back of the lorry, intent on making an early start.

The first Lee knew of Karen going missing was when he phoned home just before 6 p.m. the following day. Michelle picked up the phone – she couldn't find Karen. It had only been an hour since she had been last seen so, while her behaviour was unusual, there should have been no immediate cause for alarm. Regardless, they were both worried and Lee promised to call every half hour.

As the minutes ticked by, Michelle became increasingly anxious. She couldn't see Karen playing in the front gardens and she had told her not to be long. She usually did as she was told. She walked the few steps to ask Susan Fellows if she had seen her. Lindsay, Karen's younger sister, had told her mum that Karen had run off with Nicola so it was a reasonable assumption they were still playing together. When Susan said she had not seen them,

Michelle asked around the children who were still playing, but no one could help.

She scouted the area and bumped into a boy who said he had seen both girls over the road in Wild Park talking to the park constable earlier. By now Michelle had been joined by Susan. Together they traversed the paths and fields of Wild Park, calling out the girls' names. Dusk was falling and they struggled to see far but, ever confident that the girls had just lost track of time, they went back home in the hope that they'd sheepishly returned.

They hadn't.

Barrie Fellows had last seen Nicola the morning of the day she went missing. Around 8 a.m. he had been standing by a bus stop waiting to go to work when she sauntered past him. He'd chivvied her along as, at that pace, she ran the risk of being late for school.

His tasks for that day involved cleaning out a swimming pool and doing some gardening at a house in Woodruff Avenue, nestled in an affluent quarter of Brighton's neighbouring town Hove. He arrived around 8.45 a.m. but Dougie, who was due to be with him, only turned up at about 10 a.m., having first signed on at the Job Centre.

They worked all day until 5 p.m. when together they walked through the winding streets of Hove to catch the 49a bus back to Moulsecoomb. On the way, Barrie popped into a butcher's shop to buy some ham for his tea, but they still caught the bus they had planned to and arrived on the estate just after 6 p.m.

Before going home the men called in to see Theresa Judd, Dougie's sister-in-law, who lived close to the bus stop. While Dougie stayed only a few moments before going to visit his girl-friend, Barrie chatted with her for around fifteen to twenty minutes before his short walk back home.

When he arrived, Susan was not in but his mother-in-law Edna was. She told Barrie that Susan had gone out with Michelle Hadaway to look for Karen and Nicola. Barrie decided to have his tea and watch *Top of the Pops* before joining the search. Then he went back to see Theresa in case she had seen Nicola. Discovering she had not, he trawled the streets alone, growing increasingly worried as the night and a blanket of low mist drew in. Out of ideas and terrified, he made his way back home.

By now Susan and Michelle were back from searching and the Fellows' house was starting to fill up with concerned friends and neighbours. The unspoken realization was growing that this was more than a couple of mischievous girls breaking a curfew.

The front room had become the community's control centre. Theories of where they might be, what they might be doing, were advanced, weighed up, pounced on or dismissed. People scurried out with expectation then returned in despair.

As each option drew a blank, the more frantic the parents became.

5

At 8.36 p.m., with all other avenues exhausted, Michelle called 999, the worry leaking through her every word. WPC Esther Winner, the operator, immediately sensed this was not a run-of-the-mill missing person's call:

WPC Winner: *Where were these children last seen?*

Michelle: *Over at the Coldean shops at the bottom of Coldean Lane. I thought my little 'un had gone up to her friend's. When she didn't come back when it started getting dark I phoned her friend and her friend's mum said she hadn't been up there.*

WPC Winner: *What time were they last seen?*

Michelle: *About half past five. It's not like her to go too far away unless she's going to a friend's house.*

WPC Winner: *And who am I speaking to now? Mrs . . .*

Michelle: *Hadaway*

WPC Winner: *Who's the other mother?*

Michelle: *Mrs Streeter. Sorry, Mrs Fellows.*

WPC Winner: *Right, and they're two nine-year-old girls?*

Michelle: *Two nine-year-olds*

After the operator had taken full descriptions she promised she would send officers but if the girls returned in the meantime, Michelle was to call back.

Miles from Brighton, Lee Hadaway was also growing increasingly agitated. With no more news from Michelle, he decided to phone the police for a first-hand update. They urged him to make his way straight back to Brighton, a request that placed Stephen Judd in a tricky position. As he was expressly forbidden to carry passengers and already late with his deliveries, it meant that doing anything other than continuing his drops would surely see him dismissed. On top of this Stephen was once again almost at the limit of his permitted hours, so could not head back to the south coast, even if he wanted to.

Lee was adamant. He needed to get home and as each hour ticked by his panic intensified. Eventually, they bit the bullet and called Brighton police again, this time for advice. They were told, given the gravity of the situation, to go to a local police station, and get a senior officer to endorse the lorry's tachograph to say that Judd had permission to continue driving. They did just that and a petrified Lee Hadaway was, at last, on his way home.

Over the ensuing months and years, as neighbours scatter-gunned suspicion around, Barrie's movements – particularly his timings – came under intense scrutiny.

To some, his account did not stack up. Questions would be asked about his journeys, how long it might or might not have taken him to walk from point A to point B. Why he took so long to join the search.

In my experience as a detective, I found it is often the simple details that become blurred yet cause the biggest problems. What can appear to be suspicious anomalies are nothing of the sort. But they are a headache when pored over in a Crown Court some twelve months – or thirty-two years – later. Not everyone's life is governed by the clock. We do not all have a perfect memory of what we did, where, when and with whom. In fact, there were occasions when I became very suspicious of too great a recall of minutiae. Almost as if it had all been rehearsed.

The truth is, people make good, old-fashioned, honest mistakes. For many, life is routine, sometimes vague. Their recollections deserve some leeway, especially if they are anxious or traumatized.

In my detective days, I would try to overcome this haziness by getting people to make their evidence as accurate as possible by fixing it to known and certain events. For example, if someone said they were watching television when they received a phone call I would want to know what programme was on and what was happening at that moment.

Were the adverts on? If so which ones?

Was it the local or national news? What were they covering?

Armed with this information I could pinpoint the relevant time.

If a person reported seeing something on a road when a bus was passing, I would want to know the bus's number, in which direction it was travelling, whether it was before or after the bus stop. Then the bus company could narrow down the time for me, almost to the second. But often these anchors just don't exist and anomalies are simply down to incredibly worried people just getting it wrong.

This would not be the first inconsistency that would haunt the enquiry and each would take hours, and in some cases years, to resolve; many never were.

6

Despite having been a police officer for six years, and a sergeant for one of those, strapping young graduate Pete Coll was Brighton Police's new boy. In search of a better life, Pete took the brave step of transferring from the Metropolitan Police, accepting demotion to PC as part of the package.

He and his wife Julie had a one-year-old baby girl, Sarah. After great consideration they had decided the capital was no place to bring up a child and so took the financial and career hit and moved to Seaford, just along the coast from Brighton.

Four months in, Pete and his partner PC Paul Richardson crewed the Moulsecoomb response car, as I would do three years later. Brighton's east and west divisions had merged so new bonds were being formed. Pete and Paul were picked for this detail because of their experience and common sense but, like any officer assigned a new beat, they needed to get to know their patch.

It had been a fairly standard Thursday 2 p.m. to 10 p.m. shift, with the usual hotchpotch of shoplifters, burglaries and minor car shunts. Even for October, the weather was gloomy. Wet and cold, a swirling low fog had descended over most of Brighton, the bars of mist giving the place an eerie feel.

Just over an hour before they were due to clock off, the call came that would change so many lives. The radio message contained little detail, just that Karen and Nicola had not come home after playing. The parents had searched the nearby area but had not yet found them.

Children often go missing, especially on estates like Moulse-coomb where the streets double up as extended play parks. Most return quickly and safely and suffer nothing more than a flea in the ear for their troubles. So, when they were dispatched, Pete and Paul were not unduly worried.

However, once they drove into Newick Road from the opposite end to the Fellows' house, they quickly realized that this was anything but ordinary. As they approached, they were struck by the crowds milling around. On a night like this, most people would normally stay behind closed doors, but something had brought them out onto the streets.

All eyes turned to Pete and Paul as their car coasted to a halt and they took in the concerned faces and flurry of activity on the street. Neither had met Barrie Fellows before but they soon spotted that this swarthy, slightly scruffy man was who they had come to see.

He appeared in shock while his neighbours showed him a combination of deference and concern. Some people darted in and out through the Fellows' open front door. Others marched to and from the Hadaways' house where a similar, but smaller, worried crowd loitered.

Pete and Paul got out of the car and pushed their way towards Barrie. For once, their uniforms were respected. 'Mr Fellows, can we go inside so we can understand what's going on please?' Pete asked, hoping others would respect his privacy.

'Yes, come in,' Barrie replied, leading the way.

Despite Pete and Paul's attempts to isolate the three petrified parents, increasingly worried neighbours still dashed in and out of the house. Some seemed to defer to Barrie for their next instructions. As gently as possible, the officers slowly coaxed everyone out. This was not easy in a community who rarely saw the police as a force for good; many felt only their own could find the girls. But eventually there was some peace and quiet and the full story emerged.

Despite their fears, Pete and Paul still went through the list that kicks off any missing person enquiry. We call it 'clearing the ground under your feet', seeing what is immediately in front of you in the hope the answer is obvious. They set about capturing basic descriptions of the girls, securing recent photos, listing school friends, playmates and habits. Both houses were searched to check the children weren't hiding somewhere. So many kids do. But tragically, like Tia Sharp who was murdered and dumped in her loft in 2012, others are killed then secreted in their own homes.

The parents' trust in the officers grew as they saw their anxiety was shared. With a modicum of calm restored, Pete left Paul with the families while he drove around the area hoping to find the girls before night finally fell. Having checked the streets, where the community were still out in force, he made his way over the road to Wild Park.

With the car's full-beam headlights sweeping the terrain, he inched up the narrow roadway that skirts the playing fields with his windows open in the vain hope of catching the girls' chatter or giggles.

As he approached the park's pavilion, a couple of hundred yards up from the main road, he stopped and got out. The damp, cloying fog chilled Pete's throat. The temperature was dropping as his fear for the girls grew. He walked around the wooden shack, checking for any signs the girls could have sneaked inside. He checked underneath and, finding nothing, returned to Newick Road.

To this day, he needlessly beats himself up that had he searched just another fifty yards to his right, among the gorse and bracken, the results might have been very different.

Expectantly, Barrie, Susan and Michelle turned as Pete walked through the front door of the Fellows' house. His worried face and the absence of any sheepish children scuppered their brief optimism.

Being a former sergeant, Pete was used to responding to critical incidents and he knew this was fast becoming just that. If he did not get some support now, all his colleagues would be going off duty and into their second pint before he knew it.

A quick call to Sergeant Derek Oakenson was all it took. Having succinctly laid out his fears, Pete was assured that the late turn would be kept on duty and the night shift called in early. Derek reminded Pete to start an incident log, a document that would eventually swell to the size of a telephone directory.

Back at Brighton Police Station the cavalry was being rounded up. As well as uniform back-up, DS John Atkins had hoisted DCs Tony Baker and Ken Probert out of the bar. Knowing only that two nine-year-olds were missing, they grabbed a set of car keys from the detective sergeants' office and made straight for Newick Road. Their own instincts and the subdued buzz of activity around the police station and across the radio told them they were in for a long night.

Unbeknown to them, the duty inspector had already alerted Superintendent Dave Tomlinson, the dapper senior officer responsible for operational policing across Brighton, and he was already back at his desk.

I was that officer some twenty years later so know that it has to be very serious for somebody that senior to come in so soon into an enquiry. Dave assessed it early: the age of the girls, the weather and the failing light all eliminated the possibility they were still out playing. From his point of view, it was an incident that required immediate action.

While Pete and Paul were busy scouring for new clues and Ken and Tony were making their way to Moulsecoomb, Dave was putting a structure around the search. As is often the way, the real workers, the constables and sergeants, have little idea, nor do they care, that they are working to a higher plan.

His calm-as-you-like persona hid a deeper, sensitive soul. He had a threefold plan; first was to interview close family, friends and others who might provide some snippet to suggest where Nicola and Karen had gone. That was where Ken and Tony came in. Second was to search throughout Moulsecoomb, checking any likely place where the children might be. That would soon be

Pete and Paul's brief. The third phase was to search the wider area, including other parks, the seafront and amusements.

As any good commander would, Dave was planning ahead. He would throw everything at this until at least 2 a.m. when, if nothing developed, he would reassess the position and possibly send officers home with orders to be back at first light.

DCs Probert and Baker arrived in refreshing haste and took over the investigation, freeing Pete, Paul and their initially reluctant shift-mates to gather under a railway bridge close to the Fellows' house for a briefing.

As the mist thickened, made all the spookier by the low sodium lighting piercing its way through the gloom, Sergeant Derek Oakenson and Pete spelled out to the shivering officers their fears for the worst if they did not act quickly. While this was Moulsecoomb and girls went missing all the time, the gathered cops soon shared their concern. Among others, they inspired PC Nigel Smith, another new arrival at Brighton, with whom, a year or so earlier, I had sniffed out drug dealers at Gatwick. Nigel had originally been sceptical but as he listened to Derek and Pete beseeching them to think of their own children out on their own on this cold misty night, the gravity of the situation hit him.

As the superintendent had ordered, the two dozen or so officers searched the streets, gardens, parks and wasteland into the early hours, and many would have stayed longer if there had been the slightest chance of finding the girls. Barrie, Susan and Michelle were given places to look to keep them occupied and to help them feel they were doing something constructive. Given Karen's love for the seaside, Michelle trudged along the beach calling out her daughter's name and checking under the rows of upturned fishing boats stretching from the Palace Pier to Brighton Marina.

Back at the station, shift patterns for the following day were turned on their heads allowing Pete and Paul's section to return early the next morning and focus on the search.

Shortly after 2 a.m., Pete and his team were stood down

despite there still being no sign of the girls. As he drove home, he yearned for his fifteen-month-old daughter, Sarah, trying to put himself in the Fellows' and Hadaways' shoes.

His heart ached for them.

DC Ken Probert, the first detective deployed, knew he was in for a long night. I know Ken well. He was a detective superintendent around the time I was a DI and, during murder enquiries, his intellect, attention to detail and recall were second to none. Those qualities are born not bred and, even now, his recollection is impressive. He still remembers the frantic comings and goings, the snippets of information that emerged on that night almost by accident, like the fact that Karen had gone fishing a few weeks previously. With Russell Bishop and his teenaged girlfriend Marion Stevenson, it turned out.

Ken was conscious that, with Lee being away, Michelle's distress was aggravated by her relative isolation. He was becoming more convinced that, despite all the police activity and the searching by neighbours, this was not going to end well. He worked until dawn, gently probing, checking Michelle's recollections, just in case some deeply buried clue or even suspicion floated to the surface. Alas, his tenacity and resilience – physical and emotional – came to nothing and exhausted he headed home, hoping to wake to the unlikely news that the girls had turned up safe and well.

While some police officers were being sent home to return refreshed the next day, the Moulsecoomb community was fully deployed. Everyone did anything they could. CB radio buff Yann Svenski corralled a group of friends to search the local area for the girls. They diligently scoured the nooks and crannies others might miss.

Nestled between the Moulsecoomb and Hollingdean estates, tucked behind what was Brighton Polytechnic's Cockcroft Building, is Moulsecoomb railway station, at the time a recent addition to Brighton's infrastructure. Nearby, a network of paths and an underpass link the two areas with the station and each other. At night the seclusion of this otherwise commonly used cut-through creates an eeriness that keeps many away.

In the small hours of Friday morning, Yann and his group were searching a patch of fenced-off land next to the footpath to Hollingdean, when one of their torches picked out something through the railings.

One of the nimbler searchers vaulted over the fence for a closer look. Slightly disheartened, he saw it was just an inside-out blue sweatshirt that looked as if it had been dumped. It seemed strangely dry given the moist grass on which it lay but as it bore no relevance to the two missing girls, he left it hanging on the fence.

Back in his younger years you could have put Russell Bishop in front of a legion of forensic psychologists and not one of them would have predicted how evil he would become.

He was the youngest of five brothers and cut a pathetic figure. In the days when boys were supposed to be tough, Russell was, by any measure, stunted and puny, struggling to hold his own with the stronger lads in Moulsecoomb.

His mother, Sylvia, was, and still is, an internationally renowned dog trainer and bestselling author on the subject. She boasts on her website of being one of the most popular individuals in the dog obedience world. His father, Roy, was a jobbing roofer who kept the family together in their Coldean Lane home while Sylvia was away on her travels living the life of a celebrity trainer.

Of the five boys, Russell gave them the most problems. His dyslexia led to a virtual inability to read or write, meaning he failed at every school he attended. Coldean School first identified his learning difficulties and he was sent to a special Catholic school in Worcester. When things did not improve there, he was dispatched to board at St Mary's Special School near Heathfield, twenty-five miles east of Brighton. He was unable to settle and regularly ran away, hitchhiking back home only to be returned at the first opportunity. Eventually his exasperated parents took him out of school altogether and arranged home education.

That solved nothing and in adulthood he struggled to hold down regular employment. He hopped from one casual labouring job to another, sometimes describing himself as a roofer like his dad. But he was over-egging his skills. Dogsbody or skivvy would have been more accurate.

His brothers made their own way in life, something Russell could have done if he had applied himself, but he was too full of his own self-importance to knuckle down to adulthood. He fooled no one with his immature and compulsive lies. His boasts of being a prolific criminal hid a petty and insignificant offending history. His claim to numerous sexual conquests belied the truth that his affections were confined to young girls and his twenty-one-year-old common-law wife, Jenny Johnson. However, his voracious sexual appetite was something that the young Marion Stevenson seemed happy to satisfy, notwithstanding the whispers of being his bit on the side.

He supplemented his meagre wages the only way he knew how – through petty crime. Bishop was an unsuccessful serial car thief with convictions for minor dishonesty. He was also a small-time drug user with a monumentally inflated ego. Few saw him as a threat though. Ambulance man Michael Evans, who knew the family well, would later tell a court that he would trust Bishop with his own children. One of Bishop's more outlandish claims, which seemed to have stemmed from knowing Michael, was that he too was in the ambulance service. Another friend would tell Brighton's *Evening Argus* newspaper that 'he used to babysit for me and never took any liberties around my house. He is just a nice lad, a soft kid.'

Others who knew him said he would always be telling harmless 'porkies' and that he came out with 'a lot of rubbish that no one took any notice of'. All in all, the embarrassing son of a successful mother and hardworking father was dismissed as an irritating joke. There were no signs of the evil simmering away within.

While chasing down all sightings, police called at his ground-floor flat in Stephens Road, Hollingdean, around 2.30 a.m. It was a brisk stroll from the back of Wild Park, and a short hop over the railway line from Moulsecoomb.

His pregnant partner, Jenny, opened the door. They had cohabited for two years, flitting between a room in Bishop's parents' house to a bed and breakfast in Kemp Town, then out to the Hove border before settling in the flat where they were bringing up their toddler son. The officers asked to speak to Bishop so she showed them into the bedroom, where he was in bed. Bleary-eyed, he confirmed he had seen Nicola at the Fellows' house and later both girls at the park while they were talking to the park constable. He maintained that was the last time he saw them.

Later, at 10 a.m. the same day, the police returned to interview him further. He was one of a number of people who had seen the girls just before they disappeared so it was routine for him to be spoken to again.

He explained how he knew the two girls, mainly through their fathers, and then expanded on the brief account he had given in the early hours. He told the officers his red Ford Escort's engine had blown up earlier in the day in Ditchling Road and he had walked home. After speaking with the park constable, he crossed Lewes Road to buy an *Evening Argus* from the Barcombe Road newsagent. However, he said he discovered he had no money and so had to leave the shop empty-handed. He told the detectives he was embarrassed and the shop assistant would surely remember the incident. After this he walked home but could not remember what time he arrived, although he knew Jenny was still at work.

When asked what he had been wearing he said a blue top and jeans. Jenny produced a blue sweatshirt with a stripe across the chest which Bishop confirmed as the one.

When the officers walked away, satisfied they had interviewed just another witness, they had no idea how Bishop's hastily concocted account would unravel over the coming days.

Earlier that morning, PC Pete Coll had ridden his rickety East German MZ motorbike back along the A27 from Seaford to resume the search. He had already learned from the local radio that the girls were still missing and he wondered what the response would be. As Moulsecoomb police box, at the foot of Wild Park, came into view, he battled to stay on two wheels. Police vans stretched as far as the eye could see on both sides of the carriageway. Hundreds of police officers milled around waiting for their orders while others were already making their way across the road, no doubt to question the thousands of friends, family and neighbours of the missing girls.

As he parked up on the verge he saw Superintendent Dave Tomlinson clearly running the show, with less senior brass scurrying off at his every command. This military-style operation was in full swing not twelve hours after he had raised the alarm. The lump in his throat was a devil to swallow. How proud he was that, just like in the Metropolitan Police he had recently left, his new force knew how to respond when tiny lives were at stake.

The fog had lifted and it was turning into a balmy autumn day. Officers had shed their jackets but the bleak shadow of two young girls having vanished off the face of the earth hung heavy. Pete was not alone in quietly fearing the worst. None would voice their concerns but few police officers anticipated a happy ending.

Over the years I looked for, and commanded the search for, countless missing children. They all start with a dreadful foreboding followed by a deep, personal and not entirely irrational fear of 'but for the grace of God this could be my kids'. After the heart-wrench of dealing with a tragedy, or near miss, involving a child, I was not the only cop who would sneak into their children's bedrooms to hug them a little tighter than usual.

Superintendent Dave Tomlinson's choice of the police box as his command post was obvious; the locals treated it as their police station, rather than the actual one in John Street. However, the squat, single-storey building had neither the space nor the infrastructure for what would be Sussex Police's biggest operation since Patrick Magee had tried to blow up Brighton's Grand Hotel, and with it the government, in 1984.

Tomlinson summoned the force's Major Incident Van to be trundled down from the headquarters in Lewes. With a maximum speed of around forty miles per hour, these Bedford MK trucks were never part of Sussex Police's rapid-response capability. Yet once in place and set up, with their plug-in telephone exchange, bullhorn radio transmitters and reams of paper message pads, they were state of the art in command and control.

The superintendent needed information fast. This was the 'golden hour' – the misnomer given to the immediate aftermath of discovering or suspecting a crime; the small window of opportunity to find forensic evidence, track down witnesses and get the truth out of people. Normally it's closer to twenty-four hours but when searching for missing children this window of time is even more critical. The majority of abducted children are murdered within the first hour. For those who are not, with each tick of the clock, their chances ebb away. Only a tiny percentage survive more than a day, and that milestone was looming.

The temptation when young children go missing is for the public to arrive in droves to search anywhere and anyhow. While having 'boots on the ground' is important, frustrating as it may seem, only a methodical and logical approach works. Otherwise chaos reigns. Rendezvous points apply that control. This way commanders can prioritize areas based upon the likelihood of finding the child alive.

Nowadays Police Search Advisors determine search parameters. Their training and experience make them experts in finding missing children – always aware that time is the enemy. In the 1980s, things were not so structured. When I was deployed from Gatwick to Horsham around this time to look for a missing man, our team of twelve was given a huge forest to search and told not to come back until we had. No one gave us a search grid or a photo nor checked how thoroughly we had looked.

Back in Moulsecoomb, everyone was scouring Wild Park and beyond. All that was on anyone's mind was finding the girls safe and sound. Despite the police's best intentions, working out what had or had not been searched must have been a nightmare. Among the first who seemed very keen – almost too keen – to assist in any way he could with the search was Russell Bishop.

The Moulsecoomb kids were familiar with every inch of Wild Park's woodland. Perfect for making dens, having a crafty smoke or even some sneaky sex, it was an obvious place to apply a little local knowledge. Behind the rickety wooden pavilion where Pete Coll had searched the night before runs a hidden path leading to the roadway, through the copse and on to the back of the Coldean estate.

Still desperate and having been out all night, Michelle could not settle – who could? So just before 1 p.m., she resumed searching with a neighbour.

On reaching the entrance to Wild Park she saw Russell Bishop, dressed in a brown V-neck jumper, grey trousers and matching shoes. Standing with him were Marion Stevenson, Kath Measor and Bishop's dog Misty, a brown and white terrier cross-breed. Kath heard Bishop announce that he had seen the girls the night before and that he 'regretted going out'. This seemed an odd comment.

About fifteen minutes later Michelle saw Bishop again, this time with Dougie Judd. Claiming his dog was a tracker, out of the blue, Bishop asked her for a piece of Karen's clothing so Misty could pick up her scent. She told him to go to her house and ask the policeman there for her white coat. A short while later he returned with the garment in a Sainsbury's carrier bag. Today, this would be unthinkable. Even with no identified suspects and no certainty a crime had even been committed, disturbing victims' clothing would be regarded as catastrophic.

Then a man turned up in a car and she heard the driver, Judd and Bishop discussing going with the dog to 49 Acres Field, some way from Wild Park, in case Misty could pick up a scent there. Michelle went in the car with them but never saw Bishop give the coat to the dog to sniff.

Around three-quarters of an hour later, after what must have been the most perfunctory of searches, Bishop was back at the police box. PC Chris Markham, on instructions from his inspector, walked into the park with him, Judd and Misty to resume his tracking. As they approached the park entrance, Bishop ruffled the coat in front of the dog's nose, proudly explaining it would now have Karen's scent. Eventually they got to Jacob's Ladder, the steps leading from the park entrance to Coldean, and the dog lost concentration. The officer felt it was all a ruse and, doubtful the dog had any tracking ability at all, suggested returning to the box to join an organized search.

Bishop agreed, then unprompted blurted out, 'I'd hate to find the girls, especially if they had been messed up.' This shocked Markham as all the other helpers he had spoken to were optimistic that the girls would be found safe and well, despite the fears held by many officers. He made a mental note of this bizarre comment, especially from one who had been so keen to ingratiate himself to the police.

10

At about 4 p.m., Kevin Rowland, an eighteen-year-old hospital porter, and his friend Matthew Marchant joined the search. Being locals, they knew their way around the park and its hidden undergrowth. While they battled their way through the dense copse behind the pavilion, Kevin found an old kitchen knife, which he hung on to. They crossed the path near the top of Jacob's Ladder and saw Bishop standing at the bottom.

'Any luck yet?' Bishop called up.

'No,' they replied before heading back into the woodland.

They trudged through the cobweb of brambles for a while before Kevin spotted a clearing guarded by broken branches, as if someone had crawled through.

'Let's go up there,' he said to Matthew. As they inched through, Kevin leading the way, the clearing came into sharper focus. Although overhanging branches prevented an uninter-rupted view, a flash of pink stood out against the murky greens and browns. Kevin readjusted his position and the glimpse of what was unmistakably the side of a face on the ground, about fifteen feet away, made him recoil.

'Shit, I think we've found them,' he shouted to Matthew.

Matthew scurried up and edged a few paces further and, peering to his left, confirmed what his friend had seen. A body. Neither dared move any closer.

'Go and get the police,' Kevin ordered Matthew.

PC Paul Smith, or 'Smudge', did not fit in police cars. Six foot eight and as broad and strong as a barge, he occasionally travelled in vans but his huge presence was best deployed as a one-man deterrent, walking the town centre.

He was a gifted musician, a talent I once saw him put to an unorthodox use. We were off duty in a pub when a group of lads at the bar were becoming raucous. I could see Smudge, who had just come from a band rehearsal, become irritated. He was not going to put up with much more.

'Hold my pint,' he told the chap standing next to him.

We winced.

To everyone's surprise, instead of striding over to fling the unsuspecting troublemakers bodily from the pub, he reached down and took out his trombone.

The bar silenced to 'The Last Post' piercing the air. We all looked on incredulously as the mellow tones boomed out, pitch-perfect. As the last bars drifted away, Smudge fixed his granite stare on the would-be combatants and bellowed, 'That means it's time for bed, children.' They scurried off as Smudge put the instrument away before reclaiming his beer as if nothing had happened.

While Kevin and Matthew were searching for the girls in the woods, Smudge was into his seventh hour knocking on doors in Barcombe Road. The gravity of the task weighed heavily and he was keen for a distraction. As if on cue, a call crackled over the radio, asking for anyone free to investigate a sound, possibly of a child in pain, coming from some trees close to the front of Wild Park.

Smudge snapped his transmit button. 'Charlie Bravo 152, I'll take that,' he snapped so no one else dare stake a claim on the job.

He crossed Lewes Road, searched the copse in question and, having found nothing, took the opportunity to stay under the cover of the trees for a quick puff on his pipe. As the first clouds billowed from his briar, a gruff voice made him start.

'Oi, what are you doing?'

Smudge spun round, expecting to see a senior officer glaring, but instead it was Russell Bishop, smirking at having wound him up.

'What you doing, Russ?' asked Smudge, having regained his composure.

'I'm searching. I've got my dog,' he said, nodding to Misty at his side.

'It doesn't look much like a tracker to me,' quipped Smudge as they made their way together out of the trees into the open parkland.

'Do you think the kids are around here?' Bishop asked.

'I don't know.'

'I reckon they've either gone north or if they're here they're finished,' Bishop replied.

'Well, Brighton has some strange people in it,' agreed Smudge, slightly taken aback at Bishop's prognosis.

'Oh, well, I'm giving up soon,' said Bishop.

'No, you can't do that,' replied Smudge, surprised at Bishop's indolence. 'We've got to keep going. We've got to find them and rush them to hospital so they can then go home to their parents.'

'No, if I found them and they were dead I'd get nicked.'

Smudge stopped in his tracks. That was odd.

'No you won't,' he replied. 'You'll have to make a statement but why would you get nicked?'

'Cos I've got a criminal record,' mumbled Bishop.

Smudge was about to argue when a cry stopped him.

'We've found them, we've found them.' A young man, looking terrified, was running towards them, having burst out of the trees about twenty yards away.

Bishop took off in his direction, followed by the much larger and slower Smudge.

'If you get there before me, keep them away from the girls,' Smudge called to Bishop.

Bishop reached Kevin first and followed him into the wood.

They joined Matthew who was sitting close to the clearing. Bishop made to step over him as if to get nearer to the bodies, but Kevin blocked him, telling him to stay away.

As Smudge caught up he panted, 'How are they, how are the girls?'

'They're fucking dead,' replied Bishop, despite not having been into the clearing.

Kevin pointed, wordlessly indicating where the girls lay. Smudge stepped across to see more clearly. It was incredibly difficult to see through, but he could just make out a figure, wearing pink, lying in the clearing.

Despite his size, Smudge belly-crawled through the bracken to be sure of what he had seen and to check if both girls were there and if they could be saved. As he broke through the bushes, he saw a sight that would give him nightmares to this day.

Nicola was on her back with her legs up. The bruise to her face and frothy blood on her nostrils told him that she had died a violent death.

Karen was lying at a right angle to Nicola, with her head facing down on her friend's lap, lying on her left arm. The girls' hands were practically touching and both appeared to be sleeping. Smudge shuffled forward and felt each girls' neck for a pulse. There was none and, feeling how cold they were, he knew they were dead.

A coded message had already been agreed should any officer find the girls. These are commonly benign requests or updates that carry great meaning to those in the know but pass almost unheard by those out of the loop. Like the press.

'Charlie Bravo 152, can I have an RV with Superintendent Tomlinson in the woods by the pavilion,' Smudge transmitted, knowing the state of alert that short message would have sparked.

He stayed put but gave his helmet to Matthew, telling him to rush down to the field and wave it like mad to show the approaching cavalry where he was. Hearing the message, officers dashed towards Smudge. Little did any of them know that being driven around that very area was Michelle Hadaway. She told the driver to stop then watched in horror at the explosion of activity, which could mean only one of two things. She became distraught but thankfully a nearby policeman dashed over to her and arranged for her to be taken straight home.

Having ordered the immediate vicinity to be sealed off and for the families to be prewarned, Dave Tomlinson made a bee-line for the pavilion and, seeing the waving helmet, made his way up towards the trees.

He scrambled up the path until he came across Smudge, Kevin, and Bishop. Matthew followed on.

Tomlinson did not know any of them but was struck by how two of the young men seemed utterly devastated yet the third showed no reaction at all. He would later discover the impassive one to be Russell Bishop. Smudge pointed to where the bodies lay but, like him, Tomlinson could not see clearly. He dropped down the track, following its path in a semicircle before he could fully view the horrific scene. Both junior and senior officer hid their distress and arranged for the crime scene to be properly sealed and guarded, while they ushered away Bishop, Kevin and Matthew from the immediate area back to the park.

Barrie Fellows was walking down Newick Road towards the police box with his brother Kevin when he noticed the activity. His heart in his mouth, he stopped a passer-by.

'Have they found them?' he enquired desperately.

'Yes,' said the man, looking relieved.

'Are they OK?'

'Yes, they are cold and wet but OK.'

Barrie and Kevin picked up their pace to hopefully savour a reunion with Nicola at the police box. The inquisition could wait. As he stepped through the door, the hush hit him. Awkward looks. No sign of relief.

'Mr Fellows, would you like to come through here?' urged an officer, taking his arm to guide him into a small back office.

He did not need telling. The faces of the officers, struggling to find the words, told him all he had to know. A primal rage erupted in him and in sheer grief and despair he roared, his arms flailing at no one and everyone.

Kevin tried to grab him, restraining and comforting his brother in a loving bear hug, but Barrie was too strong, flinging him away and breaking his arm.

After the outburst of emotion, he calmed down, at least on the outside. His world had crashed around him and he still knew none of the details.

'Whatever you do,' he cried, 'don't tell Sue. I need to tell her. Promise me you won't.'

The officer nodded a promise, leaving Barrie and Kevin to stagger back home. As he was just yards from his front door, he heard the shriek come from inside. He knew, in that moment, the police could not even do that one thing for him. He dashed inside and took the shattered Sue in his arms, vowing never to forgive the police for breaking their word.

Back at the police station, a double murder enquiry was under way.

11

Just before Kevin and Matthew found the girls, someone else was making a key discovery just a few hundred yards away.

That Friday afternoon, Robert Gander, an engineer with the local electricity supplier, Seeboard, was working at the sub-station close to where CB radio fanatic Yann Svenski and his pals had been the night before. He spotted a woman pause on the footpath to study an apparently discarded blue sweatshirt lying on the grass verge. She nudged it with her foot then scurried off. Puzzled as to what had piqued the lady's curiosity, he ventured over to take a look.

The sweatshirt was dirty and he thought he could make out traces of blood on it. He knew about the search for Karen and Nicola so called the police and was told to take it to the incident van in Wild Park.

Bending down to pick it up, he was struck by the rancid body odour wafting from the garment. He pinched it between thumb and forefinger and gingerly carried it to his car, dropping it on the front seat. He must have been mightily relieved that the police van was only a moment's drive away.

When he arrived, around 4 p.m., the officers took the sweat-shirt – which bore the brand name Pinto – bagged it, pinned Mr Gander's details to the outside and left it in a corner of the van. They were still looking for the girls so did not imagine a discarded piece of male clothing was in the least bit relevant. With the discovery of the girls' bodies, the Incident Van was driven closer to the crime scene and the investigation shifted up a gear from a missing person enquiry to murder hunt. Sensing the long haul now ahead, an inspector cleared out the Incident Van and took the sweatshirt and other items back to Brighton Police Station, leaving them in their bags by the exhibit store where they would remain unnoticed for several days.

Maybe, and only maybe, a well-briefed detective would not have been so keen to rule out the importance of the clothing. CID officers live by the ABC code – assume nothing, believe no one, check everything – and this was a vivid example of why. That said, the officers who received the sweatshirt could never have known they had just been handed one of the most contentious pieces of evidence in Sussex Police's history of crime investigation.

Detective Superintendent Bernie Wells, the head of Brighton CID, would have had no idea when he received the call to say two bodies had been found that Friday afternoon, that his hunt for the killer would stretch beyond his and many of this successors' careers, mine included. Had the science and technology we all now take for granted been available, then things might have been very different. Over my police service, I saw first-hand the developments transforming crime investigation beyond all recognition. The techniques and tactics today's detectives have at their fingertips were mere pipe dreams in the mid-1980s. CCTV was embryonic, to say the least. Mobile phones were the stuff of science fiction, and the internet was confined to very specialist circles. Forensics were limited, more or less, to fingerprints, fibres, and blood grouping. DNA profiling, so widely used now, was only developed in 1985 and did not secure its first conviction until 1988; that of Leicester double child rapist and murderer Colin Pitchfork.

As when the IRA blew up the Grand Hotel in 1984, as soon as Bernie was told of the grim discovery, he made straight for the scene. His no-nonsense, old-school style exuded power and confidence and his London accent hit the mark with those privileged to follow his leadership.

As the top man, he led from the front. He needed to see with his own eyes the wretched deeds of the man he was now hunting. Others would spend longer there, poring over every inch, but as the senior investigating officer, experiencing the sights, sounds and smells of the scene was essential. First, though, he dispatched his troops.

DC John Moreton was one of the detectives called in at 7 a.m. Instantly recognizable by his upright posture, crisp suits and garish bow ties, he was well known in Moulsecoomb. A Londoner by birth, given his mother's ill-health he spent much of his childhood living with his grandmother on the estate. Having spent some time on the Special Enquiry Unit – the forerunner to the Child Protection Team – he knew only too well what wicked men could do to helpless children.

John had spent the day searching the area then interviewing well-meaning members of the public who thought they had crucial information. Around 4.20 p.m., he was just pulling up outside the Fellows' house to relieve the exhausted family liaison officer when he received the urgent call to head back to Wild Park.

As John approached the pavilion, he could see a woman with a pram, crying. To the right, up on the bank by the bushes, were two young men sitting with their heads in their hands, looking totally stunned. Beside them another young man was shuffling around on his feet, whistling. He realized that these were the three who found the girls.

John sidled up to Bishop.

'What are you doing here?' he asked, knowing the answer.

'I was with the other two boys when they found the bodies. I went across to the bodies and felt both girls' necks for a pulse,' replied Bishop. This assertion would fluctuate throughout the early days, and in the years to come.

John thought this was odd. Why would a non-medical person try the neck rather than the arm for a pulse? Aren't bodies normally 'found' by the killers themselves?

Bishop was getting bored and started bleating that he wanted to go home with his dog. John was torn – he needed to speak to Kevin and Matthew – so took the decision to arrange for a detective to drive Bishop home, telling him to wait there for someone to take a statement. I may be applying modern standards but Bishop was, at the very least, a key witness. All hands were needed on deck and he could have made his own way home. Or better still, been told to wait.

When detectives went back to see him later that afternoon, he was not at home.

Clad in blue overalls, the SOCOs – scenes of crime officers – arrived at the site about twenty-five minutes after the discovery, followed by dozens more police. And the press.

Despite the glamorous TV image, SOCO – or CSI as they're now called – work can be mundane. Much of the job entails dusting burglary scenes for fingerprints or photographing cuts and bruises. They relish getting their teeth into a murder. Although every death is a tragedy, SOCOs want to find that vital clue; a single hair, a clothing fibre or a microscopic blood spot invisible to the naked eye that might put the perpetrator behind bars for life. But the one job no one wants is the murder of a small, innocent child, let alone two. Detectives and SOCOs see terrible things over their careers and they have to get used to that quickly. But the deaths of children stay with you like nothing else. They haunt me, and many like me, every day.

This was mid-October so, while the clocks had yet to revert to Greenwich Meantime, there was less than two hours to go until sunset. There was no time to examine the scene in detail, but it was essential to snap some photographs, recover anything perishable then protect the area before night fell and the elements did their worst. A downpour or strong wind could obliterate crucial evidence in minutes. The weather forecast was benign, but no one was taking any chances.

Eddie Redman, a once-met-never-forgotten, squat, slightly dish-evelled Scotsman, was among the first to arrive. His diminutive stature belied a powerful presence. He was not everyone's cup of tea and never short of an opinion or two, his heavy accent and booming tone ensuring that all in the vicinity heard it.

I often struggled to work out whether he had just arrived at work or been out crawling around crime scenes all night. But like most SOCOs, he was a grafter. You do not choose that profession for a nine-to-five, weekends-off lifestyle. Criminals do not re-spect office hours and evidence can have an inconvenient habit of disappearing or degenerating throughout the day and night.

When Eddie and his three colleagues arrived, they began to pore over the microscopic clues the girls and the clearing might hold. Dressed in forensic barrier suits, they trudged through the woods until they found Smudge, dutifully guarding the bodies and scene against interference, be that inadvertent or deliberate.

You only get one chance to examine a crime scene. Once you have cleared it and surrendered control, there is no going back to reconstruct how the killer left it. In my time, I used to drum in to new detectives the importance of cordoning off as wide an area as possible – you can always contract a large scene but never expand small ones.

Preservation and integrity are key. Eddie and his team knew that whatever they did, or did not do, over the next hours, days and weeks would be subject to intense scrutiny in the months to come.

Every movement, every step, is planned and deliberate. Nothing happens by accident and everything is logged. When running investigations, I was a stickler for this, sometimes bawling out officers whose actions compromised the evidence. As a detective chief inspector, I turned up at one suspicious death to find the officer guarding the scene from an armchair in the lounge while a woman lay dead upstairs. I made my displeasure very clear. Luckily for him the death was not suspicious but my roasting would have been nothing compared to the cross-examination he would have suffered at Lewes Crown Court had it been a murder.

Before anything is touched, SOCOs photograph the scene and its immediate area in minute detail and from every conceivable angle – today it would be videoed too. The court will want to know, for example, exactly what Kevin, Matthew and Bishop saw and how. They will want to know how the girls lay, what was on and around them and what was visible to each witness. Sometimes this includes noting which bush *is not* trodden down, where debris or litter is absent as well as present. What is not there can be as significant as what is.

While there is just one SOCO behind the lens, this is a team effort. The photographer will be snapping away while the other SOCOs are scanning the scene, from a forensically safe distance, pointing out anything and everything that may become relevant.

The photographs taken, Eddie embarked on the painstaking process of methodically recovering what would be hundreds of tiny items that might unmask a monster. These included the seemingly obvious such as a discarded knife, pornographic magazines and fibres, to the less so, like samples of vegetation, soil and scraps of wood. As the light was starting to fail, it was vital this first phase was completed before Nicola and Karen were taken away.

Even though death was obvious, it needed to be verified. Unlike nowadays, where nurses or paramedics can 'declare life extinct', in 1986 it was the job of a police surgeon. It may seem a formality but it is critical that clinicians decide whether someone has died, or if they can still be saved. Only when death is indisputable – such as decapitation or where the body is significantly decomposed – is verification not required.

The police surgeon arrived about an hour and a half after the bodies were found. Strangely, he did not encroach far into the clearing and from a distance of about six feet, he confirmed death. As the colossal Smudge had managed to squeeze his way through, it is puzzling why this doctor could, or would, not. The police were lucky that Dr Iain West, one of the country's most respected and eminent forensic pathologists, was also on call. Thankfully he too arrived promptly. A convivial, heavy-smoking workaholic, he was famed for going above and beyond the call of duty. Famous for not only pinpointing the causes of death, but also providing inspired explanations.

Following the death of the disgraced British tycoon Robert Maxwell in 1991, West carried out the second post mortem and noted previously unseen muscle damage. From this he was able to suggest suicide as a real possibility.

Additionally, his determination of the exact angle of the bullet that killed Metropolitan WPC Yvonne Fletcher as she policed a protest outside the Libyan Embassy in 1984 made it crystal clear that it was a Libyan national who had murdered her. Other notable crimes to which he lent his considerable expertise included the Brighton Grand Hotel bombing, the Hillsborough Football Stadium disaster, the Clapham and Paddington rail crashes and the 1990 murder of Kenyan Foreign Minister Dr Robert Ouko at his country residence some 300 miles outside Nairobi.

Pathologists do not always see bodies in situ, but this was not a run-of-the-mill case. Detective Superintendent Bernie Wells returned to the scene with Dr West so he could learn first-hand what science might reveal about how the girls were killed. Bernie confirmed Smudge's account of how he found them and that of the police surgeon regarding the injuries he saw from a distance. By Nicola's left hand he spotted what appeared to be Karen's jumper and knickers – a sure sign of a sexual motive. Having seen all he needed to, West gave the order for the girls to be taken from their cold, damp dumping ground to the borough mortuary, less than a mile away.

This was a most delicate operation, as Dr West would later be looking for any minute clue that would solve the case. Moving a body from A to B can dislodge important evidence or, worse, new and misleading material can attach to it, later sending investigators up blind alleys

Satisfied that the girls had been carefully cocooned in the forensically secure body bags, Redman gave the green light to the waiting undertakers to take the small bodies away.

14

Early that Friday evening, Russell Bishop wandered over to a neighbour who was chatting with family outside the flats. In conversation he mentioned that he had been one of the people who had found the missing girls' bodies and had taken the pulse of one of them. He boasted about using Karen's white coat to track her and how his dog had sniffed out the children.

The neighbour asked him if the girls had been badly injured, to which Bishop replied that it did not appear so, before describing exactly how the girls were lying, a sight, he said, he would never forget.

At around 7 p.m. the police returned to Stephens Road to catch up with Bishop. Jenny answered the door and told them he was at the Hikers' Rest pub in Coldean Lane, just behind Wild Park.

They drove the short distance, explained they needed to speak to him again and took him straight to Brighton Police Station.

His account of his movements on the Thursday afternoon remained broadly the same, although he could not remember who the girl was that opened the Fellows' door. He also added he had originally arranged to meet Marion Stevenson at 6 p.m. that evening but headed off home instead, describing a route which would have taken him past where the Pinto sweatshirt was found. He struggled to remember what time he got home but, when he did, no one was there so he made dinner and put a load of washing on. This seemed curious. A man of his ilk, in those days, would baulk at the idea of doing anything but the most essential of domestic chores. He tried to explain this away by saying that, following a row with Jenny, he had been doing his own washing for a while and, anyway, it needed doing and he had nothing else to do. Jenny arrived home from work between eight and half past, and he maintained that he stayed indoors all evening.

So far as that Friday was concerned, his account married with those given by police officers and Michelle Hadaway. He remembered bumping into Smudge and winding him up about his sneaky puff on his pipe. Then his recollection started to deviate from everyone else's.

Instead of saying he walked with Smudge, chatting about how he would get blamed if he found them, Bishop maintained he had walked away from the officer to join Kevin and Matthew when he heard a shout that the girls had been found. He said he ran towards the pavilion and then into the woods.

He described seeing the two girls huddled together. Nicola was lying on her back, he said, and Karen's head was resting on her friend's stomach. He said he felt each girl's neck for a pulse but found none. He added that there was red-flecked foam on Nicola's lips and he was certain they were dead. Having signed his statement, he confessed to feeling worried because he believed he was suspected of the murders, something he repeated to the officers on the ride home.

Despite their reservations, the officers tried to reassure him that if he could supply an alibi or corroborate his movements for the previous evening, he would be in the clear. He suddenly blurted out that he watched television when he got in but did not pay much attention to what was on, nor did he have any callers. The details of his statement were obviously playing on his mind as the officers drove him back to Stephens Road.

15

While Bishop was being interviewed at the police station, Dr West was embarking on the saddest task of all – carrying out Nicola and Karen's post mortem examinations.

Mortuaries are soulless places. Their ethereal grey, steel gurneys and ever-present stench of blood combined with disinfectant rob the dead of any remaining dignity. I won't describe the process of a post mortem – out of respect for the families – but suffice to say most officers only attend these when they absolutely have to.

Under the watchful eyes of senior police officers, scenes of crime officers and photographers, pathologist Dr West set about his work. Both girls' clothes were covered in mud and vegetation, as were the exposed parts of their bodies. Karen did not have her jumper or knickers on but was otherwise fully clothed, as was Nicola except her knickers were inside out. Dr West lifted loose material from both girls' clothes and skin, using sticky tape and then fixing it to acetate, locking in the evidence. These tapings would become critical. On Nicola he noted some hairs and a piece of fibre on her lower abdomen.

Both girls' faces were flushed with blood and had petechial haemorrhages (tiny blood spots indicative of strangulation or suffocation) across them. Both, too, had suffered significant bruising and grazing all over their little bodies. Nicola had grazes and bruising to her face, extensively to the left side, suggesting she had been slapped or punched.

They both showed signs of having been sexually assaulted, but not raped. In Nicola's case Dr West believed she had been molested both before and after death. There was undigested food in their stomachs which would be relevant to their time of death as the girls were seen eating chips just before their last sighting.

The pathologist concluded that both had been strangled, probably by hands rather than a ligature. Karen's loss of consciousness was possibly rapid, but death would not have been instant. Nicola would have remained conscious for longer than her friend, which might only have prolonged her terror.

Given the hugely variable factors involved, and contrary to popular belief, pathologists now rarely provide times of death. If asked, they will say that death occurred sometime between when the victims were last seen and when they were found. Dr West, however, plumped for between 7 p.m. and 8 p.m.

A short while later, a completely devastated Barrie was escorted by a family liaison officer to identify and say goodbye to his darling Nicola. He could not understand why she was covered with a sheet up to her neck, but the penny dropped when he was gently reminded she had been examined. He could see her facial injuries but only imagine her horror. Not being allowed to give her a final kiss and cuddle goodbye, he slipped fifty pence of pocket money into her hand, and left a broken man.

Post mortems over, Detective Superintendent Bernie Wells was coming to terms with the enormity of the task that lay before him. The nation was horrified by what had been coined in the press as the Babes in the Wood murders. The community, not just of Moulsecoomb but of the whole of Sussex, felt horrified that such innocence could be so brutally robbed on their doorstep.

16

Everyone wanted to help, but that help, while welcome, led to Bernie and his team becoming completely overwhelmed. Within a couple of weeks, the police were to receive nearly 3,000 telephone calls, interview 2,000 people and take 700 statements. Bernie decided to put pride to one side and asked for assistance. He needed dozens of extra detectives drafted in and he needed them now.

Prior to the birth of dedicated Major Crime Teams, Senior Investigating Officers had day jobs; Bernie was busy enough as head of CID for Brighton and Hove sub-divisions. They were expected to investigate any murder, or murders, on their patch using their own officers who, likewise, were not exactly sitting around waiting for people to be killed.

While it was not unheard of to ask for more detectives, for a Senior Investigating Officer, or SIO, to put their hand up and request a deputy from headquarters would normally raise eyebrows. Not this time though. Bernie wanted a detective chief inspector on whom he could rely and who had a consummate eye for detail. He wanted Chris Page and got him. Chris was a bull of a man: bald, dour, gruff and with an intellect and drive that would, years later, make him head of Sussex CID. He and Bernie had different styles but always the same goal. They were the perfect partnership.

Another detective destined to become head of CID, DC Kevin Moore, arrived for work on 11 October expecting to be allocated whatever detritus his town of Hastings had thrown up during the previous Friday night. He knew about the missing girls and their grim discovery but, as Hastings was the furthest Sussex police station from Brighton, being seconded to the investigation was the last thing on his mind.

But he was and would spend the next three months travelling with DC Phil 'Muddy' Waters to and from Brighton working on what he would later describe as the most thorough, open-minded and intensive enquiry of his service. Towards the end of my career, Kevin was at times my boss and became a good friend but there is one thing we all agree on about him. He calls a spade a spade and has never knowingly spared anyone's sensitivities if he feels they have fallen short in some way.

Years later, Kevin laid bare his admiration for the way the enquiry was run. 'Any suggestion that Bernie and Chris were anything other than completely dedicated is, quite frankly, wrong. I've never seen an enquiry so thoroughly run. Remember, we were overwhelmed with messages and actions. Despite being swamped they kept focus and this was before the days of the all-singing, all-dancing HOLMES computer system we have now. People called in with all sorts of stuff that took us up blind alleys. Don't get me wrong, they were well-meaning, but we spent days, weeks, chasing down blind alleys. This was also the first time I'd experienced the clamour of the press. The scrutiny was intense. I'd never had to battle a path through reporters and TV vans camped outside a police station before.'

Bernie and Chris, with their combined capacity to absorb and make sense of huge volumes of information, were starting to settle on a few key suspects. There were not yet sufficient grounds to arrest any of them but they all needed looking at. As with any murder enquiry, close family and friends came under intense scrutiny with the hypothesis being the killer was probably male. Lee Hadaway was immediately ruled out as he had plenty of people to verify he was out of the county. That left Barrie Fellows, Dougie Judd, others close to the girls as well as the two boys who found them and, crucially, Russell Bishop.

Bernie had been looking very closely at Bishop, ever since his story had started to change. Had the detective not visited the scene himself, he might well have regarded the inconsistency as just another irritating anomaly that needed sorting out. Years later, Bernie animatedly shared his thinking with me. 'Bishop was so sure, so clear in his detail of what he saw and what he did that he must have seen the girls' bodies close up. But how could he? Kevin and Matthew were so sure that Bishop never went near the clearing, as was Smudge. He had tried to get into the den but Kevin had stopped him. So how did he know that Karen was lying across Nicola? That Nicola had blood-flecked froth on her lips?'

Bernie had seen with his own eyes how impossible it was to get anything more than a glimpse from where Bishop had stood. He would have had to crawl through the bushes, and he had not done that. There was only one way he would have known – if he was the killer.

Only a fool puts all their eggs in one basket though. Bernie ensured that every other possible suspect, including Barrie and Dougie, was interviewed time and again, their movements and alibis checked and rechecked, and the appeals for witnesses and information remained as broad as ever.

Only one person's story cracked under the scrutiny they all faced.

17

Inspector John Rodway was readjusting to home life after a relaxing Spanish holiday when the call came. A snapped, one-sided conversation with his boss, Superintendent Dave Tomlinson, told him his rest days were cancelled and he was to come immediately to Brighton Police Station.

He had yet to catch up on the news but knew a little of two girls having been found murdered the day before. John was from the old school and sought no further explanation. The adage of 'never being off duty' can be stretched but policing fosters a mindset that when you are called, you go – no questions asked.

John did not know the girls but, as a father, he struggled to hide his shock and horror once he heard the details. However, he knew emotion and pity never caught killers. Only steely determination, ruthless professionalism and focus would do that. As an inspector, and with his track record, he knew whatever role he was earmarked for, he had to stop this tragedy getting any worse. This was a principle I would imbue in detectives or commanders I mentored in years to come.

And he would do his damnedest to make sure it did not.

It did not take long for John to predict that the job he landed – setting up and running the house-to-house enquires in Moulsecoomb – would become a poisoned chalice; possibly the toughest and most complex challenge of his career to date.

John was a legend. A man-mountain, his entry into any room would invariably be accompanied by his thunderous voice either bringing its occupants to order or ribbing some poor unfortunate who happened to catch his eye. He saw the police as, first and foremost, problem solvers. He was too long in the tooth to expect everything to come with its own preordained and rehearsed plan. He knew that following most major incidents you just had to do the best you could and, in the absence of any other guidance, you made it up.

This is one of the reasons I have reservations about the recently introduced Direct Entry scheme, enabling civilians with no previous policing experience to join the service as superintendents. Those I have met on the scheme are highly intelligent, likeable and capable people, but I worry about their ability to innovate with no operational background.

By the time I reached that rank, when called upon to make critical operational decisions, I drew on every ounce of my experience. My judgement came from years of service – learning from my and others' mistakes – and watching better leaders than me in action. I used that grounding so those I led could trust my decisions and follow my orders. I wonder how you make up for that with a few weeks of training.

John's ability to inspire others through his self-assurance, powers of persuasion and people's downright fear of the consequences of incurring his wrath gave him a faithful following. When pressed for time, John would think up a plan, sometimes write it down, sometimes not, handpick a team and create the illusion of a well-thought-through, tried-and-tested strategy. One through which, by his sheer weight of personality and absolute self-belief, he would deliver a result. The most effective way of harnessing the support of wary communities is to deploy local, familiar officers able to build on existing relationships, rather than throwing in scores of cops from far-flung corners of the force who know nothing about them.

Some estates and communities take years of nurturing to engender anything close to confidence in the police. Even then it is often confined to one or two beat officers who would tire of hearing the back-handed compliment, 'I hate the police. But not you, you're all right. It's the rest of them I can't stand.' It is not that these officers are soft or have gone over to the other side. It is down to them investing years in befriending the locals and understanding the patch. It takes huge skill to read the psychology of the residents, work out the networks and hierarchies and then set firm but fair boundaries.

My job in Moulsecoomb, a few years later, was different. As a response driver, I raced into the neighbourhood, blue lights flashing and sirens wailing, coming down hard on criminals or suppressing the violence that would erupt from nowhere. I did not have the luxury of getting to know people. We were seen as the illegitimate force, the cops they hated, poles apart from the local bobbies, but, nonetheless, the ones they called when the need arose.

Some writers depict house-to-house enquiries as being a casual, almost incidental, affair. A couple of officers rapping on doors asking some benign questions of whoever happened to answer, then moving on. Nothing could be further from the truth. It is a methodical, painstaking activity designed to smoke out each and every person who may have been in the area on the night in question and then elicit from them every snippet of information, however insignificant it may seem.

With a killer on the loose, John needed every ounce of his creativity, guile and personality to pull it off. He had no time to ponder the what, whys or wherefores. He needed lots of officers, and quickly, to find out what the locals knew, suspected or just heard, and report back to the rapidly mushrooming investigation.

Thank goodness for community beat officer PC Eric Macintosh. Over the previous eighteen months, the diminutive 'Mac', a self-effacing, unassuming bobby, had embedded himself so well he was as much part of the community as any resident. Despite his easy style, he was tough and stood no nonsense. Any cop who ventured into the estate hoping to attract the same respect and trust Mac had built up received short shrift. Only Mac could fearlessly walk – or in his case, shuffle – alone around Moulsecoomb's streets.

Not only was he untouchable but he was a one-man database of who was who among the estate's complex and enigmatic networks. When I worked in Moulsecoomb, the formal handover file was an irrelevance. It was Mac who told the real story of what was going on and who needed nicking. He spoke in riddles and nicknames. He knew the good from the bad, the ones who were at it and those who could be relied upon, in the right circumstances, to whisper in his ear.

He quickly developed a sixth sense of the estate's mood and how best to approach its people. While I was stuck at Gatwick, friends who had been deployed to the enquiry returned with tales of this charmer who could literally open closed doors.

During Operation Salop, the code name randomly allocated to the investigation, Mac was critical to unlocking the inherently suspicious and anti-police families who might just have held the key to catching Britain's most wanted killer. Once tasked, John made sure that Mac never left his side.

Running one of the largest house-to-house operations Sussex Police ever faced presented a huge problem. There was no time to reverse this deep-rooted hatred of the force. If John had had about fifty years and infinite Macs at his disposal, then maybe he could have managed it, but instead he had to somehow convince the residents that there was no difference between the good cops (like Mac) and the bad cops (everyone else).

Winning over the residents' hearts and minds proved to be a long game. Convincing some people the mass of uniforms knocking on their doors were only there to find out who had killed the girls was a struggle. Years of bitter experience made many suspicious that, once they allowed the police over their threshold, all their secrets would be exposed.

The inconvenient truth in the wake of horrific murders is that life, in all its shades of grey, carries on. People will still be burgled, have domestics, fight and take drugs. Cars will still be stolen and some crashed. Sometimes that calls for an unwelcome robust police response amid the softly-softly approach. Not everyone comes quietly, so occasionally the police will use force either to keep the peace or make an arrest. Word of heavy-handed policing or an 'honest' thief getting his collar felt can spread like wildfire along with an 'I told you so' disaffection.

Sergeant David Gaylor, who would later become the model for Peter James' Detective Superintendent Roy Grace, was drafted in from rural Chichester. Recently promoted out of CID, David knew how murder investigations worked but had never experienced anything on this scale. David remembers John's brief clearly. His first order was to forbid anyone involved in the house-to-house to respond to emergency calls, and vice versa. It would be fatal for a bobby to be seen dragging little Jimmy off in handcuffs at dawn only to return all nicey-nicey with a clipboard as night fell.

Secondly, John made it crystal clear that while the officers were deployed, their sole focus was to find potential witnesses. If they suspected a motorbike secreted down a side alley to be stolen or saw someone wanted for failing to pay their court fines, they were to turn a blind eye. It would take just one over-zealous cop asking too many questions or checking the Police National Computer to trigger frosty receptions and slamming doors.

Many of those deployed, like David, were not local and had never experienced the complexity of policing Brighton. It was vital they understood the community and its dynamics. They also needed to know everything that had gone on since their last tour of duty. Before each shift, John briefed the whole team on each and every incident the police had responded to, its background, its outcome and the mood on the estate. Officers had to know the answers to inevitable questions such as, 'Why did your lot drag off Bill from next door last night?' or 'I hear number 42 was burgled yesterday. What did they get away with?' He also updated them on the investigation and anything, or anyone, particular to look out for.

One major problem was that many houses here were home to unofficial lodgers. All were council houses, which meant low rents but a strict ban on subletting. If caught, every tenant – legal and illegal – faced eviction. Often PCs would only be allowed into the kitchen, as the rest of the house was given over to sleeping accommodation for whoever could pay a sly tenner for a room.

This vital income stream was jealously guarded by the official householder and, as it was the only way the guest could keep a roof over their head, the last thing anyone needed was to be grassed up to the Housing Department.

'Just don't ask,' was John's brief. 'It is none of our business but you make sure you speak to everyone who lives there or was there on the night. Miss one person and this whole exercise will have been a waste of time.'

One of the biggest shocks, particularly for those who had leafier beats elsewhere in Sussex, was the abject poverty. Few had ever seen houses heated by stolen railway sleepers or their own internal doors burning in open fireplaces. Despite these and other desperate measures to provide shelter and warmth, almost without exception the cops found a proud and upstanding community prepared to do their bit to help unmask the killer.

The residents slowly warmed to the officers and began to trust them. They were proving true to their word; they really were only interested in the murders. Nothing else seemed to matter. At first, few believed the killer to be local. Maybe that was too much to stomach; the overwhelming view was the killer was an interloper. Many latched on to a ginger-haired man who had been spotted lurking around schools, despite the inescapable fact that it would have been nigh-on impossible for a stranger to cajole or drag the girls into the den. Either they knew their killer, or he knew the killing ground and found or followed them there. He had to be a local.

18

The weight of traffic crawling through and around Brighton makes it hard to imagine how much worse it would be now, had the A27 bypass not been built. In 1986, the new road had yet to be cut out of the picturesque downland that formed the city's northern boundary.

At the time the police were hunting the Babes in the Wood killer, to drive from West Sussex to East involved meandering around the North Brighton streets of Hollingbury or ploughing through the town centre and up the Lewes Road – both routes running past or very close to Wild Park. The girls' last sightings meant that literally hundreds of motorists, heading one way or the other, could have seen something which, even after the news broke, they dismissed as innocuous.

In the days before twenty-four-hour news and decades before social media, the only quick way to track down witnesses was by putting boots on the ground. The house-to-house operation was part of that, but John Rodway and his team had to find another way to speak to everyone who might have passed through Moulsecoomb on the night of the attacks. And, as ever, John was not one to do things by halves.

The gridlock John planned for exactly one week after the murders was audacious. It was also one of the biggest logistical challenges the enquiry faced. Timing was of the essence, and so was secrecy. Police were determined to exploit the human instinct of routine. Many people would drive up and down the Lewes Road on a daily basis for work or perhaps weekly to visit friends or relatives, play a particular sport or even meet a clandestine lover. These were the very people John needed to talk to. To give notice of a massive lockdown would prompt many either to change their plans or alter their route and be lost to the enquiry forever. It might also alert the killer.

To John, size mattered. The bigger the better. He knew that many of the passing public would have nothing to offer, but to unearth the golden nugget of information, he needed to throw the net far and wide. Under a veil of secrecy, he conjured up a plan to ensure whichever way people drove, no one could escape talking to a cop. Ever suspicious, as a contingency he supplemented those officers stopping the cars with a fleet of fast traffic cars and motorbikes ready to chase down anyone foolish enough to flee.

Having briefed 300 officers just hours earlier, at teatime on 16 October he gave the order which brought the whole northern fringe of Brighton to a standstill. The mammoth task of quizzing over 18,000 motorists could now begin. To free up officers and keep the flow moving, John devised a filtering system to ensure only those who had been in the area the previous week were delayed for more than a few moments. Meanwhile, police officers boarded every bus, bellowing the pre-agreed questions through loudhailers to the hundreds of passengers. Although this was less scientific than the quizzing of those in cars, it at least gave people the option to come forward for further questioning should they believe they had something to say.

Despite the massive delays, colossal inconvenience and the complete decimation of the bus schedules – a journey that would normally take fifteen minutes took closer to ninety – few complained.

One of the unforeseen problems was the number of cars running out of petrol while they waited. John, making it appear this was all in the plan, commandeered the assistance of a number of local garages to tow them away. It was all well worth the effort.

That single exercise netted over a hundred new witnesses who might otherwise have never been traced. Many were not central to the case, but some reported seeing potential suspects running from the park at exactly the right time. This gave the fledgling enquiry fresh impetus as well as helping the public feel that they could play a part in catching a child killer.

It was a huge relief to everyone that, while John was locking down the town, the Sussex Police Authority – the body which then oversaw the running of the force – accepted a recommendation from Chief Constable Roger Birch that no expenditure should be spared in solving the murders. No one, from the top down, could stomach leaving any stone unturned for the want of a few thousand pounds.

Unlocking the war chest seemed much simpler then. While I have never constrained an investigation, a firearms or public order operation on cost alone, every decision and every tactic has its price. From 2010, given the scandalous stripping-out of police budgets, I needed to keep a weather eye on the money and was forced to choose the most efficient way to get the job done.

As if having a roadblock in full swing was not enough, a reconstruction was also in progress. This was done deliberately as part of the theatre to jog people's memory as they were being questioned. Seeing what appeared to be the same girls, in identical clothing doing the same things, might just flick a switch that would bring a flood of crucial information. Two brave local girls had volunteered to play the part of the tragic playmates. Dressing as they had – one in a pink sweatshirt, the other in a green school jumper – they followed their exact footsteps. No one could have imagined the terrible irony that ten years later, one of those brave little actresses, Katrina Taylor, would herself be savagely murdered.

The courage shown by Lianne Martin's and Katrina Taylor's parents was breath-taking. How selfless to let your daughter wear the same clothes, walk the same route and speak to the same people as her ill-fated friends had moments before they were murdered? Allowing Lianne to play Karen, and Katrina, Nicola, in front of the glaring eyes of the media and the thousands of motorists caught up in the gridlock cunningly created by John Rodway, was astonishing. Few could imagine their agony as the brave mums and dads watched their daughters retrace the girls' final steps. They so closely resembled the girls that Barrie Fellows could not watch. He tried, but grief overwhelmed him and he was helped away in tears.

It was still daylight when Lianne and Katrina walked from Newick Road towards Lewes Road. PC Dadswell spoke to them, as he had to Karen and Nicola, while they swung on a tree in Wild Park before scuttling back across Lewes Road to the Barcombe Road chip shop. As they crossed back over the main road, officers pointed them out to the delayed drivers hoping for recognition. In the fading light, those witnesses who last saw Nicola and Karen appeared, again in the hope that someone might remember something in seeing the girls.

Lianne and Katrina stood at the entrance to the park and waved over to the estate, the last thing the tragic girls were seen to do. At this cue, their mothers swept in, cuddled them and led them to the safety and warmth of their homes. Two hundred yards behind this reunion, harsh arc-lights still bathed the murder scene; a stark reminder that, just one week ago, the evening ended very differently for two other children.

19

July 1996

Ten years later, nineteen-year-old Katrina was not so safe.

A £200-per-week heroin habit and providing for her baby was taking its toll. It did not take much for two local men to persuade her to act as lookout as they burgled a house in Bolney Road, Moulsecoomb, just across the road from her family home.

During their hunt for drugs they trashed Neisha Williams' house, smashed up furniture, pulled out a washing machine – causing a flood – and set fire to a pile of clothes. They stole jewellery, some of which Katrina sold for a paltry £20 to buy drugs. For keeping watch and selling the proceeds she was charged with burglary. But for some this was not payback enough and revenge was sought.

Neisha's brothers Jason and Simon, together with her ex-boyfriend, Trevor Smith, and his close friend Fergal Scollan and others who were never identified, were said to be on the hunt for those responsible.

Luckily for the first burglar, the police found him before the vigilantes did. With him in custody, the gang searched for the other. He was less fortunate.

It was a shame he could not bring himself to confirm to the police who it was that beat him up, stabbed him in the legs and viciously assaulted his innocent friend who happened to be in the wrong place at the wrong time.

Katrina's arrest the next day brought only a temporary reprieve as, despite the Crown Prosecution Service (CPS) asking magistrates to remand her in custody, she was bailed and went into hiding. It took Simon Williams two months to track her down but when he did, chancing upon her outside a seafront hotel, he forced her to go to Neisha's new house in Centurion Road, Brighton. Once there, Williams summoned Smith and Scollan from London. Katrina was held captive until she agreed to pay for the damage caused during the burglary. She must have thought them most benevolent when they agreed repayments of £10 per week.

Later that evening, however, matters took a darker turn when screaming was heard in St Nicholas' churchyard, a few yards from the house. The following morning, a shocked dog walker stumbled across Katrina's mutilated corpse, bloodied and abandoned in the graveyard. A post mortem concluded she had been restrained from behind and stabbed six times, once in the arm and five times to the chest.

During the trial at Lewes Crown Court in July 1997, Neisha and Simon Williams said that Katrina had left the flat with Smith and Scollan. They maintained the two men returned a short while later saying she was dead. Smith and Scollan denied this and said it was Simon Williams who was responsible.

The Williamses were acquitted of the murder while Smith and Scollan were convicted but, in a twist, two years later they successfully appealed and at their retrial at the Central Criminal Court the judge directed the jury to acquit them both on the grounds of insufficient evidence. Smith had admitted false imprisonment but, due to time already served, he, along with Scollan, walked out a free man.

No one stands convicted of Katrina's horrific and senseless murder. That she was killed for playing a minor part in a burglary shows how cheap human life can be. The case, like the Babes in the Wood, frustrated Sussex Police for years.

The tragedy and poignancy that Nicola and her stand-in Katrina are bound together in their untimely ruthless murders and their denial of justice for decades has remained a wretched subplot to these brutal events.

20

As Operation Salop got into its stride it became clear that it lacked a silver bullet. Most homicide enquiries, however serious loss of life is, are not that hard to solve. Many murders I investigated over the years were less a whodunnit, more a whydunnit. The suspects I met struggled to protest complete innocence if they were caught, quite literally, with blood on their hands. Their only hope was to argue provocation, self-defence or diminished responsibility. Normally such pleas are blown out of the water by evidence of pre-planning or of them picking up a weapon when they had the chance to run away.

Nowadays, with the indelible digital footprints we all leave, whether by logging on to the internet, passing a CCTV camera or just phoning our friends, let alone the staggering advances in forensic science, most false alibis do not get past first base. Eyewitnesses also have a habit of scuppering any hope of getting away with murder. It is not just the sharp-eyed passer-by with keen powers of observation who sees the slaying from start to finish that nails murderers. Many are caught by a patchwork of sightings – human and digital – which, when overlaid with other circumstantial evidence, can seal their fate.

Police forces stop at nothing to catch a killer because murder is the ultimate crime and one for which there is no possible restitution. If you steal from someone you can pay them back. But if you kill them, that is final. Not only have you destroyed them, you have destroyed the lives of their loved ones too. Forever.

The overriding imperative to stop the Babes in the Wood killer striking again meant a result could not come quickly enough. But

nothing happens in isolation and this was not the only intractable murder vexing Sussex Police at the time. Another was
already stretching Sussex CID to its limits. This one not only
lacked an obvious killer but also a complete body.

Just over a month before Nicola and Karen were killed, a
motorcyclist's early morning ride through Ashdown Forest, one
of the largest and most beautiful public spaces in the south-east
of England, was rudely interrupted.

The biker's overwhelming call of nature forced him to pull
over to relieve himself. So as not to offend the sensitivities
of other road users, he pushed his way through a bush, out of
sight.

The frenzied swarm of flies and a putrid stench made him
curious. Venturing further he stumbled across what appeared to
be barely concealed lumps of flesh wrapped in cloth. He initially
assumed it was an animal, perhaps someone's beloved pet,
dumped at the mercy of the food chain.

He called the police nonetheless. A detailed forensic examination revealed a woman's dismembered body divided into two
shallow graves, wrapped in curtain material and nightdresses.

The head, hands and feet were nowhere to be found. Despite
this, the pathologist was able to determine the sex, age and cause
of death – a slit throat. Still, the police had no idea who this
woman was.

At any other time, that investigation would have become the
single most important priority for Sussex Police. No expense
would have been spared. But less than six weeks in, still with no
idea of who the body or killer were, Detective Superintendent
Brian Grove lost half his investigation team to Bernie Wells. With
morale and resources on the floor, Brian and his team needed a
little luck.

When the case featured on BBC's *Crimewatch* – a monthly
prime-time programme consisting of appeals for information
about the most serious and puzzling crimes in the UK – the
flurry of calls led the team to look at Crawley, a busy and bustling

new town on the northern edge of Sussex, some fifteen miles from where the body was found.

A local man, Kassem Lachaal, had taken advantage of Islamic tradition and married a second wife, Fatima, in his native Morocco. His first wife, Latifa, was less than pleased but had mysteriously disappeared.

Kassem tried to convince the police she had travelled to Morocco to divorce him but neighbours and the other evidence suggested this was unlikely. Cutting-edge forensic techniques showed the body was the same age, height and build as Latifa and bore the same scars as she did. Meanwhile, investigators proved a connection between her and the curtains that became her shroud.

Kassem and Fatima were arrested and subsequently charged in connection with the murder but Brian knew that without a firm identification, he would struggle to prove the case beyond reasonable doubt. An act of God saved the day.

Following the 1987 hurricane, which wiped out thousands of acres of woodland across the south of England, a woodman clearing fallen trees near Worth Abbey stumbled across a human skull. This was quickly connected to Brian's enquiry and the team held their breath as forensic odontologist Dr Bernard Sims tried to compare the skull to Latifa's.

Two X-rays of Latifa's jaw – one from the dentist and a second from her treatment following a vicious assault by Kassem – together with an unusual sinus satisfied Dr Sims it was a match.

With this final piece of the jigsaw, Kassem was convicted of her murder and sentenced to life imprisonment and Fatima was jailed for eighteen months for assisting in the disposal of the body.

With two concurrent high-profile murder investigations, it was a wonder that the 3,000 officers in Sussex Police were able to do anything else. No force solves every murder. Sussex was no different but within a week of the Babes in the Wood killings, the local newspaper the *Evening Argus* recapped some of the force's other unsolved cases for its readers.

There had already been more than a dozen murders in 1986 and, in fairness, most were cleared up, but some from years before still waited for answers.

Among the catalogue of cases was the death of Keith Lyon, the twelve-year-old son of a popular local bandleader, who was found stabbed with a steak knife on the Downs close to his home in Woodingdean, Brighton. That remains unsolved to this day.

The one that would truly haunt Operation Salop, however, was the rape and murder of thirty-four-year-old Margaret Frame on 12 October 1978 – eight years almost to the day before Karen and Nicola died.

Margaret, happily married with a nine-year-old son she adored, disappeared while walking home from her cleaning job at Falmer High School, on the edge of Moulsecoomb. Ten days later, her body was found in Stanmer Park, less than half a mile across the Coldean estate from Wild Park. All the indications pointed to her having been clubbed over the back of the head, stabbed in the back, then raped. Attempts had also been made to sever her head. The evidence suggested the killer returned later, dragging her 500 yards to bury her in a shallow grave.

Despite a huge police investigation involving the taking of around 2,500 statements and calling at over 5,000 homes the killer was never found. Even a reinvestigation twenty-two years later, led by Kevin Bazyluk, my first DS on joining CID, using new scientific breakthroughs, failed to unmask him.

Although there were stark disparities between Margaret's murder and the Babes' – age, modus operandi, levels of violence, offender behaviour after the murder – many in the press kept returning to the coincidences in time and place to assert the two cases were connected. This was never a serious hypothesis but it was yet another unnecessary distraction Bernie Wells could ill afford.

21

Other theories would also trouble the investigation, and yet despite still being without a definite suspect, the police remained convinced the answer lay close to home.

Great store was placed on someone from the community having that credible snippet of information which would nail the killer. The girls must have been murdered where they were found and probably had gone there willingly. That would suggest they knew their killer and, given their social circles did not extend far beyond Moulsecoomb, it was someone local.

One of the most significant lines of enquiry, even before the bodies had been found, centred on the ginger-haired man who had been cruising around schools in the Brighton and Lewes areas trying to entice young girls into his blue car. Three times he had approached would-be victims but, thankfully, each of the gutsy girls refused his advances and alerted the police. Just a few days before the girls were killed, the man and his car had been seen around Moulsecoomb. This prompted the local infant and junior schools to send letters to parents warning them of the danger. Police schools liaison officers warned children of the 'stranger danger' at special assemblies, but the man had yet to be captured.

There was no doubt that someone of that description was stalking girls and it became a key line of enquiry for the team. However, there were no firm sightings at the relevant time and there was no getting away from the fact the police were certain the girls knew their killer. With great sensitivity, Superintendent Dave Tomlinson made it clear to the press that there was nothing to suggest this man had been in the area at the time. While not ruling him out as a suspect, he needed to keep the focus of the public and police on where the evidence was pointing.

Like the detectives investigating the murder of Latifa Lachaal, the Babes in the Wood team turned to *Crimewatch* for help. Winning a slot on the show often took weeks of negotiation and planning. It was a measure of how seriously the nation was taking the Babes in the Wood killings that it featured just a week after the girls disappeared.

The show featured direct appeals, reconstructions, photofits (it is credited with inventing the updated 'e-fit' of suspects) and pleas for witnesses to call the studio. Part of the deal of having your crime featured was that before and after your few minutes in front of the camera, you answered the phones to callers on each and every appeal made during that show.

I have been on *Crimewatch* twice and you got some seriously odd people phoning in. Some just wanted the opportunity to swear at a cop, others were fantasists, but many had information that cracked cases. In its first thirty years, its appeals led to around 1,500 arrests and 900 convictions. Sadly, it is currently off the air.

So, when a chap who gave his name as 'Dave' called in to describe two youths running from Wild Park at around six thirty – exactly the time the police were interested in – the team thought they were onto something. Despite giving only his first name, he promised to meet detectives in the park at lunchtime the following day. Timid witnesses are not unusual, so it was not totally unexpected when he failed to show. That did not mean he was a time-waster; he might have just got cold feet. The police appealed directly to him through the media but to no avail.

As other lines of enquiry were drawing a blank, Bernie kept coming back to Russell Bishop. His accounts flip-flopped and while some were vague and uncheckable, others were downright lies. There is a phrase we use in the police for people who are simply unable to tell the truth; they 'cannot lie straight in bed'. That was Bishop.

Clever liars devise their yarns so that they are credible, consistent and verifiable. Often they are based on truth but lack the depth which stands them up to scrutiny. Above all, though, good liars stick to their story come what may.

Bishop was not one of those.

On the Wednesday, six days after the murders, Bishop was again invited to Brighton Police Station for another interview. DC Barry Evans, a hugely experienced, gentle investigator, asked Bishop about his whereabouts on the Thursday evening. Oddly, he claimed to be in two places at once. First, that he arrived home around 6 p.m., then he said he had been smoking drugs near the police box in Wild Park at the same time. A riskier place to enjoy a joint is difficult to conceive. All along, this was when he said he was due to be at Marion Stevenson's house, but did not turn up. His account of smoking by the police box was verified by brothers Kevin and Mark Doyle who, separately, reported seeing him in Lewes Road at 6.15 p.m. and leaving Wild Park at 6.30 p.m.

Six thirty was perilously close to the time that Karen and Nicola were last seen, so the timings of who was where, and with whom, were crucial. The police could afford him no margin of error. Bishop's accounts, in all their haziness, were becoming more and more suspicious.

Jenny, his common-law wife, for whatever reason was also unable to throw any more light on Bishop's whereabouts. She told a workmate he had been at the pub all evening, not arriving home until 11 p.m. However, she would later tell the police that, having collected their son from a friend's house after work, Bishop was at home. This was about 8.40 p.m. She remarked that he had changed his clothes and had a bath.

Accepting that some people lie to the police for all sorts of reasons (and Bishop had many) and some just get confused, a simple fact remains. The girls were last seen at 6.45 p.m. and Bishop had no verifiable alibi of his movements between this time and 8.40 p.m.

He was asked to give further details about the washing he did when he arrived home that evening. This time he said he needed some clean clothes as he had fallen into some dog faeces and his trousers were covered in it. They also questioned him about the trip to the newsagent's he claimed to have made that evening. Initially he was adamant that having picked up his newspaper, he only realized he had no money when he reached the counter. If this were true it would be easy to verify. The shopkeeper and other customers would surely confirm this. After all, it cannot be every day that a familiar face presents himself at the counter with a newspaper only to realize he does not have the means to pay for it. They were asked and no one recalled it.

The police then covered his movements on the day the girls were found. Now he was adamant he had not ventured into the area where the bodies were lying. He was shown the notes from the previous interview when he had said he had checked for a pulse. He denied this, although he did say that had been his intention. He said he must have missed that part of the statement when he signed it.

When pressed, he changed his mind again, saying that he had in fact felt for a pulse. That story changed again a few minutes later and he wedded himself to the account given by Kevin Rowland, that he had not approached the girls.

Despite his best, but rather shallow, efforts Bishop had no alibi and there were no sightings of him between 6.30 p.m. and 8.40 p.m., by which time the two little girls were probably dead.

No self-respecting senior investigating officer would ever jump on such a fact as being conclusive evidence of guilt. But, with everything else that followed, it elevated Bishop to more than just a 'person of interest'.

22

In the early twentieth century, Dr Edmond Locard theorized that whenever contact is made between a person, place or object, an exchange of physical material occurs. He said that by touching or rubbing up against anything, criminals leave and remove traces of evidence. This could be fingerprints, footprints, blood or other bodily fluids as well as hair, skin cells or fibres.

Locard's Principle of Exchange, as it became known, underpins almost every forensic technique and, while finding traces of alien material is not always conclusive of guilt, when coupled with other evidence it can be. To take full advantage of Dr Locard's theory, the handling, preservation and storage of forensic material must be flawless. The chain of evidence is one of the most critical aspects of any investigation. If this is broken, even the dimmest lawyer can drive a coach and horses through the smartest prosecution case. There can be no question of any contamination, be that inadvertently or through the misdeeds of corrupt officers or scientists.

DI 'Kit' Bentham was in charge of the force SOCOs. As one of those at the post mortem some weeks before, he knew enough of the case to have been moved by it, despite not now having a day-to-day role. Exactly three weeks after the girls' bodies were found, on Halloween, while he was trawling through paperwork in his Eastbourne office, his phone rang.

'Guv,' came a gruff Scots voice, clearly flustered.

'Eddie, is that you?'

'Aye. I need to see you urgently. Can you come over? I need to show you something,' panted SOCO Redman.

'I'm on my way.'

When he arrived, he walked up the four flights of stairs to the SOCO office to find an excited Eddie holding a brown paper bag containing a Pinto sweatshirt.

'I've got this, guv, and I think there's blood on it. I'd been reading the statements and it was found on the route that Bishop took on the way home. I think it's important.'

Kit took the bag from him and sent him off to inform the incident room.

In a murder investigation, any action or enquiry has to be set by the incident room who have the overview of the case. This prevents duplication of effort and anything being missed.

For some reason, after reading the statements, Eddie had looked at the sweatshirt of his own volition. He then carried out a field test for blood which showed a weak positive result. This is a very standard procedure; it is just that prior to going ahead, Eddie should have been sanctioned by the incident room – which they certainly would have done.

Being more of a detective than a SOCO, Kit predicted what might now need to be done with the Pinto. If it was connected with the murder, then clearly it would need to be subject to the most thorough forensic analysis but also someone would need to confirm whether it belonged to Bishop – or anyone else. He took it to the SOCO laboratory, supported it on a piece of card, repackaged it in a polythene bag, making sure that there was no prospect of cross-contamination, and sealed it.

Eddie Redman has since suffered significant criticism for how he handled the sweatshirt. He was wrongly accused of exposing it to other exhibits. Some even put future events at his door. This accusation was completely misplaced. Had Eddie not had the presence of mind to read through the statements – not his job – and link this one sweatshirt to the evidence he'd read, test it and raise his concerns with his boss, the Pinto might have festered in some general property store forever.

It was Eddie who first recognized the importance of the

sweatshirt, and for that he should be praised, not castigated as he was for many years.

That same morning, DS Phil Swan and DC Dave Wilkinson visited Bishop and invited him back to the police station to go through his previous statements and provide a little clarification. They questioned him again about Kevin Doyle's sighting of him when he claimed to have been home. Bishop explained that Doyle was wrong and was, in fact, referring to the following Saturday.

The detectives then took him back to the discovery of the bodies – they were intrigued as to which version of events he would choose. He once again returned to the one in which he said he saw blood-flecked foam on one of the girls.

In a break from the police station, Bishop was taken out to confirm his route home from the park and where he had fallen in the faeces. Both locations put him close to where the Pinto sweatshirt was found. They arrived back around 11 a.m. and DS Swan went straight to consult with Bernie Wells. The case was mounting and Bernie was satisfied that a threshold had been reached.

Twenty minutes later, Swan returned to the interview room.

'Russell, I'm arresting you on suspicion of the murders of Nicola Fellows and Karen Hadaway. You are not obliged to say anything unless you wish to do so but what you say may be given in evidence,' he announced.

Bishop was stunned. 'No, no, it's not me, fuck off, leave it out,' he yelled. Despite his impassioned protestations, he was marched straight down to the basement custody block, booked in and put in a cell.

As is often the case when dealing with suspected murderers, the initial twenty-four hours of detention permitted was not enough so it was extended first by a superintendent and then by magistrates.

The next three days consisted of intense questioning. It was clear to Bishop, after trying to front it out without legal representation during the first two interviews once arrested, he would need some help. Mr Oxford, a local solicitor's clerk, was dispatched and the interrogations continued. Bishop's only respite between interviews was being subjected to a full and invasive medical examination, with saliva, blood, head, face and pubic hair samples taken from him for forensic testing, before he was once again grilled by Phil and Dave.

He accepted that he had not visited the newsagent, as he had earlier maintained, but had headed for another vendor – Angie Cutting, a local drug dealer. He said he fancied smoking some 'blow' on his own so stood Marion up and bought some cannabis which he smoked by the police box. His explanation for not mentioning this before was reasonable – he did not want to get himself or his dealer in trouble. Given he had now spilled the beans, you would have expected it to be true. The police checked. The dealer admitted she sold drugs but not to Bishop on that evening.

He then said he had gone straight home after finishing his joint, arriving at 6.30 p.m., the time he was seen by the police box. They pushed him on the clothes he had worn that night. Bishop assured the officers they already had everything he had been wearing; there was nothing left at his home. Later, he was shown the stained Pinto sweatshirt that was now in transparent packaging. He emphatically denied it was his but accepted he did own the pair of trousers they had seized, which he usually wore while repairing car bodywork, including his own Ford Escort.

Things became heated when he was told that Jenny had signed a statement that day to confirm that the sweatshirt was his. He dismissed this out of hand, putting it down to a mistake on her part, but there it was in black and white. The sweatshirt was then biked to the Forensic Science Laboratory where its secrets would be revealed.

Bishop went on to deny that Nicola had come to the door when he visited the Fellows' house looking for Dougie and denied that anyone had called anyone a slag. He tried to explain away his bizarre comment to Smudge that he would get in trouble if he found the bodies as being down to the fact he was one of the last people to see the girls. It is curious how he knew that at the time. He again denied touching the bodies to feel for a pulse. Instead, he changed his story yet again, accepting that he had tried but was stopped by Kevin from going into the den. As for the blood-flecked foam on Nicola's mouth, he said he had been guessing. A pretty good guess.

After three days of grilling, the police took the decision to release Bishop on bail, instructing him to return on 4 December 1986.

Bail is a tactical decision – the police only have a finite time in which they can keep a suspect in custody and, in simple cases, that is usually sufficient. This was anything but simple. Despite the police having burned the midnight oil from the moment the girls were reported missing until Bishop's eventual arrest, his interviews threw up many more lines of enquiry.

Detectives had to recheck his ever-fluid accounts, revisit witnesses and cross-check the forensic samples combed, scraped and swabbed from his body after his arrest as well as on the Pinto sweatshirt. All of that took time. Many believe that the crescendo of any murder enquiry is the arrest. Far from it.

23

At the point of bail before charge the hard work really starts, and this case was no exception. Even getting to the point where there was sufficient evidence to charge would take a colossal effort and far more time than was left on Bishop's 'custody clock'. Releasing a person on bail effectively freezes that clock. When they return to custody, the clock restarts. This is fair to all. The suspect has his or her liberty restored while the police can get on with their complex and intricate enquiries without rushing.

Some years after these events, in 2011, a district judge from Salford, Manchester, threw that twenty-five-year-old interpretation of the law into turmoil. He decided that, as far as the custody clock was concerned, bail time counted as if it were jail time. This meant that even with the most convoluted investigation the police had, at most, a mere four days to get their evidence in order, or their suspect would walk free.

This created utter panic among the police, courts and politicians.

All of Sussex's divisional commanders were summoned to an emergency meeting to ponder what the hell we were going to do. Our collective experience and expertise told us that hundreds, if not thousands, of criminals would be let off the hook. I drove to the meeting thinking of the rapists, murderers and armed robbers I had arrested and bailed over the years, only for them to be charged, and later imprisoned, once all the evidence was in place. How would we ever protect the public if this ruling stood?

Thankfully common sense prevailed and in less than three

weeks emergency legislation was passed to close this loophole and normal practice resumed.

Bishop's month on bail was frenetic. Scenes of crime officers continued searching key sites for whatever they might reveal. The initial forensic examination of the Pinto sweatshirt had also created a number of leads to follow. The garment had been covered in ivy spores which would become critical to the case so samples were harvested from the crime scene and where the garment was dumped. Equally, what was first thought to be blood was, in fact, different types of paint. DC Kevin Moore from Hastings was tasked with linking the sweatshirt with cars Bishop had sprayed and garages where he'd worked, seizing paint that might prove a match and dashing it up to the forensic lab for comparison.

Early on, Michael Evans, the ambulance-man friend of Bishop, described seeing Bishop in a sweatshirt, almost indistinguishable from the Pinto. The following month, when shown the sweatshirt, he said it was not the same one.

Officers also seized the clothes Marion Stevenson had been seen wearing on the day in case there had been any transference of forensic material. She was even arrested on suspicion of being involved in the murders but was soon eliminated from the enquiry.

Bishop's flat was searched once again, having earlier been examined while he was under arrest. Clothing, hairs, paint, fingerprints and microscopic samples of indeterminate origin were recovered, all of which would become as controversial as they were critical.

The public demanded progress but, until charged, police rarely release the identity of those arrested. Despite this, the rumour mill ensured it soon became clear who it was.

Bishop decided to spend some of his time on bail in Wales, fearing for his safety. While he was away, he made several telephone calls to Marion which were recorded by the police on bugging equipment placed in her family home with the blessing of her parents. They did not reveal much other than, despite

Marion's assurances to her mum and dad that the relationship was over, she was still very much in a relationship with Bishop.

On 21 November 1986, Bishop, out of the blue, visited Barrie Fellows. On answering the door Barrie was shocked. Here, on his doorstep, was the primary suspect for the murder of his daughter.

'Barrie, I just want to tell you I never topped the girls.'

Barrie was dumfounded. No 'how are you', or 'I'm so sorry for what you're going through', just a flat denial. Barrie refused to have him in the house so they walked together along Newick Road. Bishop said he wanted to clear the air and implored Barrie to believe he had nothing to do with the murders. He lied, claiming the police had cleared him and that he had sold his story to the press. At first he told Barrie he was going to keep the money from the papers for himself before quickly changing his intentions to the more palatable suggestion he would donate it to charity.

When Barrie pressed him on his movements that October evening, Bishop conjured up an insurance salesman who he said had called on him after he had arrived home. He had not mentioned this during his three days of questioning a few weeks previously.

Barrie grew concerned that they were even having this conversation so cut it short, saying he was going to speak to the police about it. They confirmed Bishop should be nowhere near him – although he had no bail conditions to prevent that – and, to prevent further calls, warned Bishop off.

The following day, Bishop reported a burglary at his Stephens Road flat. He alleged the electricity meter had been broken into. While the officers were taking details, suddenly, he reached and pulled out a blue sweatshirt from behind a cushion, saying, 'I'm guarding this with my life. I don't want the CID getting their hands on it . . . I'm sorry but this jumper proves my innocence. This is the jumper with the red paint on it that the Murder Squad say they have. I can prove this is the one.'

The officers did not know what he was talking about but he was keen to press on, urging the officers to 'tell the Murder Squad that I can prove that I was at home at 6.30 p.m. that night. I have some insurance men who will testify to that, so their witness couldn't have seen me at Wild Park.' Once again, he was up to his usual tricks, conjuring witnesses from his imagination.

24

The Pinto sweatshirt, which had almost been overlooked, was now central to the enquiry. No witnesses described it being worn by anyone, including Bishop, on the night the girls were killed. It was not found close to where they were discovered, or in any of the places where they had been spotted in the hours before their deaths. So, what was Detective Superintendent Wells' fixation with this dumped sweatshirt?

Mr Gander, the electricity worker who had spotted it on the footpath by Moulsecoomb Station, could easily have ignored it and got on with his day. Yann Svenski and his friends, as well as a woman who had prodded it with her foot, understandably did just that. The officers who Gander handed it to treated it as another piece of found property, destined, were it not for Redman, to lie unclaimed, clogging up the property store at Brighton Police Station.

Those initial forensic examinations on the clothing, however, did reveal some significant findings. There were eleven green fibres, indistinguishable from Karen's long-sleeved sweatshirt; four pink fibres, indistinguishable from Nicola's V-neck sweatshirt; and hundreds of ivy hairs matching those at the den, all now present on the Pinto, together with fibres which appeared to have come from Marion Stevenson's clothing.

The shirt Karen was wearing also bore eleven fibres that were probably from the Pinto and Nicola's top had nine. There were also some Pinto fibres found on the trousers Bishop had handed over to the police. Finally, the same tiny ivy hairs that had coated the Pinto were also found on the girls' jumpers and their bodies.

Despite the meticulous examination, the scientists were unable to find any of the girls' hairs on the Pinto. Nor did they find Bishop's hairs on the girls' jumpers.

The Pinto did have animal hairs on it but whether they came from Bishop's dog, no one could be certain.

Next the scientists turned to the paint stains on the Pinto. Under a microscope different samples of paint can be quite distinct. Bishop was forever working on, and spraying, cars – sometimes stolen ones. Furthermore, a number of outhouse doors at the block of flats where Bishop lived had been graffitied in red. He had admitted spraying the cars but not the doors.

After careful testing, the red staining on the Pinto was found to have come from a paint identical to that used to graffiti two of the outhouse doors and to paint Bishop's Ford Escort. The maroon paint also found was exactly the same as that found on one of Bishop's friend's cars which he had sprayed as well as a can of paint found at Bishop's flat. Frustratingly, the paint on Bishop's trousers was different from that on the Pinto. This scuppered the theory that he had worn both the trousers and the Pinto while spraying cars, which, if proved, would have shown that he owned both. That would have nailed him.

The shared ivy hairs suggested that the Pinto had been in contact with both girls' jumpers and probably had been at the scene of the killings. This, and the various matching fibres, made it almost certain that the killer, whoever it was, had worn the Pinto at the time. It was also very likely that whoever had worked on Bishop's friend's car and had used the paint can had worn this sweatshirt.

The link between the Pinto and the murders was extremely strong. Slightly weaker was the link between Bishop and the Pinto, but that was tantalizingly close. The key was in proving it belonged to Bishop and that he had been wearing it when the girls were killed. Unfortunately, even this amount of circumstantial evidence would only stand up if the paint, and fibres, were totally unique. Without that certainty, all it would take was a smart lawyer to chip away at each piece of the theory, bit by bit, until the whole house of cards came crashing down.

Paint and clothing fibres do not contain DNA, so, in the 1980s, cast-iron proof was rare that one item came from or had been in contact with another. The problem also remained that no one had seen Bishop wearing that exact top on the night and there was nothing on it that could be scientifically proven to show he did. It did not take Jenny Johnson long to change her almost spontaneous identification of the Pinto to DC Evans into a denial.

It seemed irrefutable that all the paint samples were from a similar source. However, a reputable owner of a car accessory shop, just a few hundred yards from Wild Park and Stephens Road, scuppered that hope when he showed that in the month before the girls were killed he had sold around thirty cans of the same red paint.

All was not lost though. During the post mortem, three hairs and a fibre were found on Nicola's stomach. An examination of these could go a long way to putting Bishop – or someone else – and the girls together at the time of the murders. It would only take a small leap to then conclude who the killer was.

But no one thought to examine them. This was a huge oversight, the like of which as a detective both junior and senior I have never come across or heard of before or since. Given the lack of hard evidence and the fact that other forensic techniques were pretty basic, it beggars belief that these fragments, which could have nailed the killer once and for all, were overlooked.

25

Bishop had originally been required to surrender, following his bail, on 4 December 1986 but at the last minute he was ordered to turn himself in at 10 a.m. the day before. Mr Oxford had, in the meantime, decided he could not act for Bishop so he was accompanied by his new dapper, confrontational London solicitor, Ralph Haeems. Bishop must have wondered why he was being brought in early.

The formalities out of the way, Bishop was marched to an interview room where DC Dave Wilkinson went through the motions required when someone surrenders to custody: 'I am arresting you for the murders of Nicola Fellows and Karen Hadaway. You do not have to say anything unless you wish to do so, but anything you do say may be given in evidence.'

Bishop, predictably, replied, 'I'm not guilty, leave it out.'

With those words he was formally back in custody. He might have guessed what was coming next but, still, it would have hit him like a thunderbolt.

'You are charged that between 8 October 1986 and 10 October 1986 at Brighton in the County of East Sussex you murdered Karen Hadaway, contrary to common law. You are further charged that between 8 October 1986 and 10 October 1986 at Brighton in the County of East Sussex you murdered Nicola Fellows, contrary to common law. Do you wish to say anything? You do not have to say anything unless you wish to do so, but anything you do say may be given in evidence.'

He was taken straight to a cell, with no prospect of bail this time.

The following morning, he was driven the short distance in a police van to Hove Magistrates' Court for his first court appearance. Arriving a full ninety minutes early, he was met with an angry crowd already gathering in the rain, hoping to glimpse the monster who had robbed two girls of their innocent lives.

These initial remand hearings are brisk and businesslike. They are no different whether the defendant is a suspected murderer or shoplifter. In front of a small audience, including two of Bishop's brothers but not the victims' families, the charges were put. He was not asked to plead but the outline of the case was read and after confirmation that there would be no bail application and a passionate assertion of his innocence by his solicitor, Bishop was remanded in custody.

As he was taken to Brixton Prison in a police convoy, in a last flex of their muscles, two of his brothers made a futile attempt to follow it. It was not clear what they intended to do but the accompanying officers from the convoy gave them short shrift and they headed off home.

Being formally charged with the murder of two little girls is as bad as it gets. Bishop knew there was no way he was going anywhere, until he had been tried – even if then. In the meantime, locked up in prison as a child killer, his life would be hell. Despite prisoners' own protestations of innocence, they are rarely afforded the benefit of the doubt by their fellow inmates. Notwithstanding the inconvenient fact that Bishop was, in the eyes of the law, still presumed innocent, his fellow lags would convict him as soon as the prison gates slammed.

His life from now on was in serious danger. Almost all sex offenders, and those accused of offences against children, spend their lives protected in segregation. Even then they are not immune from the threat of merciless beatings, faeces in their food, gang rapes, being slashed with makeshift knifes or being killed themselves.

Bishop's family visited occasionally but most of his time in Brixton Prison was spent locked up in his cell. He was scared witless. Already branded a child killer, he complained his food was spiked with broken glass or phlegm as he collected it from the grinning orderlies. He claimed prison officers threatened him and that he was beaten with a lump of wood on one occasion. On another he was lucky when a jug of scalding water narrowly missed him. He said he was attacked when he answered a warder back. He had no friends and no allies. He lived a nightmare. Convinced that there was a concerted effort to poison him, he lived on nothing but the fruit, biscuits and crisps his family brought him. The most he dared eat from the kitchens was a handful of chips.

While the wheels of justice ground on in the background, the people of Brighton and Hove breathed a sigh of relief, content that finally the police had got their man and life could return to a semblance of normality. Yet if the period between arrest and charge is frenetic, the year before trial is frantic for police, prosecutors and defence alike.

26

In the 1980s, before a case could be heard at the Crown Court it needed to clear an 'Old Style Committal'. This involved bringing all the witnesses along to the magistrates' court for the Justices of the Peace to hear their evidence and decide whether there was a case to answer. Then, and only then, could it be heard at the higher court. In the meantime, the defendant had to be brought, often weekly, to appear just for progress to be monitored and the committal hearing set. All this generated an eye-watering mountain of paperwork and huge inconvenience and stress to civilian witnesses. Thankfully these events are confined to the judicial history books. Now murder charges are invariably 'sent' to the Crown Court the day after the charge is laid and the defendant appears there a few days later. Thereafter, all appearances are by video link saving time and cost for the hard-pressed criminal justice agencies.

In February 1987, Bishop appeared for the start of his committal hearing. All the prosecution evidence was laid out, tested and evaluated, a process that strung out over a whole month until the magistrates, quite predictably, decided there was sufficient evidence for Bishop to be tried. Meanwhile Ralph Haeems, the lawyer, was going to great lengths to muddy the waters. He regularly appeared in the media appealing for various anonymous people who had called his office to get back in touch. They never did, or if they did they were never called as defence witnesses. We will never know whether they actually existed.

In the small hours of one morning, while Bishop was on remand, Detective Superintendent Bernie Wells was woken by his ringing phone. The inspector on the other end sheepishly told him that Ralph Haeems had turned up unannounced at the police station demanding to see him. He was with two witnesses who had spoken to a third who could unequivocally testify to Barrie Fellows being the killer.

Sceptical as he was, Bernie knew he had to turn out. This was bound to be yet another smokescreen to cast doubt on Bishop's guilt but to ignore a line of enquiry recommended by the defence would be judicial suicide. So, Bernie called DCI Chris Page and told him to meet him at the police station. They arrived around the same time and walked into the interview room together. They were met by an angry Haeems, with two teenage girls sitting meekly beside him.

'I told you, you had the wrong man. These girls know someone who knows it was Fellows. I demand you interview them then arrange for my client to be released.'

'We will interview them,' Bernie assured the seething solicitor.

'And I'll be present while you do.'

'No, you won't. Mr Page will interview one and I will interview the other. They are our witnesses.'

Haeems tried to protest but Bernie was adamant. Both girls came out with the same bland story. They had been chatting to a girl who said that she had seen Fellows kill the two girls and could prove it. Bernie and Chris told Haeems they would see this other girl straightaway. His assumption that he would be allowed to go with them was quickly quashed.

Having tracked her down, at around four in the morning, they soon realized that this was either a set-up or she was a fantasist. It was immediately very clear to Bernie she had learning difficulties. Thankfully her parents were there so, with them by her side, he gently probed.

'I'm told you know who killed Karen and Nicola.'

'Yes, Barrie Fellows,' she barked.

'Oh, did he? How do you know that?'

'Because he's ugly,' she snapped.

'I see,' said Bernie, turning his gaze to the parents who looked as confused as he did.

'Any other way you know he killed them?'

'It's obvious isn't it. He's ugly. He must have done it.'

'Did you see him kill them?'

'No but he must have. He's ugly.'

Bernie and Chris made their excuses, apologized and left promptly.

When they returned to the police station, Haeems was eagerly waiting to hear the news. Bernie built him up by solemnly inviting him into his office.

'You're right, Mr Haeems, it seems it was Barrie Fellows after all,' he said, poker-faced.

'I told you, Superintendent. I knew all along. What did she say?'

'She said . . . "*It's obvious. He's ugly*",' Wells roared as he watched Haeems crumple before scurrying out and away.

With the pre-trial preparations still occupying a huge team, Bernie was told he was being considered for promotion to Chief Superintendent. However, as was the way in the 1980s, he would need to move to a uniformed posting before that could happen. Having been a detective for most of his service, the thought of working in uniform in a more rural division did not appeal. But the prize at the end of it was tempting so, just before Bishop stood trial, Detective Superintendent Wells became Superintendent Wells and began running policing in Horsham. A change of leadership at such a crucial stage never bodes well, however proficient the replacement.

While Bishop was enduring a private hell in prison, the Fellows and Hadaway families were suffering far more on the outside. It was nearly four months before the girls could be laid to rest. Wednesday 4 February 1987 will be etched in the families' hearts forever. The whole community turned out to say goodbye. The cortège set off from Newick Road, flowers adorning the hearses' roofs. As they crept the short distance to Bear Road Cemetery, onlookers stood silent.

The eulogies broke every heart and Barrie, Sue, Michelle and Lee were comforted by friends and family, while they consoled their own distraught children. The floral tributes talked of sleeping well, precious daughters and the love and pain that had been left behind. Their white coffins were buried in graves side by side, so they could comfort each other as they rested in peace, a white stone angel between them.

27

On 11 November 1987, after nearly a year of incarceration, a pristine and miraculously unmarked Bishop stood flanked by prison officers in the dock of Court One, Lewes Crown Court.

The nineteenth-century building stands majestically at the top of School Hill in the shadow of the ruin of Lewes Castle. It faces the opulent White Hart Hotel, less than a hundred yards from the spot where seventeen sixteenth-century Protestant martyrs were burned at the stake by order of Queen Mary I. A fitting place to dispense today's fairer and more humane justice.

On the narrow steps, outside its white-fronted facade, nervous defendants puff a last cigarette as they wait apprehensively for the jury to announce their fate. They jostle for space with gowned barristers frantically scanning their papers or taking instructions from clients or the Crown Prosecution Service.

Over the years I have seen many of my cases won, and a few lost, within these walls. During murder trials I practically lived at the court, either waiting to give evidence or as Queen's Counsel's gofer.

Whatever you felt about Bishop, it is understandable why, when faced with a lifetime of looking over his shoulder, he would do anything to secure a not guilty verdict. A life sentence would not be worth living. No other suspects had emerged in the thirteen months since the murders. Bishop, in the eyes of the police, was the only person who could have possibly committed these dreadful crimes. His equivocal accounts of where he was and what he was doing over those critical hours between the girls going out to play and their deaths had remained conveniently confused. Clearly someone was lying.

Jenny was vague too. Was he at the pub when she got home, or was he indoors doing the washing, having just had a bath?

Then there was the Pinto sweatshirt. While there was no definitive evidence that Bishop was wearing it when the girls were killed, it seemed almost certain that it had been worn by whoever killed them. With the variety of paints on both the sweatshirt and his trousers, it was incredibly likely that the top was his, as Jenny had said then denied. And crucially, how did Bishop manage to describe the girls' repose when he simply did not see them well enough after they had been found? Time would tell.

Prosecutions rarely rely on one irrefutable fact. Some testimonies and some forensic results are stronger than others but even if a case is built on a cornucopia of circumstantial evidence that can sometimes be enough.

As Bishop stood in the dock, the packed courtroom hushed as the indictments were read out. None of the jurors who would hear, assess and interpret all of the evidence for and against him could have been oblivious to the murders. However, they would never have expected to try the sole suspect a year later. Would they have made their minds up already? The judge warned them to ignore everything but the evidence they heard in the courtroom – but would they? Could they?

Bishop had appointed a formidable state-funded defence team. All he could do was trust their skill in seeding the tiniest doubt in the jurors' minds. Achieve that and, assuming they heeded the judge's warning, he would walk. His barristers would have reassured him that there was, indeed, no 'slam dunk' piece of evidence to nail him so they could methodically chip away at the patchwork of suspicions.

It is the prosecution's job to prove, beyond reasonable doubt, that the person in the dock is guilty. The accused has to prove nothing, only inject uncertainty. If just three jurors waivered, Bishop would walk free. Scanning their faces, he would be trying to read which, if any, would wobble. He could not go back to that hellhole where he had miraculously survived since he was charged.

Brian Leary QC, for the prosecution, was an accomplished orator and his opening statement was sound. He did what great barristers do best in hooking juries. He set out the whole sordid story as simply but as vividly as he could. He talked of play-mates, worried mothers, swirling mist. He painted the picture of hundreds of cops and locals frantically searching until Kevin Rowland and Matthew Marchant stumbled across the pitiful bodies.

Carefully avoiding language or detail that would shock the jury – that would come later – he described the girls' injuries and the signs of their abuse. Then he moved on, cataloguing Bishop's fluid accounts, the sightings of him and the Pinto sweatshirt. Leary drummed home that it was Bishop, and only Bishop, who could possibly have killed the girls. Any suggestion they had been killed by anyone else was a ruse to deflect from the man sat in the dock.

Drawing on his brief summary, he insisted that Bishop had become overwhelmed with sexual desire and tried to molest Nicola. Then, struck with the realization that he was doomed if there were any witnesses to his perversion, he strangled both girls with his bare hands. If the trial had stopped there, Bishop would have been finished.

But his wily lead counsel, Ivan Lawrence QC MP (it is almost unthinkable that today a sitting MP would be the lead barrister in a major criminal trial), reclined expressionless, taking it all in; he was plotting where to aim his arrows. Trials are never won on opening statements and Lawrence was convinced this one was based on a devastating flaw.

On the second day, the trial was sensationally halted. A woman juror fell ill with a stomach upset. Reluctant at that early stage to continue with just eleven jurors, Mr Justice Schiemann QC – adjudicating his first murder trial – adjourned, warning that they may not resume for a few days. Recognizing the jurors' curiosity had been piqued, Schiemann drummed home his grave warning that they were not to visit the scene, nor turn private detective in the meantime.

The jurors must have been devastated when, on what would have been day three, the judge instructed that the trial would start again but with an all-new jury. When it resumed the next day, an emotional Susan Fellows revealed that some on the estate had accused her husband of being the girls' killer. Whispers had grown until their house was daubed with 'Fellows Out', 'Murderer', 'Child Killer' and 'Child Molester' in white paint. As if they were not suffering enough.

She went on to take the jury through her recollections of that devastating night. In cross-examination she was quizzed to verify Barrie Fellows' and Dougie Judd's movements. Mr Lawrence was laying the foundations for what would become a drip-feed of suggestions – and only suggestions – that the killer was even closer to home than Bishop.

When it was Barrie's turn to take the stand, he resolutely confirmed his movements on the night and rebuffed accusations that he had previously broken Susan's grandmother's nose. The pressure increased when Mr Lawrence challenged him about what happened when Bishop visited him while on bail. He also alleged Barrie had shown flashes of temper towards Nicola. Barrie held up well, but the seeds of doubt were being sown. For Bishop and his team, it was all going to plan.

Karen's parents, on the other hand, were never in the frame. Like the Fellowses, they were hugely protective of their daughter but had a lower profile than Barrie so attracted less ire. Michelle poignantly told the court she would forever be telling Karen to stay away from Bishop and Marion Stevenson. She took exception to their relationship given the age gap and Jenny, like her, being heavily pregnant. She described the dreadful night, calling out along Brighton seafront, then how hope was cruelly ripped away as she saw the officers running into Wild Park's woods.

As with every witness who knew or saw Bishop, she was asked a simple question, 'Have you ever seen Russell Bishop wearing this sweatshirt?', as the Pinto was lifted aloft.

'No,' came her reply. Of course she had not. Mr Lawrence already knew that. The first rule of advocacy is to never ask a question you do not know the answer to.

Sometimes juries have to be shown gruesome and distressing photographs. Be it dismembered corpses, injuries inflicted on the helpless or hardcore pornography, they must study the images of cruelty or depravity that are central to the trial.

When I was running a major child abuse image investigation in 2002, we provided our investigators with regular counselling, such was the volume and nature of the revolting images they viewed day in, day out. I have known many SOCOs suffer breakdowns following years of poring over countless brutal murder scenes and mutilated bodies. The police are only human and they bleed on the inside like everyone else. What chance was there then for a juror whose experience of horror was confined to the odd hour-long TV crime drama or World War II movie?

The pictures of Karen and Nicola were dreadful. How do you prepare twelve ordinary people for seeing the bruised, grimy and grazed corpses of two sexually abused playmates? Despite having the nature of the charges laid out for them, hearing the eloquent prose of counsel and the more down-to-earth testimony of witnesses, seeing it with their own eyes would scar them for life.

If the jury struggled it was hardly surprising that, as Lawrence brandished the explicit photos while cross-examining Kevin Rowland, Barrie Fellows stormed out of court. It would be disingenuous to claim that counsel was trying to shock, but it was rare that a judge would feel compelled to instruct a barrister to put pictures away as Mr Justice Schiemann did.

The finding of the bodies was central to the prosecution case. For Bishop to describe so accurately how the girls lay it was clear he must have seen them before Rowland did. After that, he simply did not get close enough. He must be the killer. The defence therefore banked on being able to render young Rowland and Marchant so unreliable that the jury would take their recollections of Bishop's movements at the den with a pinch of salt. It was put to nineteen-year-old Rowland that with 'all his experience as a hospital porter' he would surely have gone closer to the body than the fifteen feet he claimed. Wouldn't he have checked in case she was still alive?

Next in Mr Lawrence's sights was the discrepancy between Rowland's original account to the police, that he saw both bodies, to now, that he saw just the one. An *Evening Argus* interview he had given shortly after finding the bodies also came back to bite him. In that, he repeated that he had seen two bodies who appeared to be sleeping in each other's arms. He explained he had told Barrie Fellows that just to provide him a little comfort and had therefore repeated it to the journalist for consistency. The coincidence of this fabricated tableau matching the reality, despite, like Bishop, Rowland not having been in a position to see, was left for the jury to ponder.

Marchant had no option but to admit to lying to the police in the same way as his friend. If he had also lied to the police, why was it only Bishop in the dock?

It is a big ask to expect traumatized witnesses to present evidence that is perfectly faithful to their first account. Witnessing crimes, finding bodies or hearing confessions are, thankfully, alien to the average man or woman. Memory can become tunnelled so that part of the event is recalled in fine detail while peripheral information is blurred. Despite the expectations of investigators and lawyers, it is virtually impossible for a shocked or stressed witness to give untainted testimony.

Kevin and Matthew had known that they were looking for two girls. Is it not reasonable, either through their own minds conflating what they expected to see with what they actually saw or by an inadvertent slip made to an interviewer, that they claimed they saw both girls? Over a year later, with all they now knew and under the glare and scrutiny of bewigged and learned gentlemen, scrutinized by dozens of journalists, family and friends, and a jury hanging on their every word, it was no wonder their recollection was shaky.

But that is how the adversarial system works. Ignoring the natural frailty of the human mind and its inability to recall like a mainframe computer is grist to the mill.

In fairness, the prosecution similarly exploited Bishop's inconsistencies. That is counsel's job, to shed doubt and influence juries, but it can make an honest witness appear dissembling, with major consequences for the verdict.

The first real drama came on day five.

28

It was hardly surprising that, despite being called by the prosecution, the combative Jenny Johnson was no help whatsoever in proving her partner was a killer. Nor was anyone shocked that she blamed a police fit-up for Bishop being on trial. She painted a picture of a harmonious relationship with its normal ups and downs. During sex on the night of the murders she said she saw no scratches on Bishop's body. She maintained he was neither violent – Marion Stevenson later refuted this by recalling him punching Jenny – nor prone to any 'tendencies to perversion'.

It was during the questioning over her original statement that her mood changed. In her initial version, she had identified the Pinto as Bishop's, having previously described a similar top he owned and even recalling him struggling to wash the paint out. By now she'd had a rethink. She wanted the court to believe this was all concocted by the detectives who had kept her up all night and behaved 'like animals' towards her. She blamed her apparent poor eyesight for mistaking the garment they showed her for another. She now insisted he had never owned a sweatshirt like the Pinto after all.

She put her signing of the statement, she allegedly never read, down to her rage that Bishop was still carrying on with Marion Stevenson. She then said she would have signed anything to get rid of the police. Despite being eight months pregnant and under extreme stress, it might be thought that having her partner incarcerated on suspicion of murder could have prompted a modicum of diligence in checking what she was signing. When specifically asked in court which account was true, she stuck by her current version rather the one at the time when events would have been fresher.

For the defence, it was critical she kept to the new narrative. Jenny knew that were she to put that Pinto sweatshirt in the hands of, or rather on the back of, Bishop he was doomed. If, as the prosecution maintained, she had unambiguously confirmed it was his then he would never see the light of day again. She had to deny it and keep denying it until her dying breath.

With the sweatshirt being so central to the case, Dr Anthony Peabody, the forensic scientist, was never going to be in for an easy ride. If he were able to convince the court that Bishop had worn it – despite the plethora of witnesses for both the defence and prosecution who denied seeing him ever do so – that should be job done. The jury would have little choice but to convict.

Bishop had accepted that he owned the blue–grey trousers on which four fibres from the Pinto were found. He never denied that he had worn those trousers on the day of the killings. But he did not, and would never, accept those Pinto fibres had transferred to the trousers when he had worn both garments together.

The only option open to the defence therefore, however dangerous, was to allege police conspiracy or cock-up. It was far safer to blame the latter and here it was handed to them on a plate. The chain of evidence from when the sweatshirt was handed in to the police to being taken back to the police station was incomplete. Any potential exhibit coming into the hands of the police should have been put into a forensically sterile bag, sealed and signed by all who touched it. Its integrity and continuity would then be set out plainly for all to see. Instead the Pinto had sat outside the exhibits store until Eddie Redman examined it for blood. But, removing the hindsight spectacles, this sweatshirt came to the police as found property, not an exhibit. To all intents and purposes, it was preserved. The police just could not show that. It certainly never came into contact with the girls' clothes.

Court advocacy, particularly in cross-examination, is a real skill. Defence counsel aims to foster doubt in the jury's collective mind that a witness is telling the truth, stopping short of branding them a liar. Blinding the court with science is also an own goal; a jury needs to be able to follow an argument. So, a good barrister will proffer alternative hypotheses as to why a witness is saying what they are. Perhaps they did not see things as clearly as they thought. Perhaps the passage of time has fogged their memory. Perhaps an alternative explanation makes their assertions less than certain.

By leading the witness down a particular path, encouraging him or her to admit other, seemingly innocuous, possibilities and by gradually increasing the sum value of their concessions, the inquisitor can bring it all to a climax that hopefully will hit the jury like a steam train and make them question all they have assumed to be true.

That should be easier with non-professional witnesses, those for whom it is their first and only time in the witness box. But professionals can become complacent in their ability to parry these attacks. They can assume that, given they are in court three or four times a year, they can spot an ambush coming and head it off at the pass.

That can be fatal. They may be no stranger to the witness box but their opponent – the barrister – is there every day and holds all the cards. Overconfidence or, as in the forensic elements of this case, failing to cover all the bases, can crash-land an otherwise decent case. Any worthy defence barrister will approach a case as if he or she were prosecuting and vice versa. The same should be true for detectives.

Forget any of the seven Ps – Proper Prior Planning Prevents Piss Poor Performance – and, despite all your efforts, defeat looms.

Pinto sweatshirt aside, if any forensic evidence could link the girls, their clothing or the murder scene to the trousers Bishop said he was wearing, then a conviction must follow. Prim Dr Peabody found no such link.

When questioned whether he could, on a scientific basis, say that the Pinto sweatshirt was worn by the murderer, all he could say was, 'it *could* have been.' He might have tried to be a little less aloof.

Lawrence had the scientist on the hook. He just needed to keep him there to induce enough doubt over those crucial links that were so central to the Crown's case so that the jury would have no choice but to acquit. He followed up with another question he knew the answer to. Scientifically, could Peabody say that the Pinto was ever actually worn by Bishop? 'No, but it *could* have been.' Then came a stream of questions designed to test whether the scientists were charged with finding the killer, whoever it may be, or just to build a case against Bishop:

'Have you examined Dougie Judd's clothing?' Mr Lawrence asked.

'No,' replied Dr Peabody.

'Have you examined Barrie Fellows' clothing?'

'No.'

'Have you examined Marion Stevenson's clothing?'

'Yes, twice.'

'Why?'

'To see if I could link Bishop to the murders through her.'

'Not to see if she was linked to the murders?'

'No.'

'So, the purpose of examining the Pinto was not to see who it was linked to but just to see if Bishop was linked to it?' the barrister concluded.

'Yes,' conceded the scientist.

Another line of attack was the presence, or otherwise, of Bishop's dog's hairs on the Pinto. Initially none were found but after the defence scientists discovered other dog hairs on the sweatshirt, Peabody also found three that could belong to Misty. He explained he left that particular examination to last as he felt it was 'low priority'. Lawrence went to the brink of accusing Peabody of interfering with the evidence. His observation that it 'just so happened' the hairs were subsequently found and that this was an 'interesting coincidence', prompted the most robust challenge from the judge.

'Are you suggesting the witness tampered with the evidence?'

Obviously, Lawrence could not assert that and neither did he want to. Just airing those thoughts in front of the jury was enough to suggest all was not squeaky clean. Peabody was furious. He stopped giving his evidence to scribble the insinuation down. I have never seen a witness whip out a pen and paper to make their own notes while giving evidence. Neither, it seemed, had Lawrence, who challenged him before the judge followed suit. Peabody was unrepentant. He was determined to record what had been said so that 'I can remember it has been said for my own purpose.'

Dr Peabody's evidence did not cover the prosecution in glory. It seemed the police were furious too. Years later, Peabody would admit to having been pinned up against a wall by a senior police officer as he left court as, in his words, 'emotions ran naturally high.'

The challenges and counter-challenges between the two leading barristers had become a distraction. Leary, for the prosecution, called on the judge to stop his opponent asking hypothetical questions. Lawrence mocked Leary for getting dates wrong. This particular spat prompted Bishop to shout from the dock, 'My lord, I am innocent of these charges and my defence has the right to question this bloke.'

The judge had had enough and reminded the experienced barristers, 'This is a very serious trial. It is very nice to have games between the two of you, but don't.'

This must have been most unseemly to all sides. The victims' families must have wondered how Nicola and Karen's memory had been allowed to descend into such a petty squabble. Bishop's mother, Sylvia, took the debacle to new depths when she stormed out of court sobbing, 'I'm sorry, I just can't take any more,' pausing just before she disappeared through the door, to turn and shout 'Bastards'.

29

Examining rural crime scenes pays no respect to conservation. Awful as it may seem, when murder strikes in a copse or the open countryside, trees, shrubs and bushes that have been there for years are razed to the ground.

Sending lines of booted cops wielding sickles into a wood may seem at odds with the careful, systematic scientific harvest of other evidence but the methods are meticulous. The search for and retrieval of potential evidence that *is* there, together with proving what *is not* present, requires trees to be felled, bushes stripped and forest floors raked.

Just one month before the trial, Wild Park and its woodland were devastated by the same storm which unearthed Latifa Lachaal's skull.

While the landscape may have changed, both sets of counsel argued that seeing the park, its surroundings and topography would be invaluable for the jury to get a real sense of the evidence, enabling them to determine for themselves how credible each version was.

Given that, technically, the court was still in session during the visit, its planning and the security of the judge and jury was a top priority. It was unthinkable for this trial to falter a second time. The entire area had to be prepared, secured by officers and cordons and the whole process recorded. Judge, jury and counsel travelled in a private coach with motorcycle outriders warding off anyone inclined to disrupt their sanctity. The jury needed to see and appreciate, in this barely recognizable wood, exactly where the girls had lain. The simple white cross depicting the fateful spot was a sombre reminder that, amid all the highbrow legal argument and brickbats, this was all about two young girls robbed of their innocence and lives.

Having taken in Wild Park, they moved to the path by Moulsecoomb railway station where the Pinto sweatshirt was dumped. The short distance from the first place to the other, together with its convenience as a thoroughfare to Bishop's home, would not have been lost on the jurors. Once back in the courtroom, the graphic description of the girls' injuries moved some jurors to tears, so much so that the judge briefly halted the trial to allow them to regain their composure.

The interactions between Bishop and the police prior to his arrest were critical to defence and prosecution alike. As he had yet to be considered a suspect, there had been no need for him to be read his rights. That was only necessary when the police had enough to think he was the offender. Until then, they could ask him what they liked and his answers could still be used to support a prosecution.

That may seem unfair, but suspicion has to come from some-where, and the jury needs to know its origins. Crucially, this evidence allowed the jury to hear, in Bishop's own words, his lies, his changing accounts and his selective amnesia.

Bishop was not the only person to receive extra attention in those early days, one of the investigators, DC Doug Penry, reminded the jury. Dougie Judd, Barrie Fellows, Kevin Rowland and Matthew Marchant had all come under scrutiny. But it seemed that Bishop was the only one paranoid enough to believe that he was going to be put in the frame.

Wisely, the defence chose not to put Bishop on the stand. Without doubt he would have been tied up in knots during cross-examination – the jury would see the real person. Mr Law-rence had excelled in casting doubt over the forensic evidence which purported to nail him. He painted Bishop as a hapless, harmless Walter Mitty, but no killer. Even an incompetent barrister would see the dangers in putting Bishop at the mercy of the prosecutor. Lawrence was the best of the best. He needed his client to stay silent and for doubt to ferment in the jury's mind.

30

Lawrence must have been amazed when the prosecution boxed themselves into a corner by asserting the girls must have been dead by 6.30 p.m. – especially as Dr West had suggested the time being between 7 p.m. and 8 p.m. – as that was when Bishop was seen walking home. But was he walking home? No one saw him actually arrive in Stephens Road. Here, Lawrence would play his trump card.

The defence called several witnesses who could either further muddy the prosecution's waters or perpetuate the image of Bishop as a blameless lamb who, aside from being a rascal, could do no wrong. Some fared better than others. One young boy could pinpoint the timings of seeing the girls, then forgot where he was for nearly five hours around the critical time. Another witness could not be sure if it was Karen or Nicola he saw by the roadside.

A few defence witnesses were granted anonymity, as they claimed their lives had been threatened after talking to the police. It was odd that little had been known of these threats until the day they gave evidence. Nowadays, with notice and the leave of the court, some intimidated witnesses can give evidence from behind screens, remain anonymous or speak from a video link. In this trial they were simply assigned pseudonyms based upon the colour of their clothing.

So, Mrs 'White' stepped into the witness box. She struggled with why she had not mentioned to Barrie Fellows, when he came around to her house with the police on the evening the girls disappeared, that Nicola had waved to her just two hours previously. However, her timings were crucial as she saw the girls at 6.30 p.m, when the prosecution said Bishop had headed home. By which time, the jury were told, he must have killed them.

After yet another witness had declined to be named, the judge was uncompromising in his warnings to those doing the threatening. He described 'enormous penalties' and that those responsible would find themselves in prison 'for a long time'. Who knows how many witnesses had been successfully scared into silence.

Understandably, potential witnesses as well as victims are often terrified after being threatened with some terrible revenge should they give evidence in court. In those days, sharing court-waiting facilities with the defendant's friends and family was commonplace and only compounded their fears.

Most people give their evidence without incident, but convincing an intimidated witness they will be safe takes some doing.

As the trial drew to a close, all that remained was for each side to press home the main tenets of their case. Summing up is a skilful balancing act. For the prosecution it is about reminding the jury of the bricks of evidence their case is built on. Regardless of it having been questioned during the trial, or that the evidence may be only circumstantial, their job is to leave the jury with just one conclusion – they must convict the person in the dock. The defence on the other hand just have to suggest alternatives. If there is damning evidence that blows the Crown's case out of the water, then they will drive that home. If not, all they have to do is hint.

The prosecution emphasized Bishop's lies and inconsistencies; his whereabouts, the links between him, the Pinto sweatshirt and the murder scene. His inexplicable fear that the finger of blame would be pointed at him, even before the bodies had been found. How he knew exactly how the bodies lay, even though he could not possibly have seen them when they were discovered. These simple facts pointed to only one killer. Russell Bishop.

For the defence who, aside from the judge, always have the last word, it was much simpler. With no burden of proof, Ivan Lawrence QC MP just cast doubt. Bishop had no alibi, far from it. There was no exculpatory forensic evidence nor was there proof of someone else being the killer. But there was more than enough for Lawrence to work with. He questioned the assumption that only Bishop could have been responsible by reminding the jury of all the points Barrie Fellows, Dougie Judd, Matthew Marchant, Kevin Rowland and even Marion Stevenson could not answer.

He asked whether it was unthinkable that one of those individuals could have been the killer. On hearing this, Barrie Fellows stormed out of court, only for Lawrence to then clarify that he could not have actually been the killer. He maintained that he was just making the point that there was as much evidence and suspicion around him as there was Bishop; that is, not enough.

While others had long since dismissed the 'ginger-haired man', Lawrence resurrected him for the jury. Given he was never traced, they were free to hypothesize over his guilt. No eyewitnesses put Bishop with both girls after PC Dadswell saw them. There was no confession and the forensic evidence fell short of proving Bishop wore the Pinto sweatshirt on the night of the murders.

The very last person to have his say was the judge. His was a precarious task. Not only did he have to sum up the key evidence, and direct on the law itself, but he also, very carefully, had to suggest which points the jury might wish to dwell on. It is never the judge's job to favour either side but by posing questions around specific points, his or her thoughts can often be inferred. Crucially though, a judge has to be fair and accurate, and direct the jury properly and according to both statute and case law.

This was Mr Justice Schiemann's first big criminal trial and he summed up fairly. He was clear that while no one ever suggested Bishop had previously sexually assaulted or abused children, it was perfectly understandable why he was arrested. He said they had to decide whether the case had been proved beyond reasonable doubt. He drummed this in by saying, 'Our law provides that the burden of proof is on the prosecution. They have to prove their case and our law provides that you are not to convict any individual of any crime, be it never so grave or never so petty, unless you are sure that he is guilty of that crime. I cannot emphasize that too much. It is most important.'

While all judges in every trial up and down the country will make this point, his words were particularly notable. He was not suggesting whether he thought Bishop was guilty or not. That was irrelevant. What he was saying was if they could not be one hundred per cent sure they must acquit. He was reminding them that the bar has to be high – very high. Had the prosecution reached it?

To help them he set the jury three questions:

If you are not sure that the girls were dead by six thirty, acquit.

If you are not sure that the Pinto was worn by Bishop that night, acquit.

If you are not sure that the Pinto was worn by the murderer, acquit.

With those words ringing in their ears the jury, when he sent them out on the morning of 10 December 1987, was very unlikely to come to any other conclusion than they did.

Despite the evidence and judge's directions, juries can be fickle beasts. I gave up trying to read them long ago. They are untrained. They come from all walks of life. They are affected by the same biases and prejudices as the rest of us.

And you never know what is going through their minds or what they are discussing. Because of that, they are the jewel in our criminal justice system.

It is pointless pinning your hopes on 'the Colonel Blimp chap second from the end in the front row', as he seems to be glaring with impatience every time the defence counsel rises to their feet. The 'tweedy woman far left at the back' could just as easily be on your side as the defendant's, regardless of her bearing a striking resemblance to his mum.

The time a jury takes to consider its verdict is also no predictor of the outcome. I remember a two-week trial of two defendants charged with attempted murder during which, with no proof, officers were accused of sprinkling the victim's blood on the defendants' clothing.

When we entered the fourth day waiting for the jury to return, we were starting to believe that they actually thought we were corrupt. That would be the only basis upon which they could acquit. However, shortly after His Honour Judge Michael Coombe allowed them to return a majority verdict – one upon which at least ten of the twelve were agreed – they promptly and unanimously found both thugs guilty.

We were baffled as to what on earth they were doing for all that time. Still, we got there in the end. It is hard to explain how important the right verdict is in a big case. Especially if you have been close to the victim or their family. You feel you owe them the right result and the burden of that lies heavily on the shoulders. There is nothing sweeter than a guilty verdict to validate the months of hard work and expectation and to give the victim some form of closure. If things do not work out as you had planned, though, as a professional you have to move on quickly.

The case against Bishop was strong but not unassailable, as Ivan Lawrence had shown. The time of death was a huge problem, especially with it being the first of the judge's three questions. The police and press remained confident, however. Perhaps the journalists missed the end of the summing-up, or at least the direction of what to do if the jury believed the girls were alive after 6.30 p.m. as it was never reported.

The police briefed Jon Buss, the crime reporter for the *Evening Argus*, in advance. They shared all the background that could only be made public once the guilty verdicts had been delivered. This was common practice in those days and, in their optimism, the *Argus* did not believe the pages of copy that Buss and his colleagues Jim Hatley and Phil Mills had prepared would be wasted.

In 1987, the first edition of the *Evening Argus* came out at noon, another around 4 p.m. and then a final version would hit the streets about 6 p.m. It sold around a hundred thousand copies a day, with an estimated 2.4 people reading each copy across Sussex. That was nearly a quarter of a million people who, well before the days of rolling news channels, could read that day's headlines before they sat down for tea.

To stay ahead of the game, journalists needed to do their homework and these background briefings were as good for the police as the newspapers. They provided all the detail the court may not have heard and, with it, reassurance the right person was behind bars.

The journalists checked and rechecked all they had. They burned the midnight oil so that when the guilty verdicts rang out, a quick phone call to the office would flick a switch, the presses would roll and the truth would be in the shops, on the news stands and in the readers' hands within hours.

Of course, there might be an appeal, but Bishop was going down for these horrendous crimes and their sales would soar. If he did challenge his inevitable conviction, that would be another red-letter day for the hardworking hacks. Another chance to tell the whole grim, sordid but utterly gripping story, and another chance to celebrate Bishop's conviction.

31

'Not guilty.'

Two words that rocked the nation.

Two words repeated a second time by the foreman – once for Nicola and once for Karen. The packed courtroom was stunned. Some were elated.

In just a shade over two hours of deliberation, after one false start and four weeks of evidence, Bishop was to walk free. One juror wept. Lee Hadaway, after all the dignity he had shown throughout, buried his head in his hands and also sobbed. Sylvia Bishop collapsed in tears as one of her other sons vaulted the dock-rail to embrace his brother. In the melee, he was dragged off, shouting and cheering, by three prison officers as they bundled him out of court. Sylvia, while being subdued by a policewoman, shouted, 'If my husband has a heart attack I'll kill you.'

As for Bishop, he looked stunned. He remained in the dock, blubbering with his fists in his eyes. Taking in the mayhem around him he suddenly snapped, banged his hands down on the dock and bellowed, 'Shut up, shut up. Take it easy.'

Alec Bishop, Russell's brother, ran from court, burst out onto the street and, with a punch in the air, yelled a jubilant 'Not guilty, lads,' to the dozens of onlookers blocking the road as they waited for news. The street fell silent.

As the uproar in the court abated, the judge formally released Bishop, who was whisked away in his solicitor's Mercedes. He then thanked the jury for their efforts and, given the emotional strain of the case, excused them from further jury service for five years. One notable absentee from court for the verdict was Barrie Fellows. His brother, Nigel Heffron, explained that he could not bring himself to be there on such a day.

Outside the building, Jim Hatley and what seemed to be half of the UK's press were eager to elicit quotes from all the key players.

Before he left with his client, Ralph Haeems put in his two-penny worth. 'An innocent man has been locked up for over a year. He's been treated very badly. I just hope he is able to recover from this. I could never bring myself to believe that young Bishop could have done it and I was never happy with the way the police conducted the case.'

Bishop's father, Roy, was delighted. 'We knew all along he was innocent. It is absolutely terrific. We just don't know what we are going to do when we get home,' he told the waiting journalists.

Some of the family could not wait for that though. They dashed across to the White Hart Hotel and started the party straight away.

For Sussex Police, the mood was sombre. 'This case was thoroughly investigated by us at the time. No new information emerged during the trial and we have no plans to reopen this enquiry. But obviously any fresh information that was put to us would be carefully looked at.' That was about as far as the police could go short of saying the jury got it wrong. Following other acquittals, the investigating officer will grudgingly add that they 'respect the verdict and the decision of the court'. Not this time though. They were seething.

Back in Moulsecoomb, residents feared scores would be settled.

In an interview with the *Evening Argus*, the North Moulsecoomb Residents' Association chairman, Colin Bradford, warned, 'Whichever way the verdict went, there was bound to be problems. There are a lot of rumours and threats flying around.' The police responded, 'After everything that happened, the last thing we need is more trouble.'

The news travelled around the force like wildfire. I was still living at Slaugham Manor, with many colleagues who knew the estate well, having pounded the beat in Brighton prior to their posting to Gatwick. I recall sitting in the Manor's small canteen, aghast at the acquittals. I chewed it over with friends. How could this be? He had to be guilty. What had gone wrong? Had the jury been nobbled?

Unable to use their prepared background pieces, reporters Jon Buss, Jim Hatley and Phil Mills cobbled together some hasty interviews and perspectives. To his credit, amid all the shock and elation, Buss's piece reminded readers what this was all about. Two little girls had been snatched, sexually assaulted and murdered just yards from their doorsteps. Whoever was responsible and irrespective of whether the case was strong enough, there was no escaping the fact their killer was free to strike again.

As for Bishop, the press could only paint him as a loveable clown. During an interview with Jim Hatley, Bishop's own mother labelled him a fantasist, trapped in his own world. It frustrated her that he was branded a killer rather than the attention-seeker he actually was. She admitted, 'We know what a wally he is really, and we can see why the police made him a suspect right from the start.'

Others described him as a petty, but popular, thief who was well known around the estate. In an instant his whole image changed from convicted-murderer-in-waiting to misunderstood scallywag.

With great care, the press highlighted the contradictory character that was Barrie Fellows. He had never hidden his criminal past, nor his shortcomings. Bishop's defence had set them all out but, at the end of the day, he was a bereaved father. His lifestyle might have been unconventional, but parents are not supposed to bury their children.

Shortly after the verdicts, Owen Lee-Winton, a private investigator, claimed in the press to have dossiers that would name the real Babes in the Wood killer. Lee-Winton was originally hired to track down a mysterious woman known only as 'Christine'. She told Ralph Haeems she had vital evidence that would clear Bishop.

It was strange that Lee-Winton did not think to reveal this trump card before the trial. It was no surprise that this woman turned out not to hold the key to the murders after all.

The Sunday after the acquittals, the *News of the World* printed an interview with Marion Stevenson, who claimed to have walked in on Barrie Fellows while he was watching a video of Nicola being raped by Dougie Judd. In hours of interviews, even while under arrest, there was never any record of her having mentioned this to the police. Only to the cash-wielding journalists was she happy to describe a father complicit in his child's abuse.

32

The acquittals bewildered Sussex Police. Their public stance hid an inner fury that a guilty man had got off the hook; they resolutely believed Bishop was the killer. No one accepted they had put an innocent man in the dock. But their response remained clear; there was no intention to reopen the investigation. Not unless new evidence came to light. And no one was expecting that any time soon. Some members of the public hoped this position shrouded a clandestine reinvestigation already in progress.

The law at the time prohibited Bishop being charged again, but what about the 'ginger-haired man', or maybe one of those whose names Mr Lawrence bandied about at the trial? The last thing the police needed was for any new leads to leak out. That would spark a furore, with the press crawling all over every snippet of gossip, scuppering all attempts at a measured and methodical reinvestigation of the facts. Maybe that's why the police were playing their cards so closely to their chest. Regardless of this speculation, there was no secret team of detectives crawling over the case looking for a second suspect. They honestly believed they had their man and had let him slip through their fingers.

The new year of 1988 was a hiatus period, with a community plunged back into the fear of a child killer at large and aching for the day they would pick up their *Evening Argus* to see the headline, 'Babes in the Woods Murders – Suspect Arrested'.

The Fellows and Hadaway families, however, were just at the start of their campaign. They knew the law but these were not people to be deterred. They quietly, and then not so quietly, resolved to fight for justice.

Bishop, on the other hand, moved back to Stephens Road as if nothing had happened. Buoyed by the acquittals he milled around as before, naively believing he would be welcomed back as a prodigal son. But people had heard the evidence and read the accusations – they were making their own minds up and their reaction was predictable.

A little over a year after Bishop walked from court, in January 1989 I earned my long-awaited posting from Gatwick to Brighton.

Those four years policing the airport did have its upsides. Given the time on my hands, I kept busy in other ways; I got chatting to a beautiful, blue-eyed British Caledonian check-in agent called Julie. She would later become my wife and mother of our triplets.

Soon after I met Julie, despite having stepped on the property ladder by buying a flat with a friend, Shaun Robbins, I realized that Julie and I were likely to stick together so, after just a year, we looked to buy a place of our own. I persuaded Shaun that we should put the flat on the market while Julie and I eyed up an end-of-terrace new-build on the other side of town.

I have no idea how we managed; we were still trying to sell the flat when the time came to close the deal on the house. So, with two mortgages, a wedding to plan and all the bills that go with that, Julie and I were like ships in the night. We worked stupid hours, barely clawing in enough money to pay our crippling debts.

Starting at Brighton was a rebirth. I took to street policing as if I had never been away. It was like riding a bike. After my probationary years in Bognor Regis, Brighton was not so different. Over the course of a year, policing Bognor was like working two completely different towns. Between Easter and September, it was mayhem. The huge Butlins holiday camp drew in thousands of visitors and casual staff, and the town buzzed 24/7. The staff were committed to helping guests unwind on their week-long holiday, in any way they could. Some went further and prided themselves on how many guests, and colleagues, they could steal from, copulate with or fight. Come September, someone flicked the houselights on. The mass exodus turned Bognor into a ghost town providing us with some well-earned catch-up time.

The only difference with Brighton was that it had no closed season.

Soon after being posted there I was allocated the Moulse-coomb response car. This was prestigious and a recognition of the way I had knuckled down since arriving. My crew mate, Dave Leeney, had less service than me but had served in Brighton longer. His local knowledge and my experience made for the perfect blend.

We knew about the Babes in the Wood murders. We knew of the acquittals. Dave had been in his probation at the time. The folklore of Inspector John Rodway's house-to-house enquiries and roadblocks was still regarded with fondness. Some even remembered the police being tolerated by the locals for a few short weeks.

When we cruised the estate, though, the bubble had well and truly burst. If the frostiness started after Bishop's arrest then a year on from him walking free and no sign of the killer being caught, a deep freeze had set in. I never recall actually being told to 'leave me alone and go and catch that child killer', but that was the mood and it was made very clear that we, the police, had let Moulsecoomb down. Bridges needed building and, despite Mac still working his magic, we yearned for the trust that had crumbled alongside the Bishop case.

While no one was reinvestigating the murders, some were poring over how, one way or another, the police had got it so wrong. After extensive lobbying by the furious families, the Home Office had commissioned a review into the Crown Prosecution Service's handling of the case. Local people were awaiting its findings with baited breath. While many were determined to paint Bishop as the innocent victim of police incompetence, others were not so sure.

Shortly after midnight on 11 April 1989, while Bishop, Jenny and their three young children were fast asleep in their Stephens Road flat, the sound of breaking glass jolted them awake. Bishop crawled out of bed and searched for the source of the noise. Unsure whether it was even in his flat, he checked outside. He happened to glance back through his own window and was terrified to see his lounge ablaze. He dashed back in, grabbed Jenny and the kids and led them out to safety. The two adults watched agog as the fire brigade raced into the road and battled to douse the flames. Both could only wonder how much worse it would have been if the fire had started in one of the bedrooms.

It did not take long for investigators to determine the root of the fire; a Molotov cocktail – a firebomb – had been hurled through the window. Catching it so quickly, Bishop and the fire brigade saved his family and their neighbours from being burned alive. Bishop was determined not to be bullied out of Brighton. Returning to the gutted flat was out of the question though so he put the ball firmly in the council's court to find him an alternative, safer, place to live. Eventually they moved a few hundred yards away to a house in Preston Barracks – terraces of council homes overlooking a disused Territorial Army base.

The police condemned the attack and Detective Sergeant Don Welch was tasked with finding the would-be killer. Many were interviewed – even Barrie Fellows was arrested as he might have had motive – but, despite Bishop's brother David putting up a £1,000 reward, the arsonist was never found.

Moulsecoomb's Councillor Gordon Wingate took up the fight. His outrage that Bishop and his family were attacked only strengthened his resolve for answers over the failed investigation. The Home Office told Wingate the CPS review would take four to six weeks. However, seventeen months later, in May 1989, it was still to surface. This silence sparked him to go public and seek justice for the families himself.

He fired off a letter to the then Home Secretary, Douglas Hurd, demanding answers. He reminded Mr Hurd of his own timescales that had long since expired, that two bereaved families were still looking for answers and that a child killer was still on the loose. He promised that if the Home Office could not intervene, he would push for a public inquiry. In a press interview, he hinted that a mystery caller had provided information that made publication even more vital. He was coy about revealing what had been said, but it was another suggestion there was more to the case than the public knew.

In June that year, an author and criminologist hit the local media claiming to know with one hundred per cent certainty who the killer was. Christopher Berry-Dee who, with Robin Odell, wrote about the case in his 1991 book *A Question of Evidence*, announced that six months working with the Fellows, Hadaway and Bishop families and speaking with around 500 people while re-examining case papers and forensic evidence meant he had traced the real killer.

He never has publicly revealed who he suspected. He did tell the *Evening Argus* and briefed the police about his suspicions but, after investigations, the CID dismissed it as nothing new. Many still wonder why Berry-Dee never named his suspect, even in his book published some four years after the killings. Perhaps he was not so sure after all. Perhaps his claims being rejected made him think again. Maybe we will never know, but his silence is deafening.

Undaunted, Berry-Dee remained a constant voice during the emerging campaign. On Sunday 30 July 1989, at St Francis' Hall in the heart of Moulsecoomb and just yards from where Nicola and Karen were last seen, in a distasteful alliance, their families, Councillor Wingate and the Bishops – including Russell – held a public meeting which would mark the beginning of a concerted push to force the police, once and for all, to reopen the case.

The families were stuck. Of course they wanted the investigation reopened. Of course they wanted the killer brought to justice. They had been knocking down every door they could to make that happen. In their hearts, though, they knew who the killer was, but what could they do other than be seen to support the campaign, even if it was orchestrated by Bishop and his family?

33

Since the trial, the Fellows and Hadaway families had all moved from Brighton but this was one of their many trips back. Only seventy people turned up to the meeting, which must have been disappointing. Nearly three years had passed since the murders and about a year and a half since the trial ended. Were people trying to put the tragedies behind them and just getting on with their lives? Or maybe it was the presence of Russell Bishop himself. The jury may have cleared him but many in the community remained uneasy over the verdict and, although they kept silent, there was barely a Sussex Police officer who believed it was a sound one. Neither did the girls' families, but they felt compelled to share the platform to seek justice.

Councillor Wingate announced plans to post leaflets through every door in Brighton and to collect thousands of signatures on a petition. This would culminate in a massive march from Wild Park to Brighton Police Station, three weeks later.

The march was to be led by the families and Russell Bishop. They resolved not leave the police station until the Chief Constable, Roger Birch, came out to meet them. The battle lines had been drawn and those present declared their support. Michelle Hadaway made a dignified and tearful plea for justice later at the meeting, expressing her frustration that she was still waiting for answers to her questions. This composure was in contrast to the behaviour of Sylvia Bishop who stood up and ranted to the gathering that 'it is about time we started shouting our mouths off to get something done about it'.

Councillor Wingate focused attention on finding the person

who wore the Pinto sweatshirt. He intended to deliver a photograph of it to every house in Moulsecoomb, convinced that its wearer was the killer. Lee Hadaway considered taking the protest to the House of Commons should Sussex Police not acquiesce to their demands. One of the most bizarre – perhaps tasteless – acts of that afternoon's events was the sight of Russell Bishop handing out the very petition forms that it was hoped would lead to the unmasking of a child killer. When interviewed on TV, wearing a fluorescent bib to denote his organizing role, he calmly said, 'I hope this march goes ahead and the police do not try and intervene. This case has got to be solved and there is more than enough evidence to get the investigation reopened. But the police are too embarrassed to do that, and we will have to keep up the pressure until someone is brought to justice.'

Of course he knew wherever any new evidence led, it could not be to his door. That would take a change in the centuries-old law which protected acquitted defendants from retrial, and no one was predicting that might happen.

Roger Birch had made it clear he would not be at the police station on the day of the march. His policy was to receive petitions in his office at Lewes Police Headquarters and he was not going to change that. However, he ensured that Dave Tomlinson, by now a Chief Superintendent and the divisional commander, would be there together with his deputy, Superintendent John Albon.

These were different times but I feel sure that in my time as a senior officer, given the profile of the murders and the strength of the case, the Chief Constable would have made an exception. Sir Roger, as he would later become, was a fine leader but the campaigners, including the bereaved families, wanted to make a public show of delivering the petition. There is nowhere less suited to that than the quiet, suburban backwater of the Police HQ campus in Lewes. Had Mr Birch acceded to wishes and been at the police station, it may have shown compassion for the families. Perhaps, with hindsight, he could have negotiated that he only met the Fellowses, Hadaways and Councillor Wingate.

Despite the knowledge that the Chief Constable would not be there, the march went ahead. At noon on 19 August 1989, forty men, women and children, fewer people than at the public meeting, displaying signs demanding a reopening of the enquiry, set off in the sweltering heat to walk the two and a half miles from Wild Park to the John Street police station. It turned Barrie Fellows' stomach to march with Bishop but his brother persuaded him he must show his face, so he reluctantly joined in.

Again, in what I would suggest was a bit of an own goal, the police refused to escort the march, so it fell to Councillor Wingate to keep the marchers safe from the busy Saturday lunchtime traffic along Lewes Road as they headed into the town centre. During the march, Russell Bishop, clad in an orange high-vis vest as if a steward, leapt on buses to hand out leaflets and lunged at a taxi driver who accused another marcher of scratching his car. He was the poster boy so far as the press were concerned.

By 3 p.m., exhausted and with the press in tow, the march finally arrived at John Street armed with their 5,000-signature petition. They crammed into the cool of the lobby, their banners and leaflets proudly displayed. Despite knowing he was not in the building, they demanded to see the Chief Constable, making sure onlookers could hear their demands being rebuffed.

When Tomlinson came out to receive the petition, wearing his uniform of white shirt, black tie, epaulettes and cap – no tunic in this heat – Councillor Wingate, with Russell Bishop at his shoulder, flatly refused to hand it over. The Divisional Commander explained the Chief Constable's stance, but despite already knowing this, Sylvia Bishop and Jenny Johnson seethed at the officers, and the group threatened to hold a sit-in and demonstrations until their demand to see Mr Birch was met.

Chief Superintendent Tomlinson explained that he was senior enough to take the petition and would ensure it reached Mr Birch, but they would not budge. He promised to convey their strength of feeling, and to arrange a meeting with the Chief Constable in the coming week. The stalemate persisted but eventually, knowing that Mr Birch was not going to appear, the protestors drifted off with their petition, vowing to continue the fight. Michelle Hadaway was 'disgusted' and Barrie Fellows felt 'no one cared'.

Dave Tomlinson must also have been feeling it. After all, he had led the search for the girls, was one of the first to see their bodies and gave evidence in Bishop's trial. This was certainly not just another case for him. He had lived and breathed it for three years and still does to this day.

So much could have been done differently to make this event a dignified and purposeful protest. It is not for me to criticize the decisions and actions of my predecessors, but had the approach to protest that I established in 2012 been in place in 1989, things would have been so different. The march would have been escorted. The Chief Constable may or may not have been there but we would have negotiated that with the protestors beforehand. The petition would have been received with appropriate opportunities for the media to get their pictures and interviews. And one of my conditions would be that Bishop would have been nowhere in sight.

If Wingate, the parents of the girls, and the Bishops thought they had secured some progress with Tomlinson's promises, they were to be sorely disappointed. Four days after the abortive attempt to face down the Chief Constable, the deputation returned to Brighton. Despite Birch previously insisting he only accepted petitions at his Lewes office, common sense prevailed and he met them at the more accessible police station.

During the tense hour-and-a-quarter meeting, Mr Birch repeatedly turned down requests to bring in an outside force to review the police's handling of the case. Although the long-awaited Home Office report which examined the CPS's role had still not materialized, the families were now focused on what local officers did or did not do.

These days, in a case with such a high profile and unsatisfactory outcome, it would be unthinkable *not* to commission another force to review the investigation. But in the late 1980s, what the chief constable said, went.

And he said no.

In denying an outside perspective, he drew attention to the huge effort of the initial investigation and that the decision to charge Bishop was taken, not by him or his officers, but by the Director of Public Prosecution (DPP) after a painstaking analysis of the evidence. He said the case was first tested during the committal proceedings at the magistrates' court before being committed to the Crown Court where, of course, it was scrutinized every which way. At none of those points, he said, was there the slightest criticism of the investigation other than by the defence counsel. He remained resolutely confident in the diligence and competence of his officers. That was it. No new investigation.

In my view, even with that faith in his officers, considering the magnitude of both the crimes and the verdicts, the Chief Constable should have taken a step back and considered what would have been the harm in having the case reviewed. His force, and every other force in the country, could have learned so much from a second look.

The review of the evidence by the DPP and the courts was just that – a review of the evidence. External reviews go far deeper and look at every aspect, from the initial call-handling through to the big decisions, the budget and all points in between. Something might have been unearthed that may have led to another suspect.

The Chief did eventually accept a package containing 'new evidence'. The nature of this has never been revealed but Mr Birch promised the meeting attendees that it would be investigated and acted upon if, as was claimed, it was truly new. This seemed to satisfy at least Councillor Wingate, who described the meeting as fruitful – unlike Barrie Fellows who felt he was 'being stalled.'

There was one more surprise for the Chief Constable. The march, the sit-in at Brighton Police Station and now this meeting had all been about the 5,000-signature petition that Mr Wingate was determined to hand over. This petition was to be the show-piece. However, at the last minute, Wingate refused to present it. Was it all a ruse? Were their fewer signatures than he claimed? It baffled the police as much as the press. What was going on? Maybe it was just a device to get airtime with the Chief Constable. If that was the case, it worked. Petition or no petition, finally the families could look him in the eye and say their piece. But they came away disappointed, seemingly no closer to justice than three years earlier.

34

Even though the march and the meetings failed to spark a new enquiry, they certainly triggered renewed vigour from both the press and public to get the police to do something, anything, to catch the killer.

In September 1989, almost three years after the murders, a brand-new community centre, St George's Hall, opened in the heart of Moulsecoomb. Planning had started long before the girls' murders but it seemed the deaths pushed it up the development agenda, as the dearth of facilities on the estate for young and old alike was becoming an embarrassment.

In tribute to Karen and Nicola, two memorial clocks were installed either side of the main hall. All these years on, it is hard to remember Moulsecoomb without St George's Hall, let alone that it was tragedy that finally prompted its building.

There was no doubt that Councillor Gordon Wingate was still the driving force behind the quest for justice for the Fellows and Hadaway families. He led a Brighton Borough Council debate calling for a motion to demand the reopening of the enquiry. The matter became intensely political with accusations coming from the Conservative opposition that Wingate was police bashing; that he was using the deaths as a political pawn. He countered by insisting that Bishop was innocent. Despite the challenges, his motion was passed and the council were forced to urge the police to reopen. Regardless, this was not legally binding. UK police are, at least on paper, operationally independent of party politics.

A flurry of activity over the next six weeks saw campaigners seeking out their own legal advice to force the police to reopen the case. Bishop's uncle, Mick Dawes, threatened to privately prosecute an unnamed man he was convinced was the real killer. Meanwhile, the police's announcement that the package of apparent 'new evidence' was not new at all only served to rile those who were convinced that justice could still be delivered. Councillor Wingate stormed out of a meeting with Chris Page, by then a detective superintendent, describing him as 'subtly hostile and openly dismissive', alleging others were playing politics and there was a cover-up.

By now Bishop was preparing to sue the police for wrongful arrest. The *Evening Argus* described the campaigners' demands as 'shrill' and the police 'aloof'. They rightly pointed out that while the police were being sued by Bishop, their public response had to be circumspect, but who can condemn the families for being so angry?

As the three-year anniversary loomed, press coverage once again intensified. A vigil lasting twenty-three hours – the time from the girls going missing to their bodies being found – was held at Wild Park, as there would be every year going forward. Cutting a cold and lonely figure, Michelle Hadaway, who had since moved away from the city that brought her so much sadness, sat on a bench just yards from where her daughter was slain. Periodically she was joined by friends and supporters, but her husband Lee was too distraught to be there. So too was Susan Fellows, but Barrie and his brother Nigel Heffron turned out to pay their respects.

In *Argus* interviews to mark the occasion, Michelle reflected on how her once-active life had been reduced to a mere existence since Karen's murder. 'There just doesn't seem to be any purpose to things. It doesn't get any easier at all,' she told the newspaper. She had been prescribed drugs to help get her through, yet had received no professional grief counselling. Some mornings she could barely get out of bed and found each day a struggle to believe Karen was dead. 'I still lay the table for her,' she said.

Through her unimaginable grief, she said she kept strong. Despite the insensitive advice from some less than helpful friends, she told journalists, 'They don't really know how it feels. You just take each day as it comes and hope to get through, and at night sometimes you don't sleep.' She channelled her grief into keeping Karen's and Nicola's memory alive. However, she opposed a return to capital punishment, even for her daughter's killer, which surprised many. 'I don't want to be barbaric. I'm not particularly religious, but I think you could run the risk of lowering yourself to their level.' That did not mean she did not crave justice. Once new technologies emerged, she searched for ways to have Karen's blood-stained clothing DNA-tested, but was never successful on her own.

On the same day as Michelle's anniversary vigil, Councillor Wingate led a four-hour silent vigil outside Brighton Police Station. This culminated in a 5,000-signature petition being presented to Chief Superintendent Tomlinson. The flurry of campaigning concluded with another high-profile Labour Councillor and Sussex Police Authority member, Ken Bodfish, demanding another force be brought in to reinvestigate the murders.

At a meeting of the Sussex Police Authority, Chief Constable Roger Birch eloquently explained how thorough he felt the investigation had been. He described the levels of external scrutiny it had already received, before and during the trial, and the absence of independent criticism. Little would be gained, he said, by reopening the case. He reassured members that he would keep the matter under review and reminded them of Councillor Wingate's new evidence that was currently sitting with the Director of Public Prosecutions. He went on to acknowledge the immense public concern of there being a double child murderer still at large and the parents' dreadful grief. Then, changing tack, he took a swipe at what he called 'ill-informed comment, unwarranted criticism and unforgivable speculation' over the handling of the case.

This briefing did the trick, as a now reassured Councillor

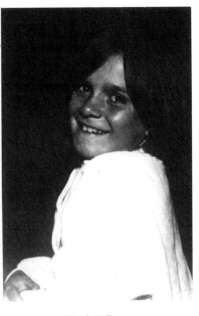

Nicola Fellows

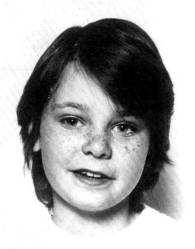

Karen Hadaway

Barrie Fellows with Nicola as a toddler

20 and 26 Newick Road, the homes of the Hadaway and Fellows families

Scenes of crime officers prepare to go into Wild Park woods, where the girls' bodies were discovered

The 'den' where the girls' bodies were found

Barrie Fellows faces the press following the discovery of Nicola and Karen's bodies

Michelle and Lee Hadaway at a press conference in 1986

Russell Bishop in a school nativity scene

Russell Bishop in 1986

The Pinto sweatshirt

The path and fence close to Moulsecoomb where the Pinto sweatshirt was discovered

Jenny Johnson, Bishop's partner, in 1986

Sylvia Bishop and family leave court following the not guilty verdict in 1987

Russell Bishop leafleting for the Babes in the Wood case to be reopened in 1989

The search of Devil's Dyke following Claire Perkins' kidnap and attempted murder in 1990

The makeshift police base at the scene of Claire's kidnapping

The Preston Barracks house where Bishop was arrested for Claire's kidnapping

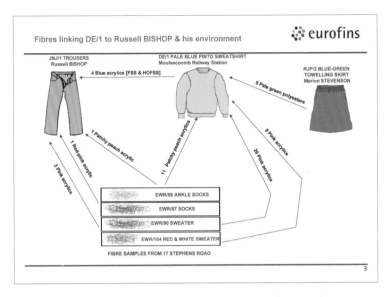

eurofins

JNJ/1 TROUSERS
Russell BISHOP

DE/1 PALE BLUE PINTO SWEATSHIRT
Moulsecoomb Railway Station

RJP/2 BLUE-GREEN
TOWELLING SKIRT
Marion STEVENSON

4 Blue acrylics [FSS & HOFSS]

5 Pale green polyesters

1 Patchy peach acrylic

11 Patchy peach acrylics

8 Pink acrylics

1 Red-pink acrylic

28 Pink acrylics

3 Pink acrylics

EWR/86 ANKLE SOCKS

EWR/87 SOCKS

EWR/90 SWEATER

EWR/104 RED & WHITE SWEATER

FIBRE SAMPLES FROM 17 STEPHENS ROAD

3

A chart showing how the fibres found at 17 Stephens Road
linked the Pinto sweatshirt to Bishop

Detective Superintendent Jeff Riley,
the senior investigating officer who
finally brought Bishop to justice

Russell Bishop in 2018

Michelle Johnson (Hadaway), Barrie Fellows and Sue Eismann (Fellows)
after Bishop was found guilty

The entrance to Wild Park after Bishop was found guilty

Bodfish dropped his demand, noting the Chief Constable's genuine concern that the case remained unsolved.

The last weeks of the 1980s brought no more hope for the families or for the police. The relevance of the new lines of enquiry fizzled out and justice was as distant as two years previously when Bishop walked out of the dock a free man. Gordon Wingate's tenure as a Moulsecoomb councillor was overshadowed by the murders and their aftermath. He had been elected just five months before and was masterful in keeping the case on the front pages and in the minds of the police and his fellow councillors.

The accusations that he was playing politics were unfair, but predictable given the partisan council; there was no love lost between the Conservatives and the more extreme left-wing elements of the Labour group. Brighton has always been fiercely political and entrenched battles have raged there for years.

In my time as Divisional Commander, I had to stand firm against one council who demanded that we ban all protests, evict all travellers and clamp down on the World Naked Bike Ride. We had no powers to do any of these but it was down to me to tread a fine line between acquiescence and dissent.

Then, after an election, the new leadership argued the polar opposite. I again needed to explain the political independence of the police and that sometimes our interventions would be unpopular, but necessary. My job was to face up to criticism when justified but defend our approach when it was operationally essential. I held our ground and somehow managed to avoid falling out with leaders or their parties

While waging his constitutional battles, Councillor Wingate fought tooth and nail against any obstruction to his resolve to deliver answers to the Fellowses, Hadaways and the rest of his community. But in January 1990 he announced that he would not be standing for re-election that May.

He had not run out of steam, far from it, as he pointed out in announcing his difficult decision. 'There is nothing political about this, but the leading politicians in the town have ignored Nicola and Karen. I can in no way be part of the council as long as the girls continue to be ignored. The best thing I can do is to devote all of my energies to the campaign. I will not rest until natural justice has been done. My position in the Labour Party is to defend the working class, and I shall continue to do that. But Karen and Nicola must come first.'

On 1 February that year, author Christopher Berry-Dee announced that he had written to Prime Minister Margaret Thatcher and the Leader of the Opposition Neil Kinnock in frustration at what he perceived to be a lack of police action. Along with copies of his research, in a curious – arguably repugnant – gesture, he enclosed colour photographs of Karen's and Nicola's bodies. He threatened to send the same package to every MP if no action was taken. It is unclear whether the imminent publication of his book dictated the timing of this announcement.

The following day, having received advice from the Crown Prosecution Service, Sussex Police invited the Hadaway and Fellows families to a meeting at Brighton Police Station. There, over a tense ninety minutes, the police broke the news that there would be no new investigation. In a statement that marked the end of the road for the campaign, the police said they had thoroughly examined the apparent new evidence. The Crown Prosecution Service, after considering this, had decided that the material did not warrant further investigation.

Denying the case was closed, Assistant Chief Constable Rodney Lind stressed the police were very sensitive to the public concern, and would continue to investigate any fresh evidence that might arise.

Michelle Hadaway was furious. She would not rest until the investigation was reopened. All the family members demanded to put their questions directly to the CPS. Barrie Fellows' brother, Nigel Heffron, recalls being thrown out of their offices and threatened with arrest when he tried to do just that.

These cases are never truly closed, but in light of no new statements being taken, no fresh scenes being examined or no arrests made, the Fellowses and Hadaways could be forgiven for thinking this one was. The police were true to their word in diligently following up all new leads. Christopher Berry-Dee had provided the police with his evidence, and the name of the person he thought he was the killer. All this had been carefully considered but did not take the case any further forward.

It seemed relations with the families were deteriorating, and rather than working with them to seek an achievable solution, the police became entrenched in the merits or otherwise of relaunching an investigation which, all knew, would reach the same conclusions as the first. All the evidence still pointed to the one person on earth who could never be charged with these killings. The one person who had put himself front and centre of the campaign to reopen the enquiry was safe in the knowledge that the prohibition of double jeopardy made him untouchable.

But that person had just over forty-eight hours of free air left to breathe. Little did we know that his secret, sickening and brutal appetite would rise up again, and this would be momentous in the pursuit of the Babes in the Woods killer.

PART TWO

35

Weaving through Brighton's backstreets early that Sunday evening, 4 February 1990, I was on top of the world.

Barely seven years into my police career, I had finally started working for Brighton CID. For now, I was only a temporary detective constable – just a month into my trial posting – but the first few weeks of the 1990s felt like a new beginning. Alongside my new job, Julie and I moved into our new house and a diamond sparkled on her ring finger.

Making the most of a surprisingly 'Q' – we never said 'quiet', that tempted fate – late shift I had grabbed the opportunity to spend a few hours tracking down witnesses to a large-scale fraud at a local furniture shop. Not the most adrenaline-pumping crime to investigate but, for me, it was the work of a proper detective so I threw everything I had at it.

Back in my car and cruising into the dimly lit backyard of Brighton Police Station, even the prospect of spending the rest of the evening ploughing through the mountains of reports and prosecution files piled up on my desk could not dampen my ardour. I wormed around the crammed patrol and CID cars searching for a parking space, when I was suddenly forced to stand on the brakes.

Three police cars, lights strobing and sirens blaring, sped across my bows. I swore under my breath, watching in the rear-view mirror as the convoy squealed out of the yard and away towards East Brighton.

I stole one of their parking bays, jumped out of the tiny Mini Metro and marched to the back door, tapping in the security number before heaving it open. Having just come from uniform I knew the call that spawned their urgency could be anything from a struggling shoplifter to a murder in progress. But as I narrowly avoided being bowled over by three more PCs sprinting down the stairway, I guessed this was no cat stuck up a tree.

I was still getting used to the lag between the rush of the emergency 'shout' and CID getting a look in. So, having leapt up the stairs three at a time and burst into the capacious open-plan CID office, the serenity of the room took the wind out of my sails.

'What's going on?' I panted. 'I've just nearly been wiped out by three response cars on blues and twos. What's the job?'

'Calm down, boy,' murmured my wily tutor, DC Dave Swainston, not even looking up from the statement he was reading. 'If it's one for us we'll find out soon enough.' Suitably chastised, I slumped into my battered swivel chair, contemplating my ever-growing workload with considerably less gusto than five minutes before.

Was it a mistake moving to CID after all? Was I going to miss the cut and thrust of dashing around on uniform response, fuelled by adrenaline and fast food, literally not knowing where I would be headed next?

I settled down and scanned a couple of new crime reports which had been mysteriously gifted to me while I was out, resigning myself to perhaps never knowing what all the fuss had been about.

A short while later I glimpsed a uniformed inspector sliding quietly into the detective sergeants' office just across the corridor, closing the door behind him.

I pricked up my antennae.

What was going on? Was it connected to the speeding police cars?

I tingled in the hope of my first big job as a detective.

DS Kevin Bazyluk – Baz – strode into the DCs' office. Baz was the most tenacious detective I knew. For him there was only one way of doing things – the right way. While he was not in the least bit scary, you crossed him at your peril. Every cog of every investigation that hit his desk had to be followed up to the nth degree. Try as we might, we could never get anything less past him. An utter professional, he was the perfect DS for a trainee detective like me. Some of the more seasoned detectives would sneak over to his desk while he was out to cross tasks off his notorious 'to do' list that related to them.

I was never that brave.

'Right, everyone, listen in,' he barked. 'Stop what you're doing, finish your phone calls.'

The silence he demanded descended instantly.

'I'm not sure what we've got but I'm guessing none of us will be going home on time,' he forewarned us.

'Baz, get to the point,' pleaded Dave Swainston who, with just a few years to retirement, was the only one bold enough to answer back.

'Dave, wind your neck in for a moment, please.' Baz paused. 'Right. Two jobs have come in. First there's been a call to Whitehawk – a seven-year-old girl, Claire Perkins [her name has been changed to protect her life-long anonymity], is missing. She'd been out roller-skating but now she's vanished. That was two hours ago.'

No banter now, just rapt attention. Fathers thinking of daughters and everyone fearing the worst. No one needed reminding that nearly a quarter of a million people go missing in England each year. Most either turn up or have made a rational choice to disappear, but a seven-year-old girl vanishing late on a winter's afternoon – that was as bad as it got.

'Added to that,' continued a sombre Baz, 'a couple have just come across a naked young girl wandering along the Devil's Dyke Road, covered in blood and mud, crying her eyes out. WPC Debbie Wood and a DS from Hove are dealing with that.'

'Shit, Baz, it's pissing down and freezing. It'll be worse up there on the Downs,' observed DC Steve Bowers.

Undeterred, Baz glanced at his notes. 'They are meeting the

little girl's parents at the Royal Alexandra Children's Hospital. We are on standby to pick up any urgent actions that come from there or the scene.'

The events of a little over three years before and the catastrophe that followed were written across every face. Surely this could not be happening again.

36

Just the thought of the frail seven-year-old wandering Devil's Dyke naked, scratched and frozen evoked fury in everyone. I had abandoned any thought of my furniture fraud investigation while others were swiftly bailing prisoners they had left languishing in the cells. The decks were being cleared to catch whoever this bastard was.

None of us realized that today was the third anniversary of Nicola and Karen's funerals and, while we were rushing around, the Fellows and Hadaway families were making the sombre journey home from their gravesides.

Baz was farming out fast-track actions based on seniority and experience. I was bottom of the ladder, several rungs below the exciting tasks that would, hopefully, crack these harrowing events. I felt as if I had been picked for the Cup Final, knowing I would only be warming the substitutes' bench. My time would come, but I wished it were now.

'Research likely suspects,' I was told. *Suspects for what? We don't even know what we've got yet.*

It was years before computers could serve up all we ever needed, so I sloped off towards the shadowy Local Intelligence Office on the ground floor, dreading the hours ahead of me flipping through thousands of index cards hoping a name might pop out. I could only imagine the adrenaline rush those picked for more exhilarating assignments were experiencing.

Spotting my disappointment, Baz grabbed me as I passed his office.

'Graham, two things. First, there is no such thing as a crap job on enquiries like this and second, it's not always the glory hunters who crack the case. What you are doing is crucial. Do it well.'

Wise words, which I would repeat to many a rookie in future years.

Wading through index cards but still unable to locate the needle in the haystack, I was relieved when a tannoy boomed, 'All CID to the detectives' office. Briefing in ten minutes.'

During the 1980s, Brighton CID was a bit of a closed shop. *Who* you knew, rather than *what* you knew, seemed to be the predominant entry criterion. The competition to win a place in the department was fierce and youth was sparse. Relationships with uniformed officers were strained, leading some to malign what they unfairly saw as a culture of hard play – time spent apparently cultivating informants in local pubs – interspersed with a few hours of work. No one could have accused the CID of that during the Babes in the Wood or Grand Hotel bomb enquiries though.

Then, at the end of the decade, Detective Superintendent Gordon Harrison, a former rugby league professional and a wise veteran of over fifty murder enquiries, brought in the flamboyant, hard-drinking DCI Tim O'Connor to take over the city's detectives. Known as ToC, the proud Irishman, sadly now dead, did not look good in suits but his sartorial awkwardness was overlooked given his career in surveillance units. His infectious personality, passion for grass-roots policing and his inability to complete a profanity-free sentence won the hearts of the purists who would normally berate such an unconventional route into CID. His love of Jameson's whiskey did not mean he was going to acquiesce to a drinking culture. He knew there was a job to do in Brighton and he was determined to draw in the sharpest talent to help him do it.

One of his earliest and most inspired appointments was an ex-drug squad officer who had recently been promoted to uniformed inspector, pounding the streets of rural Hailsham.

Unlike ToC, Malcolm 'Streaky' Bacon was dapper and immaculately groomed. His pencil-thin moustache and ramrod posture gave him the air of a formidable yet affable Regimental Sergeant Major. ToC snared him just days before Eastbourne CID pounced and soon he was ensconced as the detective inspector for West Brighton.

Bacon's respect for ToC, and Gordon Harrison, was immeasurable and he relished the move back to Brighton. By the time I started my CID attachment, ToC had reformed it into a hard-working, dedicated squad of men and women who were committed to getting the scum off the street. Streaky's welcome to me was warm, but to the point:

'We want young blood in the office, Graham, but you will work harder than you ever have before and you will be judged on results.'

Mountains of files rose from my desk. Frauds, burglaries, robberies; all bread-and-butter enquiries to cut my teeth on. While a little overwhelming, I was in my element. As my sergeant, Baz provided me with a grounding that would last my whole career. To this day, when serving and former senior detectives gather, we still thank Baz for his tough love that made us the investigators we became.

My place in the pecking order was made clear though. Any potentially fruitful jobs would go to those who already bore the qualified detective status that I craved. I quickly immersed myself into this new world, loving the ramshackle working environment, each battered and bruised piece of mismatched office furniture resembling a boot-sale bargain. Every desk appeared as if the occupant had abandoned it in haste and would return shortly. Each, however, was the nerve centre of dozens of investigations into man's appalling inhumanity to man.

Despite the new house and impending wedding, Julie knew CID was the job I craved even though it would mean long, unpredictable hours of hard work. She was no stranger to that herself. She had been promoted to check-in supervisor at Gatwick

Airport. Sixteen-hour shifts juggling multiple flights, anxious passengers, last-minute delays and stressed staff was just another day at the office for her. Her support and encouragement kept me grounded and confirmed that, in her, I had landed one in a million – someone who would understand and tolerate the crazy hours my career would demand.

37

On my return from trawling the index cards, I was stunned that the throng of bosses, detectives, scenes of crime officers and civilian support staff had swollen even more in the detectives' office. It was standing room only. Everyone seemed to have answered the call that Sunday evening.

Briefings are the centrepiece of any investigation. Information is shared, intelligence verified, updates provided and priorities set. Good SIOs deftly retain control and structure yet enable even the most junior officer to speak up. It is often they who have the gem everyone has been waiting for but can be too timid to mention it.

Just two years later, I had my own moment like this when I plucked up the courage to suggest Ian McLaughlin as a suspect for a homophobic murder. I had arrested him for robbery a few weeks previously and the modus operandi and make of aftershave stolen at both crimes suggested to me it was him. It was, and he had killed before. He would go on to take another life when, on day release from prison in 2013, he stabbed Graham Buck to death while he tried to stop McLaughlin robbing an elderly neighbour. He will now die in prison.

Baz, now massively outranked, stood next to a stern and immaculate 'Streaky' Bacon, the perfect foil to ToC who seemed to have taken his usual route to work – through a hedge backwards. Detective Superintendent Harrison, who had been called from the golf club, completed the formidable trinity of Brighton CID big guns. I felt privileged to be part of whatever was unfolding.

'OK,' barked Streaky, bringing us to order. 'This is what we have so far. At three thirty this afternoon a seven-year-old girl, Claire Perkins, was roller-skating with four friends near her house in Whitehawk. They all went their separate ways about 4 p.m. and Claire skated back to her house and asked her dad for some money so she could go to the shop. He gave her a quid and she skated the 200 yards or so to the shop but it had shut at 2 p.m. When she didn't return, her dad went looking for her, knocked on neighbours' doors, asked around, that sort of thing, getting more and more worried. Eventually, everyone was out on the streets and Dad called 999. Uniform got there within five minutes.'

'Has she gone off before, guv?' came a voice I did not recognize from the back.

'No. She doesn't like the dark and normally stays within sight of the house,' replied Streaky. 'OK, so uniform put the balloon up and a big search started.'

'What was she wearing?' asked someone else.

'She had a maroon and pink jacket over a white patterned jumper, black leggings and her roller-skates were pink and white. She's small and has fair hair. By all accounts she's a bright, perky and sensible little girl.'

'Any sightings at all, boss?' called a SOCO standing near me.

'No, not that we know of. No one had seen anything by this stage.'

An uneasy mumbling reverberated around the crammed office.

'So as the search intensified,' continued Streaky, 'about five o'clock, a couple on the Dyke, near a place called Summer Down, saw a young girl emerge from the bushes. Realizing she was naked, the woman rushed over to her and saw she was covered in blood and mud, freezing cold and crying her eyes out. She must have been deep in the gorse as she was cut to ribbons. The lady wrapped her in a cardigan and jacket, put her in the car and went to the nearest building, which was the Dyke Golf Club. That's when they called us.'

'That's gotta be about ten miles from Whitehawk by road. How did she get there?'

'It's early days but she has said she was put in the boot of a red car. Possibly a Sierra.'

Never mind a pin, you could have heard a feather drop. Every man and woman present struggled to keep it together. All were trying to raise their emotional shields to prevent horror permeating the steely professional side of their minds. Sentiment could wait; we had a would-be child killer to catch.

Snapping us back to the job in hand, Streaky boomed, 'So, here is the hypothesis we are going to work to for now. Someone has been roaming the streets, snatched Claire, driven her to the Dyke, stripped her and left her to freeze. What's happened on the way or up on the Dyke is anyone's guess but we need to throw everything we've got at this. Whoever did this may have done it before, but worse, may do it again.'

'Why would anyone do that, guv?' came a voice from the back.

'That, sunshine,' Streaky quipped, 'is why we let you wear that smart Marks and Spencer suit and call you a detective. Go and bloody find out.'

With that, the briefing ended. We had heard all there was.

True detectives come into their own on jobs like this. Our collective intuition and tenacity would crack this and none of us would rest until we had. Someone commandeered some space in the lofts of Brighton Police Station and designated it the incident room. In those days, there were no Major Incident Suites; the SIO had to grab offices normally occupied by others. Being a Sunday evening, we had our pick. Possession being nine tenths of the law, we asserted squatters' rights when, the next day, the rightful tenants protested. These co-opted rooms had far more character than their modern counterparts. They evoked an esprit de corps that bonded the whole team with one aim – to catch a paedophile.

WPC Debbie Wood, a fresh-faced child abuse investigator, reached the hospital in record time, just as the ambulance containing the blanket-clad, terrified victim arrived with a uniformed

PC comforting her. She looked every bit as bad as Debbie had been told: cold, dirty, crying, her flesh flayed.

Gordon Harrison was mentoring ToC and insisted that Claire's interview be video recorded to guard against any allegations of inducements or leading questions.

Claire's courage was breath-taking.

She confirmed that she was the missing roller-skater and, despite what she had been through, was able to give her name, age and address. Debbie never asked, but Claire insisted on reciting her mum and dad's wedding date too.

Debbie's training drummed into her the dangers of asking too much of an abused child so soon after her ordeal. But this was the golden hour. Time was of the essence if we had any chance of catching the monster who had done this. Following some gentle coaxing, Claire volunteered some crucial facts. She told Debbie where she had been snatched from, that a man had put her in the boot of a red car, that he had a moustache and that she had found a 'tool like Dad uses' and bashed the inside of the boot lid with it.

Her attention to detail was a godsend.

Elaine [also a pseudonym to protect Claire's identity], Claire's mum, reached the hospital very quickly. Debbie met her outside and did her utmost to prepare her for the trauma she was about to face. As a seasoned child-abuse investigator, Debbie knew the irreparable harm that could be done to a child should their parents appear shocked.

Thankfully, despite her distress, Elaine listened and understood. As if nothing was wrong, she breezed into the side ward and greeted her injured, dishevelled, and bewildered child with a simple 'Hi darling,' masking her total relief and absolute horror.

38

In 1990, the Sussex Criminal Records Office at HQ was the closest we had to a force-wide intelligence system. Four veteran detectives beavering away, surrounded by filing cabinets and walls papered with mug shots, was as good as it got. But what they lacked in gadgets they more than made up for with decades of local knowledge all stored in their razor-sharp minds. Nothing could get them in to work quicker on a Sunday evening than a potential child killer at large.

In the blink of an eye, they churned out a hit-list of twenty or so potential suspects from Fareham to Folkestone. I was on the team that would work through them. But, being the trainee, I knew I was getting nowhere near the names at the top. Those visits were for the big boys. I ended up eliminating a sex offender from Worthing who was as angry at being knocked up so late on a Sunday as he was desperate to provide far more checkable alibis than we would ever need. Tedious as this was, it would prove essential in the months to come.

Meanwhile, snippets of information were still being fed back from Claire. This was going to be a long process, employing what were then cutting-edge techniques to slowly encourage a young and vulnerable little girl to speak. However, to catch this monster, we needed her to give us a starting point.

Elsewhere, others were doing their bit.

Superintendent John Albon, who was in charge of uniformed operations, had been called in and was co-ordinating the response beyond the CID's role. He had driven past the Devil's Dyke scene and had a good idea of how perilous it was for Claire.

He pulled together a briefing of his senior team, including Gordon and ToC. Streaky updated the bosses on the information they had scraped together so far.

It is not often that commanding officers trawl through intelligence logs but this was no ordinary night. Chief Inspector John Pearce, a quiet, intelligent and likeable leader and another newcomer to Brighton, was as keen as anyone to play his part. On mention of the car used in the kidnap he asked, 'Streaky, did you see that information about Russell Bishop having a red car?'

All eyes fell on him.

'No. What type?' asked Streaky.

'A Cortina I think.'

'Sierra? Cortina? Could be the same to a seven-year-old. It's definitely worth a look but let's also keep an open mind,' said Gordon.

Despite the apparent caution, John's eagle-eyed spot triggered a frenzy of activity and a fair degree of anxiety.

If it was Bishop, we had to get him now. His burglary convictions, not to mention the Babes in the Wood enquiry, gave him an edge in forensic awareness. Even if he had not murdered Nicola and Karen, he had witnessed the dissection of every scrap of scientific evidence during his trial.

As the clock ticked away, so would the chances of catching him with damning evidence. But if we nicked him and he turned out to be innocent, the force could kiss goodbye to a few hundred thousand pounds in compensation and for those involved, their careers.

The 'nine o'clock juries', as the morning meetings of the oh-so-wise senior officers are called, could be brutally judgemental. At their worst, from the warmth of a plush conference room, while sipping piping hot coffee and with twenty-twenty hindsight, the assembled brass would dissect decisions made by their minions in the heat of the moment. Thankfully, in Sussex, such officers were rare but if this arrest went wrong, you could bet some smartarse would take the opportunity to carpet those who had been faced with making the immediate and difficult choices.

Despite this Gordon Harrison felt no pressure, but few would have been brave enough to question him in any case. There was no one more experienced at investigating major crime, and his quiet, withering stare would have been enough to ward off any critics.

DS Don Welch and DC Ian Walker were picked to pay Bishop a visit straightaway. Don had investigated the Stephens Road arson the previous April and was about the only cop who had anything approaching a rapport with him. He was a rugby-playing, marathon-running giant, who deliberately gave the impression of being half a step behind everyone else. He never was; it was an illusion he created to lull the gullible into a false sense of security. Playing dumb brilliantly belied his razor-sharp instincts.

Walker was the svelte fifty-something grandfather of the CID office, with a heart of gold. Always there for the big jobs, and deft at dodging the mundane, he had a wicked sense of humour from which no one was immune, but he was nobody's fool. He had been around the block a few times and could sniff out a liar, and the most interesting investigations, better than anyone I knew.

As they pulled up outside Bishop's Preston Barracks council house, close to Moulsecoomb, they saw him valeting his red Ford Cortina outside. Immediately, alarm bells rang. There could be only one reason for him to be doing that on a freezing February evening – and it was not because, despite the notice in the window, he was trying to sell it for £750, or the nearest offer. The only incentive to get him off his butt to scrub as if his life depended on it, was that it probably did. Blood, fibre, hair, paint, semen: it all needed to vanish and he seemed to have made a good start. This was gold dust and Don and Ian had to stop him before he finished the job.

They approached, very low key, and coaxed Bishop back into the house, explaining they just needed to find out where he had been that day. No problem. Nothing to worry about. All routine. Having negotiated their way in, both Bishop and Jenny Johnson were very wary. Jenny went straight on the offensive, immediately screaming he was being fitted up for something. He, on the other hand, effortlessly reeled off a string of alibis covering the previous hours. He seemed to have it all worked out, listing his various visits to siblings, parents and friends, all conveniently timed to explain his movements and prove his innocence.

Unconvinced, Don and Ian stepped outside to radio the incident room. On hearing the update, Streaky grabbed Baz and they sprinted down to the car park via the uniformed response office to grab PC Pete Cook and his partner for back-up. As they did so, news reached them of a witness seeing Bishop in his red car in Whitehawk that very afternoon.

Sometimes it does not help to overthink the next steps.

The ability and sometimes the bloody-mindedness to just do what is right, to hell with the consequences, is fundamental to policing. Arresting Bishop might appear to the ill-informed as payback for his acquittal. It could seem like clutching at straws. The top brass would, at the very least, raise an eyebrow, and questions would be asked, but to hell with that, thought Streaky as he raced northwards.

If he and Baz were expecting a welcoming party as they pulled up at Preston Barracks, they were to be sorely disappointed. Don and Ian had already bluffed their way back into the house to preserve what evidence remained. The two detectives invited themselves in. It was plain that the presence of two more officers clearly told Bishop and Jenny that the game was up. Sylvia Bishop had arrived by now and ordered her son to say nothing without a solicitor. Faced with the inevitable, Bishop suddenly grabbed a fire poker and lunged at the officers.

'Just you fucking try it,' Streaky warned in a quiet, menacing voice, as the hulking frame of DS Don Welch stepped forward. The cowardly Bishop immediately dropped the weapon as Streaky said, 'I'm arresting you for kidnap and attempted murder.

You do not have to say anything unless you wish to do so, but anything you do say may be given in evidence.'

Jenny launched at Streaky, shrieking her hatred, raining punches onto his head and shoulders. His colleagues quickly subdued her and Bishop was whisked off to the Brighton police cells.

39

Arrests are made on 'reasonable suspicion' and convictions secured on evidence 'beyond reasonable doubt': two legal tests
that are poles apart. In layman's terms, a justifiable hunch is
enough to feel a collar. The toil to convert that into the absolute
certainty the courts demand can feel like scaling Mount Everest
in a diving suit.

The police remained convinced Bishop was guilty of the
Babes in the Wood murders. But that was history. The two cases
were totally separate. What happened to Claire was horrific,
every parent's nightmare. If it was Bishop, then the proof needed
to be airtight. If it was not him, we needed to find who *was*
responsible and damn quickly.

An early decision was taken that, as far as possible, no one
who worked on the Babes in the Wood murders would be on this
enquiry. This was not a reflection of anyone's conduct or competence, just a very wise precaution to avoid unhelpful suggestions
of old scores to settle. Detective Superintendent Gordon Harrison, ToC and Streaky knew it would take just one ill-informed
sniff of a conspiracy to scuttle any subsequent prosecution.

Harrison insisted on structure to the CID team and, un-
usually, had to turn down offers of staff from elsewhere. He
needed a relatively small, handpicked group of detectives who
met his overarching criteria. I was in the right place at the right
time.

Another decision was that the face of the enquiry should be
a senior officer with flawless integrity and a squeaky-clean discipline record. Whoever this was must have the backbone to field

the flak that would no doubt come. They did not have to look far. Streaky had it all and was the perfect embodiment of a thorough, objective and ethical investigator.

The enquiry would be run by the book. Nobody so much as breathed without an action generated by the Home Office Large Major Enquiry System – HOLMES – telling them to do so. Everything we did, and did not do, was driven from the top and documented to the letter. No well-meaning mavericks, no short cuts and no initiative were allowed. For some of the old school this stuck in their throat, but for me, with this being my first major enquiry, tracking down witnesses, taking statements, dotting Is and crossing Ts, I knew no different. Instead I would take this rigour with me as I climbed the promotion ladder.

40

A massive operation was soon under way. Claire and some of the locals pinpointed the exact location she was snatched from as the junction of Haybourne Road and Limney Road in White-hawk. A sharp-eyed neighbour, Lesley Brooks, quickly answered the original appeal for sightings of a red Ford Sierra. She and her ten-year-old daughter had been out walking when she saw what she thought was a bright red Sierra inching along close to the junction. At the same time, her daughter spotted Claire washing her roller-skate boots in a puddle. Then, while her back was turned, Lesley heard the scream of an engine and the spin of tyres trying to grip the tarmac. She turned and saw the same Sierra speeding away, the driver leaning over to slam the passenger door shut as he wrestled to control the fleeing car. At the time, she had put it down to the boy racers who blighted the estate. It was not until she heard what had happened on her doorstep that, with horror, she realized what she had witnessed.

Police descended on the Whitehawk estate in droves. Like the influx of cops in Moulsecoomb just over three years previously, the huge presence unnerved a community not known for its love of law enforcement.

Whitehawk, a huge council estate which sprawls in the shadow of Brighton Racecourse, overlooks one of the UK's most prestigious girls' school, Roedean. It felt different from Moulse-coomb. Less neighbourly. More of an edge. The estate was origin-ally developed in the 1930s but much of it was torn down and rebuilt in the 1970s and 1980s as part of a slum clearance programme. This left a hotchpotch of high-rise and low-level flats interspersed with suburban avenues and cul-de-sacs connected by warrens of dimly lit alleyways. Once a suspect ran into those, their local knowledge would surpass ours and they'd be lost to us.

Due in part to regeneration but mainly because of the sheer determination of its residents to shake off its unjustified tawdry reputation, it has award-winning facilities for young and old alike.

The estate also had its own Mac. PC Dudley Button – 'the Squire', as he was affectionately known – was proud to live on the estate despite its misrepresentation as being rife with crime and violence. The son of a former Mayor of Brighton, this portly, jolly cop was the only one of our number to do so.

For twenty years he had pounded its streets knowing every family, their personal and criminal history, their friends and enemies. He was a governor at the local infants' school and ran the community kids' disco every Thursday night. His recent move to the Special Enquiry Unit gave him a unique blend of local knowledge and an understanding of child abuse that we needed for the investigation.

A caravan, loaned by a local garage, was parked at the very place Claire was snatched from and became the makeshift police office. Scores of officers used it as their base while they laboriously knocked on every door in the area, making repeat visits when there was no answer.

PC Button waited in the van having invited any resident who had the smallest snippet of information to pop along and tell it to his friendly, familiar and trustworthy face. For twelve hours a day, every day for over a week, the Squire sat and chatted to all comers. He may have been professionally sympathetic but he was also personally horrified by this act of depravity that had tainted the community he cared so much about.

As in Moulsecoomb before, mums and dads kept their children close. No more playing on the streets, popping to the shop or walking to school. The morning after the attack, columns of uniformed children, guarded by stern and vigilant parents, marched along Whitehawk's narrow pavements in a show of strength and unity. 'Stranger Danger' assemblies were held, and our schools liaison officers spent hours both reassuring youngsters and cautioning them of the perils of talking to people they did not know, and what to do if one approached. In a sad and bizarre coincidence, just two days before she was snatched, Claire's school performed a play warning of the dangers on the streets.

Elsewhere, the nearby Sheepcote Valley refuse tip was locked down in case the offender had dumped evidence there. Bishop's house was swarming with SOCOs looking for evidence, and a huge chunk of the South Downs was a no-go area for the public.

Adopting the principle when searching open ground of starting big and working in, the searchers rose to the challenge. Devil's Dyke is enormous – about 2,000 acres of windswept, wild and open grassland. As crime scenes go they do not get much bigger or more challenging. Just north of Brighton, it offers spectacular panoramas and a stunning gorge: the longest, deepest and widest 'dry valley' in the UK. Legend has it that the Devil dug this chasm to drown the parishioners of the nearby Weald. Scientists, though, suggest it was formed naturally just over 10,000 years ago in the last ice age. It is one of the area's most beautiful National Trust sites.

For now, though, it was destined to become a wasteland as teams of officers foraged for evidence.

Every single police officer in Sussex was determined that if it was Russell Bishop, he was not going to escape justice for a second time. Not by a whisker, not by the skin of his teeth and not by a single blade of grass.

The national press was all over the story. It was a news sensation that eclipsed everything else. A pretty, bright, loveable seven-year-old snatched from the street in broad daylight, horrifically and brutally abused and then left to die on a bleak hilltop. The story provided rich pickings for tabloids and broadsheets alike.

Had social media been around in 1990, this would have been trending worldwide with armchair critics and commentators suggesting what we should and should not be doing.

We were used to dealing with the press, and in particular, one reporter from the *Evening Argus*. Phil Mills had an excellent relationship with Brighton CID, as he'd taken the time to get to know us and understood just what he could and could not publish.

As nearly 500 officers crawled across the Dyke, intent on finding anything that might prove who was capable of such evil, others were wading through hundreds of pieces of information generated by the unprecedented publicity. This was always going to be a harrowing investigation but ToC, being unfamiliar with the concept of live TV, provided a rare moment of light relief.

With his tatty wax jacket buttoned up against the cold, he stood shivering close to where the search was drawing to a close for the second night. Having been miked up, he saw the cameraman cup his ear, waiting for his cue from an unseen producer down the line.

'Tell us when that fucking thing is filming!' ToC demanded in his chirpy Irish brogue, prodding a stubby finger towards the camera, as he prepared to appeal to nation from the freezing crime scene.

'We are live on air now, Detective Chief Inspector, so what would you like to say to the *teatime* viewers?' implored the horrified interviewer back in the studio.

Watching the broadcast in real time in the makeshift incident room, we missed the rest of what he said, drowned out by the deafening guffaws.

That appeal, despite its comic opening, prompted hundreds of phone calls, all from people wanting to help. The challenge was to separate the genuine lines of enquiry from the numerous well-meant distractions.

41

Almost as soon as Bishop had been arrested, his name was plastered all over the papers. It was not the police but his own legal team who leaked it in what appeared to be an attempt to reignite their doused 'Bishop is Innocent' campaign. That played to our advantage as, since his previous acquittal, he had become unable to move around the city unnoticed. His stupidity and vanity worked against him. Rather than realizing his profile might, one day, come back to bite him, he revelled in it. He would strut around, playing the local hero; the guy the police tried to fit up for murder but could not.

Bishop's profile meant that not only were people desperate to help catch the monster who had violated Claire, they also had a focus: Bishop and his red car. The 'For Sale £750 ono' sign in its window differentiated it from dozens of similar red Cortinas cruising the city streets at the crucial times. He had been spotted on several occasions: in Whitehawk, heading towards the Dyke and finally driving back to town. Not quite the ANPR of today but enough to blow a hole in his alibis.

Meanwhile, back in the dank interview room adjacent to his cell in Brighton Police Station, Bishop was probably kicking himself for saying so much about his alibis prior to his arrest. He was now refusing to respond to anything DSs Brian Smeed and Don Welch asked. He knew it was our job to do all the proving. His time in custody was dragging on. He must have felt we were being deliberately slow – prisoners always do when they have been locked up for hours on end. However, the frenzy of activity just a few floors above him was equivalent to the investigation following Bishop's previous arrest and the Brighton Bomb enquiry.

Time being against us, in accordance with the law, thirty-six hours after he had been detained he was brought before the magistrates' court for them to authorize us to keep him longer. Bishop's solicitor protested that his client was innocent – what else would he say – but also highlighted that he had a Cortina while we initially said we were looking for a Sierra.

We still were. We were not sure if witnesses were mistaken or there was, indeed, a Sierra in the Haybourne Road area at the time. We were following all lines of enquiry whether they pointed towards or away from Bishop. We just needed more time. Thankfully, the magistrates granted the extension.

42

Over the following days, the weather was holding over Devil's Dyke and nothing was allowed to get in the way of the hunt. Fingertip searches by hundreds of officers stretched across the downland as they continued to scour the mud and undergrowth for clues. In the quest to find any minute piece of evidence that bushes, hedges, and grassland might conceal, everything was chopped down just like at Wild Park previously. The rich vegetative landscape was reduced to a wasteland.

The search had been thorough but it was becoming desperate. Claire's roller-skates and a Cortina floor mat had been found discarded in bushes but there was still no sign of her clothes. Meanwhile, Claire's interviews were surprisingly fruitful. Any adult with her powers of recollection and description would have been a godsend, but for a seven-year-old, through hours of interviews, to reveal as much as she was able to was exceptional.

She knew a man had done bad things to her. She knew she had to stop him. She knew the grown-ups now talking to her, although strangers, were nice people who wanted to help. She was safe and she had to tell them what happened.

She was out on her roller-skates and had been to the shop but it was closed. She had seen the man mending a red car; he was younger than Daddy. He was wearing a watch. He had grabbed her around the waist, lifted her off her feet and thrown her in the boot. She had taken her skates off so she could run away if she got the chance. It was dark and smelt horrible in there. There were some little holes to see through. Only tiny. Maybe the man had made them so she could breathe.

She knew she needed to get out or at least make a noise to get some help. She found a tool, maybe a hammer, so she thought if she hit the boot lid her mummy or daddy might hear and come and get her. She started banging but then had to stop. It wasn't Mummy who heard her, it was the nasty man. He shouted, 'Shut up or I'll kill you.' She was scared. She felt around and found a can. It smelt like the stuff Daddy sprayed in the engine when the car wouldn't start. The man was driving really fast now and the car radio was so loud. He shouldn't drive like that, he might crash. She was being thrown around the back. She wanted to shout again but thought that if she stayed quiet and was a good girl maybe he would let her go. After a while the car stopped. Perhaps he would let her go now. It was cold when he opened the boot. He helped her out.

It was dark. There were lots of trees. Where was she? She was frightened. She couldn't see anyone. She was so scared.

He put her in the back seat of the car then took her clothes off. Like Mummy did at bedtime. But then he started doing things to her. Things she didn't understand. Things she was sure he shouldn't do. He was hurting her. She wanted him to stop. He squeezed her throat. She couldn't breathe. She panicked. She wanted to shout but couldn't. Then she fell into a deep sleep.

When she woke she was cold, lost and her neck hurt. She was in a prickly bush. She knew Mummy wouldn't find her there. She needed to get out. She'd be in trouble with Mummy and Daddy but still she wanted to go home. Then another car came. A lady got out. She checked whether she was a kidnapper too. She seemed nice and there was a man with her. They gave her a cardigan and coat to keep her warm. She didn't mind that they were too big. They put her in their car and drove to a building with lots of people. Then the police came.

There were so many lines of enquiry just from that initial simple account. We knew the offender's rough age and we confirmed the car was red. Bishop was twenty-three and had, as we knew, a red car which was now safely in police possession. Claire had hammered on the inside of the boot and he had threatened her. A hammer was in the boot of the car and the boot lid had tell-tale dents on the inside.

She had found something that seemed to be a spray lubricant in the boot. We had recovered a can of WD40 from where she said. She described the place where they stopped as being cold with trees. That was Devil's Dyke to a tee, although we already knew that.

Her description of him removing her clothes was telling. Any parent would know that they pull them over the upstretched arms of their toddlers, with the clothes ending up inside out. Would only a parent naturally remove a child's clothes this way?

Bishop was a parent.

Things were coming together.

After the interview, Claire just wanted to get back to normality as quickly as possible. As a special treat she was allowed to stay up to nearly midnight playing Care Bears with her best friend. She was adamant though that she did not want to go to sleep in case she forgot the man's face; she knew how important it was to remember it. Heart-breakingly, she kept apologizing to her mum for losing her clothes.

Understandably, but for absolutely no reason, her dad was racked with guilt. He went over and over how he should not have let her out. 'What if' this and 'If only' that. Despite his family's reassurance, he could only blame himself.

Forensic pathologists are normally brought in only to examine dead bodies. However, occasionally their skill and experience in hypothesizing how injuries have been caused, especially if the victim has been left unconscious or amnesiac, can be vital.

Once again, the brilliant Dr Iain West was called upon to lend his trained eye and discerning mind to a case involving Bishop. The policy of not using officers from the Babes in the Wood enquiry did not apply to pathologists; they are deployed regionally according to their rota.

His gentle yet methodical forensic medical examination of

Claire a few days after the attack revealed more detail. While he could not be sure whether she had been raped, the bruising around her neck and the scarlet pinpricks speckling the whites of her eyes revealed how close to death she had been. This petechial haemorrhaging was the same sure sign of strangulation or smothering that he had found on Nicola and Karen. A clear indication that Claire was meant to die.

Dr West said that she had been only seconds from death. He concluded that, in his attempt to kill Claire, the attacker had used a technique developed among the Special Forces nicknamed 'the Sleeper.' This involved squeezing a pressure point in the throat between the knuckles of the first and second finger until the victim passed out.

Claire's age saved her life. During testing in the USA, most adults passed out after ten seconds of being subjected to this death grip. Any longer would kill. Her tender years meant that her brain was more resilient and able to survive longer. She was a very lucky girl.

43

Although the case was slowly coming together, we still needed help. We told the public as much as we could. The use of the press was a key tactic and this time we were not going to allow Bishop's side to hog the front pages. Everything you read or hear from the police in a major enquiry is the result of a conscious decision of how and when to release it; nothing is left to chance.

It was only right that people understood why Devil's Dyke was out of bounds: we were still looking for clothing. As a consequence, with the best intentions, every rag and discarded shoe was phoned in. One call gave us the break we were after.

Stuck in rush-hour traffic, an observant taxi driver glanced to the grass verge along Mill Road, one of the natural routes back from Devil's Dyke to Moulsecoomb. On any other day the crumpled fabric would not have registered. Even if it had, he would have forgotten it in a heartbeat. But not that day.

His call started with the usual preamble: 'Sorry to bother you. It's probably nothing but . . .'

But it *was* something. It was the most significant find so far.

What might have seemed like a discarded pair of men's blue jogging bottoms was, quite simply, a parcel of evidence carelessly dumped on a grass verge. This was sounding familiar to those who remembered the Pinto sweatshirt. They were carefully photographed, plotted on a map and forensically packaged before being removed to Brighton Police Station and then rushed to the Forensic Science Service. These were very early days in the use of DNA evidence but Gordon and ToC were clear; all avenues would be followed. It would be one of the first times this breakthrough technology was used in a major crime enquiry in Sussex.

The scientists eventually proved what none of us had dared hope for. Splattered across the dirty fabric was sufficient blood, semen and flecks of red paint to provide a cast-iron link between Claire, Bishop and his red Cortina.

Investigations into Bishop's car revealed that it was stolen. It was a ringer – made to look legally registered – and a clone of an identical car. Damningly, the boot lid originally came from a different-coloured Cortina and had been resprayed a number of times. Most paintwork comprises three coats. This had six layers, making it collectively unique. The chances of finding paint flecks in that combination trapped among Claire's blood and Bishop's semen on the fabric were incalculable. This damning cocktail of evidence trapped on the discarded trousers would nail Bishop.

The interior of the car contained even more evidential gems.

Debris from the mats and carpets contained fibres that would later be matched to Claire's clothes. The holes that Claire had noticed appeared to have been drilled through the boot lid. Had they been created deliberately to preserve a young girl's life just long enough for Bishop to assault and then dispose of her?

As well as trying to find any trace of Bishop or Claire through the discarded clothing, the scenes of crime officers sought to uncover other evidence on the Dyke. Tracking back from witness sightings of Claire, the car – including one describing steamed-up windows – and the bush where one of Claire's roller-skates was found discarded, the focus homed in on a narrow muddy track.

Given the time of year, the ground had the consistency of stodgy porridge. Firm to the touch but soft enough to hold an imprint. Road tyres come in all sorts of shapes and sizes. Each manufacturer boasts that its new state-of-the-art ridge pattern ensures maximum safety and the ultimate driving experience. To me they all look the same but they are distinct and, with a little wear and tear, unique. Depending on how a tyre is fitted, when and how the car is driven, each wears out differently and thus, after only a short while, the tread pattern becomes almost as distinct as a fingerprint. If there is an assortment of tyre types fitted to the same car then this combination, together with their unique wear and tear, renders any tread impression in soil, sand or across paint or blood unique evidence.

A close examination of the track revealed fresh tyre marks with the contours plain to see. Realizing their potential significance, the SOCOs took great care in making plaster-cast impressions of each, ensuring that every pit and ridge was reproduced faithfully.

The experts at the forensic lab later concluded that three of the tyres were manufactured by Tigar, and the fourth by Uniroyal. Those who knew about these things had not seen this combination before, bar once. On Bishop's Cortina.

While the weight of evidence was mounting against Bishop, Claire's clothes eluded the searchers. Of course, the attacker might have taken them with him but time was running out. The weather was due to break and the search teams were needed elsewhere. After nearly 5,000 officer hours and three days, the search was starting to draw to a close. As swathes of downland had been cleared and searched, the cordon had been reduced from its original all-embracing perimeter to a much tighter area.

'Sarge, I think I've found something,' came the cry from an exhausted PC Chris McNeill, at the foot of one of the few trees left standing.

'Line stop,' came the order to the rest of the searchers.

Photographers, SOCOs and the search supervisor were called forward to the hopeful PC's position. There, wedged deep in the hollow of the tree, almost invisible, was what appeared to be a ball of child's clothing – a maroon and pink jacket, a white patterned jumper and black leggings – secreted so that no one could find them.

Methodically and with meticulous care, after it was photographed from every imaginable angle, the bundle was removed in a manner that allowed it to retain as much of its shape as possible. Regardless, the teams of searchers glimpsed enough of it to convince them this was what they had been looking for.

Their hopes were soon confirmed. This *was* Claire's clothing. The eventual forensic examination revealed not only irrefutable DNA evidence, but also an amazing corroboration of her testimony. Just as she had said, Bishop had taken all her upper clothes off together over her head and arms. *'Just like Mummy does at bedtime.'* They were in one bundle, inside out. Unable to shake off his more innocent parental habits, he had inadvertently captured and preserved another perfect blend of bodily fluids and the telltale paint in a cocoon of inside-out textiles. It even still contained the pound coin her dad had given her for the shop.

With this last crucial find on that final day of the search, Devil's Dyke was reopened to the public and the weather, which had been so kind to us, did its worst. PC Rain, as we called it, due to its effectiveness in keeping drunks and petty villains off the streets, had dutifully held off until the windswept South Downs beauty spot had given up its last secret.

Now no one cared when the seasonal storms hit. We had what we needed.

44

The forensic results trickled through over time, but so far everything seemed to confirm that the murderous paedophile we were looking for was the man sitting silently in his basement cell. His solicitor, Ralph Haeems, was doing all the talking, denying everything on his behalf and, in a last throw of the dice, asking for an identification parade. This desperate move was possibly in the hope that Claire would be too scared or damaged to pick Bishop out.

The makeshift ID parade was set up in a social services centre, ironically in a room normally reserved for providing therapy to abused children. Adhering to the principle of employing as many independent people as possible, Inspector Phil Deith from Hove was selected as Identification Officer, with Inspector Les Templeman from Chichester assisting. Anyone with the remotest connection to Bishop or the enquiry was ordered to stay well away.

Unconnected officers were dispatched to find nine innocent volunteers to sit alongside Bishop on the parade. They were to look as similar to Bishop as possible. Watching a live link, Streaky vowed vengeance on the over-zealous PCs charged with this task; even he had difficulty distinguishing two of them from the suspect.

Even so, Bishop's solicitor still complained about the appearance of the stooges. He felt they looked nothing like his client and told Bishop to wet his hair down to give it a darker hue. Inspector Deith was having none of this and delayed the parade until it had dried. Deith collected Claire and took her to the viewing room while a legal representative and Inspector Templeman remained with Bishop and the stooges on the other side of a two-way mirror. With Ralph Haeems standing close by, Inspector Deith reminded Claire of the horrific abuse she had suffered just days before and asked her if she could see the man who assaulted her anywhere on the line-up.

After scrutinizing the ten men, she bravely announced, 'I think it's number nine.'

'Are you sure?' checked Deith.

'Yes. I'm sure,' she confirmed.

Number nine was Bishop.

Superintendent John Albon and the senior team, also watching on the remote link back in his office, on hearing her clear and certain identification were moved to tears.

Deith left Claire with her mum while he and Haeems stepped into the makeshift parade room and broke the news to Bishop. He was swiftly returned to Brighton Police Station where he was formally charged with kidnap, indecent assault and attempted murder.

45

The following morning, 8 February, the day before his twenty-fourth birthday, Bishop appeared at Brighton Magistrates' Court. His journey through the underground tunnels that linked the police cells to the court avoided the baying crowds outside. Interestingly, Sylvia Bishop was not in court. She chose to honour her entry to Cruft's Dog Show at Earl's Court in London with Magic Sunday, her sheepdog, performing in the obedience category.

Dressed in a grey patterned sweater, light blue jeans and blue canvas shoes, and handcuffed to a police officer, Bishop stood silently in the dock while the clerk of the court read out the charges. Allowing him to finish, Bishop replied, 'I'm innocent of all them charges.' The Chief Prosecutor for Brighton, Geoffrey Clinton, then outlined the details of the attack. In response, Ralph Haeems made no application for bail or for reporting restrictions to be lifted but did, once again, assert Bishop's innocence. He asked that the prosecution produce its evidence quickly which, of course, was in everyone's interest.

At the end of the nine-minute hearing, Bishop was remanded in custody and led to a waiting prison van in which he was whisked away to London's Wormwood Scrubs Prison. Lewes Prison would have meant a death warrant and there would have been no shortage of local inmates only too happy to carry it out.

Given the sub judice rule – which regulates what can and cannot be published once legal proceedings become active – the media were stymied in what they could print until the trial. Several news outlets carried interviews with psychologists hypothesizing how Claire would be supported through her trauma and how it might affect her. Others discussed the profile of offenders who could commit such crimes. All very interesting, but they did little more than fill column inches, while we were beavering away.

Our work rate never waned over the next nine months. Our drive and determination to bring justice for Claire drove the much-reduced team on. We knew we were in for the legal fight of our lives. Bishop's previous defence team had been ruthless and given their success and the continued presence of Mr Haeems it was pretty certain they would adopt the same confrontational approach now.

Those of us left on the enquiry spent hundreds of hours taking statements, checking property and eliminating other possible suspects. We checked and rechecked that every forensic exhibit was meticulously accounted for and that every line of enquiry had been exhausted, every detail verified.

During this period, I took a statement from a young girl, strikingly similar to Claire, who had told her parents that a red car with a 'For Sale' sign had twice followed her home. Her description of the driver was Bishop to a tee and the registration number she remembered was just one digit out.

This could well have been him cruising for a victim a few days before he snatched Claire. Unfortunately, it was ruled out, on the grounds of it being prejudicial to the defence. The jury would never hear that testimony.

WPC Debbie Wood was tasked with receiving, recording and then presenting to Claire the hundreds of gifts and a small fortune in cash that poured in from the public desperate to show their sympathy and support. In an extraordinary gesture of solidarity, the entire inmate population of Lewes Prison donated their weekly chocolate allocation to this brave little girl.

46

When Mr Justice Nolan QC opened Bishop's trial on 14 November 1990 it was the only show in town. The *Evening Argus* contained little else for the next four weeks. The drip-feed of the horrors of that February evening gripped its readers as the evidence was revealed, day by day.

The pressure for a conviction was intense but, unlike today, the media were more focused on reporting the facts rather than a sensational scoop or scandal. They did not have to wait long to hear the horrific details of Claire's ordeal and how she miraculously survived. The second day centred on her evidence. She could have testified via video link but, in an amazing display of courage, she chose to be present in the courtroom, speaking from behind a screen. Propped up on two cushions so she could see the judge, jury and counsel, her confidence and clarity impressed everyone – except one who was probably terrified. He had not faced live victims before.

The judge checked with her if the wigs and gowns worried her. 'No,' she said, 'that's fine.'

Nowadays there are far more protections afforded to young victims but in 1990 this was as far as it went. We were so grateful she had such backbone. The judge then quizzed her about her favourite lessons, 'English and maths', and what sports she liked, 'cricket and rounders'. These led to the crucial question: whether she knew the difference between telling the truth and lies. When she had convinced him she did, he allowed her to give evidence but ruled she need not swear the oath.

She recounted what happened that day as clearly as in her

interview. She left no one in any doubt; she knew what she knew and she saw what she saw. Nothing was going to divert her from that. She described her attacker, including his wristwatch. She told of how she was snatched, how she was thrown into the boot of the car, the sound of gravel, the car radio. She remembered being driven scarily fast, and how she had been thrown around in the boot as the car sped around corners. She even remembered being strangled on the back seat.

She was resilient to Defence Counsel Ronald Thwaites QC's gentle but thorough cross-examination. He was wily enough not to goad her as he would other witnesses. She stuck to her guns on every point, including that it was definitely number nine who had attacked her. She told Mr Thwaites about a dream she had during her ordeal. 'I was talking to someone else. I dreamt he gave me a little toy and said, "If you lose it I will kill you". He thought I was dead but I wasn't. I was in a deep sleep.'

Once again Claire's composure and resilience astonished the onlookers, not least the learned judge. Next up were the couple who rescued her and then other witnesses who saw Bishop driving on his heinous journey. They all corroborated Claire's account.

The mood changed over the next few days. Mr Thwaites' brutal attacks spared no one. The scatter-gun defence left no professional prosecution witness immune from ferocious and scandalous accusations over their motivation, expertise and integrity. Scientists were accused of contaminating exhibits with samples from Bishop's murder trial. Detectives faced allegations they had hoodwinked Bishop upon his arrest. Everyone was a target.

Bishop took the stand and if the case had not been so grave, his explanations would have been laughable. At their most bizarre, he alleged police had stolen a used condom from his bedroom and had then splattered his semen over the recovered clothing.

He also attributed the hammer marks on the inside of the car boot to a previous load of roofing tiles in another imaginative attempt to evade justice. His efforts to provide himself with alibis were equally pitiful with the witness evidence blowing them out of the water.

He denied even owning a wristwatch, let alone wearing one on the day.

Undeterred, Mr Thwaites told the court, 'The police collectively, and the scientists, have strained every fibre and sinew of their being to bring home Bishop's head to you, which some of them regarded as the missing trophy they failed to get when they were last here. In other words, did some officers set out in this case to ensure that they did have sufficient evidence to persuade any jury, regardless of how they got it and even if they had to arrange it or manufacture it themselves?'

Posed as a question, he could distance himself from owning that scurrilous accusation.

47

The judge summed up flawlessly. In his nimble yet thorough synopsis of all the evidence he not only reminded the jury of its weight but also the caution they should apply. Claire was very intelligent and articulate but how reliable could a seven-year-old be in recounting events from ten months ago? How easy would it have been for those who said they saw Bishop driving towards the Dyke to be sure it was him? Who did you believe between the police, who said the forensic samples were retrieved in accordance with strict guidelines, and the defence, who said it was planted?

It was his job to point out both sides of the story even if one touched on the ludicrous – such as the police planting the tyre tracks at the Dyke.

He was equally fastidious in spelling out the law. Walking them through each count on the indictment, he asked them to consider whether they were sure the acts that supported each charge had actually happened. Once they were satisfied they had, were they then sure it was Bishop who committed them? Nothing less than a yes to both of those questions would do.

Some of my former colleagues would speculate from a summing-up whether a judge was pro-prosecution or pro-defence. This naivety infuriates me. Judges are neither. They are simply pro-fair trial. Often, they will bend over backwards for the defence, knowing that to come down too hard on them could provide grounds for appeal.

In the 2008 trial of those responsible for shooting dead eleven-year-old Liverpool boy Rhys Jones, the judge appeared to tolerate horseplay between the defendants while asking Rhys's mother to reconsider attending court if she could not stop crying. In what could be seen as outrageous double standards, the judge was just letting the jury see the yobbish killers for what they were, while preventing accusations down the line that they were swayed by an emotional grieving mother.

In Bishop's case the judge allowed, and repeated, the defence's extraordinary explanations and accusations and reminded the jury only they could judge the facts – did they *really* believe this?

The jury were not fooled. Having sat through twenty-one days of evidence, with tractor-loads of mud thrown in the hope some would stick and so many outlandish alternative explanations proposed, it took them just four hours to deliver their unanimous verdict – guilty on all counts.

Bishop crumbled. Head in his hands, he sobbed, knowing what was coming next.

48

The judge wasted no time in issuing a crushing attack on Bishop, before condemning him to a life sentence, with a minimum term of fourteen years. No one but his closest family shed a tear as he was whisked, sobbing, down the court steps and away to begin his incarceration, where he was to become the longest-serving non-murderer in any British jail.

The press coverage of the convictions was as full as it was celebratory. It even, quite by coincidence, added to the certainty that Bishop was guilty. Despite his protestations, a family photo emerged showing, very clearly, a watch upon his wrist.

Normally we would celebrate convictions such as this. After all, we had worked so hard to secure it. Not in this instance. ToC and Streaky had already quashed any suggestion of that.

There were no winners here, no cause for joy. At the centre of it was a young child, lucky to be alive, but brutalized in a way that time could never completely heal, and the Fellows and Hadaway families still had no justice.

While we all worked to the point of exhaustion, some came close to a breakdown. The pressure had been unimaginable, made even worse by the scandalous accusations thrown around at the trial, but there was to be no gloating, no celebration. For the horror of Claire's ordeal, and in recognition of justice denied to Nicola and Karen's families, a dignified statement confirming we were 'satisfied with the outcome' was all we supplied.

Three days after the conviction, the Bishop family feared for their own lives.

Just after 10 p.m. on Sunday 16 December, Bishop's parents Sylvia and Roy were in their Coldean home, trying to come to terms with having their youngest son exposed as a child sex attacker. They were snapped from their gloom by the distinctive tinkle of breaking glass. Too muted to be a window, they looked out in the direction of their dog kennels to see flames licking the patio. They dashed out to rescue their prize dogs, praying that none had been hurt. Thankfully the firebomb had caused little damage and only a few dogs had been splashed with petrol.

Five minutes later, in Haybourne Road, Whitehawk – close to where Claire was snatched – a second Molotov cocktail exploded by David Bishop's van. Luckily a neighbour, who saw the flash, extinguished the flames before they could spread.

With impressive speed the police attended not only both seats of fire but also Preston Barracks, knowing that Jenny and the kids could be the next target. After all, it would not be the first time someone tried to burn them out of their home.

As they arrived, they found four youths loitering outside. They were swiftly arrested and taken to John Street Police Station. After intense questioning, it was established that they had played no part in the attacks so were released. The investigation was thorough but, once again, with only snatched sightings of a light-coloured car close to both areas, there were no clues and the culprit was never found. ToC went on television to issue a dire warning to anyone who thought they could take out their anger on Bishop's innocent relatives. They would be charged and prosecuted.

The following day the editor of the *Evening Argus* received a scrappy handwritten note urging him:

Please tell the Bishops and Jenny Johnson to Get out of Brighton. Last night was just a warning on them (i.e. Sunday 16th December) [sic] *Tell the liars to get out and stay out, they all lied to keep a sex monster on the street. Yours A. Team.*

They were the last attempts to hound the Bishops out of Brighton but Sylvia took the opportunity to tell the *Evening Argus* that, while she still believed her son to be innocent, people should appreciate what she was going through. She paid tribute to Claire but described her shock and her struggle to come to terms with the last year's events, insisting she was serving a life sentence too.

People like Gordon Harrison, Streaky, ToC and Debbie Wood, who had supported Claire from day one, rarely become household names. These four, who personify all that is good about policing, popped up for their fifteen minutes of fame. They then slipped quietly back below the radar to carry on giving their heart and soul on behalf of the vulnerable, to protect them from the few truly evil predators that prowl our streets day in, day out.

I saw at first-hand how their skill, dedication and tenacity – not to say compassion – delivered justice for a little girl who was lucky to escape with her life. I spent the rest of my career trying to emulate those values. I hope I was, at least in part, successful.

49

With Bishop securely incarcerated and with little likelihood of seeing the outside of a prison wall for many years, if indeed ever, a quiet understanding for the police's reticence to reopen the Babes in the Wood enquiry emerged. Karen's grandmother, Maisie Johnson, sobbed as she told journalist Phil Mills, 'I knew he did it all along. He wanted to kill that girl and left her for dead. Life should be life for a man like that. For the first time in four years I can say I am happy.'

At last, Karen and Nicola's parents could openly voice their suspicions too. Plans were afoot to use a recent precedent to allow bereaved families to sue those acquitted of their loved ones' murders in the civil court. This was a long shot but probably the last hope anyone had of getting any sort of justice for their unimaginable loss.

Devastatingly for them, in November 1991, their lawsuit was quashed as its wording implied Bishop's culpability for the murders – a matter that, then, could not be resurrected in the courts. They did not know which way to turn but one thing was for sure – they weren't giving up.

Lee Hadaway had descended into depression, becoming homeless and dependent on prescription tranquillizers. He blamed the murders for the breakdown of his marriage and his falling on hard times. He described the tragedy as a cancer eating away at him. He tragically died in 1998, twelve years after the girls' murders.

The Babes in the Woods horror remained a scar on both Moulsecoomb and the whole of Brighton and Hove that would never heal. However, the calls for justice were hushed a little, perhaps because people finally agreed who the killer was.

Few could believe that, in the wake of Bishop being exposed as a would-be child killer, he still went ahead with his legal action against Sussex Police for wrongful arrest, malicious prosecution and false imprisonment. The case was listed for the High Court in November 1993 but, due to a shortage of prison staff to escort Bishop from Whitemoor top security prison in Cambridgeshire, it was adjourned until February 1994. The previous year he had been denied the right to appeal against his conviction and sentence for the Dyke attack. His mother, Sylvia, was typically upbeat about the civil action against the police, seeing it as a precursor to a second appeal. She claimed he had been working on his case since his incarceration and he had some strong evidence to support a bid for freedom. She called for heads to roll.

Understanding the vagaries of the civil law is one thing but navigating one's way around the time-honoured conventions of the High Court is another. For someone with Bishop's intellectual limitations to think he was up to conducting his own case was naive bordering on arrogant. In fairness, Bishop had been denied legal aid and certainly could not have afforded to fund his own case so his options were limited. Perhaps even a modicum of research might have provided him an inkling of what was to come.

Two days before his twenty-eighth birthday, as Bishop stepped into the grandeur of Court Nine in London's Royal Courts of Justice, having served three and a quarter years in prison, he was barely recognizable. Dressed in a grey suit, patterned shirt and blue striped tie, his youthful looks had been erased by the prison pallor so common among convicts. With his pasty complexion and close-cropped receding hair, he looked closer to forty than his actual age.

Prison does that to long-term inmates. The diet, drugs, lack of fresh air, outbreaks of violence and general ennui takes its toll. Despite the occasional misinformed shrieks in the press about the cushy life in jail, for most convicted criminals, the sentence is far more than just the number of years they are deprived of their freedom. It is a corrosion of their spirit and their soul, and there is a no more disliked prisoner than a sex offender.

Bishop's guards outnumbered his friends and family, with only his mother Sylvia turning up to support him. She was allowed to sit close to him as his unofficial scribe – a task she undertook with gusto.

This was the first time Bishop had testified about the Babes in the Wood murders. He had opted not to in 1987 but now he had no choice and was woefully ill-prepared. He called his first witness – himself. This was the moment the police had been waiting for.

His tearful opening, delivered from behind the security bars of the dock, centred on how the police had scapegoated him on no evidence, charging him only in the absence of a more likely suspect. His snivelling cut no ice.

Richard Camden Pratt QC, defending Sussex Police, launched straight into the facts of the brutal sex attack for which Bishop was serving life, leaving the court in no doubt about the sort of man they were dealing with. Camden Pratt then went on to establish the basic facts: Bishop knew the murdered girls, he was one of the last to see them alive and he had been banned from taking Karen on outings. This last fact, apparently, was a surprise to him. The ground being set, the gloves came off. For four hours Bishop was barracked with question after question about his sex life, his movements on the night of the murders, his relationship with the dead girls and his description of their bodies. All the questions the prosecution had been itching to ask in the 1987 trial.

Bishop was dumbfounded. At one point he pleaded, 'I didn't expect to come to this court to face allegations myself.'

Really?

Even material deemed inadmissible at Lewes Crown Court was in play here. Under fierce cross-examination, his story about whether or not he went to the girls' bodies in the den see-sawed once more. He finally conceded that he had not. If he had been honest before, there might have been a different outcome six years previously.

He must have been relieved when the proceedings were adjourned for the night. His solace was short-lived. First thing the next morning, Camden Pratt QC limbered up to resume, this time armed with colour photos of the dead girls.

In a dramatic moment, Sylvia interrupted and asked for a break in proceedings to regroup with her son. No one really knew what was going on and everyone, except the Bishops, were salivating for more brutal cross-examination.

When they returned a short while later, Bishop asked to drop the case, citing the overbearing display of wigs and gowns. The same wigs and gowns he had been prepared to inflict on Claire, and every other witness, in both cases. He made a futile attempt to turn this into an adjournment but the judge, Mrs Justice Ebsworth, swatted that submission down, ordering that he could not bring the case again, before awarding £75,000 costs against him – a sum he had no hope of paying.

Despite the case being withdrawn, senior officers were raging. Both Detective Superintendent Bernie Wells, by then retired, and Assistant Chief Constable Elizabeth Neville rued the lost opportunity to finally expose the truth and let the public know what they knew – that Bishop was a killer.

The *Argus* turned on Bishop and the cost, in time and money, he had effectively robbed from Sussex Police. A conservative estimate of £100,000 – over a quarter of a million in today's terms – was given as the outlay to prepare and defend the vexatious case which was destined to fail. This was in contrast to the £100 it cost him to apply for the summons in the first place. The police are always stretched so the six officers and a solicitor who worked full-time on the defence could certainly have been better used elsewhere. Bishop, on the other hand, had all the time in the world.

50

Through sheer dedication, both families made sure the vigils at the hawthorn tree memorial, which had been set up yards from where the girls were killed, continued every year and they never allowed the police to forget their loss. Annual phone calls from the families ensured that detectives would always be looking at new developments with Karen and Nicola in mind. Barrie Fellows along with his brothers Ian, Nigel and Kevin Heffron, as well as all their adult children joined Michelle Hadaway and her family in knocking on every door they could find and were resolute in keeping the murders in the news and high on the police's agenda over the decades.

There were, from time to time, efforts to revisit the forensic secrets held in the Babes' clothing, but all to no avail. The Hadaways and the Fellowses both talked of returning to Brighton but sadly both couples separated in 1992. Marriages rarely survive the trauma of a murdered child and with all they had been through – the accusations, the acquittal and the unanswered questions – the strain on them must have been all-consuming.

51

Thursday 22 April 1993 should have been like any other day for black London teenager Stephen Lawrence. The popular extrovert had everything to live for. The events of that day would not only devastate his family, friends and community, they would change policing and the law forever.

While making his way home with good friend Duwayne Brooks from an evening with his uncle, he was jumped by a gang of five or six youths who forced him to the ground and brutally stabbed him to death.

The police response and investigation into this racist murder was pitiful, with police corruption very seriously looked at as a factor. Suspects were identified within three days of the murder but no arrests were made for weeks, as the senior investigating officer did not believe he had the grounds to detain them earlier. Two, Neil Acourt and Luke Knight, were charged but the Crown Prosecution Service discontinued proceedings citing insufficient evidence and the charges were dropped.

The Metropolitan Police reviewed the case and resubmitted it to the CPS who, just days before the first anniversary of the killing, once again announced there was insufficient evidence. Almost immediately, Stephen's family initiated a private prosecution against the two originally charged, together with three others: Neil Acourt's brother Jamie, Gary Dobson and David Norris. Before the case came to court, the charges against Jamie Acourt and David Norris were dropped and, at the trial, the remaining three defendants were acquitted.

In the public inquiry that followed, Sir William Macpherson

made seventy recommendations. These were far-reaching and one, which sat outside policing, was specifically included given the real worry that should more evidence be found against any of those acquitted at the private prosecution, justice could still not be delivered. Recommendation 38 asked that '*consideration should be given to the Court of Appeal being given power to permit prosecution after acquittal where fresh and viable evidence is presented.*'

This relatively short sentence proposed, in specific and serious cases, to sweep away 800 years of the common law principle of autrefois acquit, meaning that no acquitted person could be tried for the same crime twice.

The Stephen Lawrence murder had, quite rightly, the highest of profiles. But the campaign to change the law to allow double jeopardy had already begun long before Sir William Macpherson made his ground-breaking recommendation. He just thrust it onto the political agenda. The Fellows and Hadaway families had been tirelessly campaigning behind the scenes for this for years and describe working closely with the Lawrence family once the recommendation was published. Other cases provided momentum.

Following two trials in 1991 for the murder of twenty-two-year-old Julie Hogg, both resulting in a hung jury – where a decision cannot be reached – the judge formally acquitted William Dunlop. However, while serving a term of imprisonment for an unconnected assault, he admitted the killing to a prison officer, gloating that the law could not touch him. This enraged Julie's parents but, in the only step that could be taken, he was jailed for six years for his perjurous evidence at the trial. This was not good enough for Julie's mum and dad, so they too campaigned for a change in the law.

It is impossible for a government to ignore the findings of its own public inquiry. Certainly not one with such a high a profile as the one into Stephen Lawrence's death. That, together with the families' campaign to change the law, led to the Law Commission, the independent body which researches and consults on proposed systematic changes, consulting on a change to the law which would allow defendants to be retried despite their previous acquittals, but only in murder cases.

A parallel report on modernizing the criminal justice system felt that the Law Commission was being unduly cautious and sought to open the possibility of retrials following acquittals in other very serious cases.

Section 75 of the Criminal Justice Act 2003 was born. It allowed for a reinvestigation and possible retrial where there was compelling new evidence indicating an acquitted person may well be guilty. Examples of new evidence might include DNA, fingerprint tests or new witnesses to the offence coming forward. The types of cases to trigger this, as well as murder, would include those at the top of the scale such as rape, kidnap and arson.

Cross-party support meant that this historic change in the legislation took effect in April 2005. To prevent miscarriages of justice, the process to trigger this new provision was made deliberately long and intricate, requiring various personal authorizations from senior police officers and the Director of Public Prosecutions to even start an investigation.

Therefore, against these labyrinthine rules, it was with relative haste that it only took until November 2005 for William Dunlop's acquittal for the murder of Julie Hogg to be quashed by the Court of Appeal and a further ten months for him to be the first person convicted under these new arrangements. He had no choice but to admit the offence, as he had six years previously to his prison officer. He received the mandatory sentence of life imprisonment with a recommendation that he serve at least seventeen years.

The cases put back before the courts in this way are few and far between but over the years more and more were presented, with juries feeling confident to convict on the wall of evidence before them. In 2012 Gary Dobson and David Norris were finally convicted of Stephen Lawrence's murder. They are now serving life imprisonment.

Following the change in the law, Karen and Nicola's families eagerly anticipated an announcement by Sussex Police that they would be able to apply to the DPP for permission to reopen the case.

Four days after the new Act became law, the families called for a private prosecution if Sussex Police could not reach the required threshold. Given the role of the DPP and CPS in the new process, this would not have been possible. Their authority over these new proceedings meant that there was no short cut to reach the phenomenally high bar set for a retrial. However, the families' demands did show their determination and that of the Brighton public to see Bishop back in the dock. Over the years, with great dignity, they would consistently lobby to reopen the case. The once-only provision of the new law, however, meant that the police could not risk triggering it too early.

While not required, most new cases relied on fresh developments in scientific evidence and this had not yet reached the sophistication to convince prosecutors they had enough. In one secret meeting, in 2006, scientists explained the ins and outs of the forensic opportunities to Nicola's cousin Lorna, a biology graduate. This satisfied her that then was not the time but provided hope for the future.

The same act also allowed evidence of defendants', and sometimes witnesses', bad character to be heard. This included previous convictions or anything that might have suggested they were prone to behave in a certain manner, such as outbursts of temper, using certain unusual phrases or hiding evidence in a particular way. This could relate to any time, including since any conviction. There were thresholds and safeguards built in but it meant juries could be privy to all sorts of relevant wrongdoing previously kept from them.

The announcement a whole city was waiting for was not to

come for years. In the meantime, the police were constantly reassessing the forensic and other evidence to consider whether new scientific breakthroughs, emerging technologies or new witnesses would enable a rerun of the 1987 trial.

By 2005 I had risen to become detective chief inspector and the head of Brighton and Hove CID, a position once held by Detective Superintendent Bernie Wells. The force structure had changed though and now all murders and major crime were the remit of the newly formed Major Crime Team, based at headquarters. As a result, I watched the work on the Babes in the Wood case from the sidelines.

The police and the CPS had to judge the right time to strike and to fully make use of their one chance. Too soon and they might not reach the threshold. Too late and the court may decide they could have brought the application sooner, and rule this as an abuse of process. In either case that would be their one chance lost. Unhelpfully, alongside all of this hope, was the fear that Bishop might be released from his life sentence. His fourteen-year minimum tariff had expired in 2004, so he was eligible for parole at any time.

When I eventually became divisional commander for Brighton and Hove, I heard and read the rumours, repeated in the press, that he might be freed and return to Brighton. I was privy to secret briefings which reassured me this was highly unlikely. I still had to plan though, in case we were all wrong. We needed to be certain that we were prepared for any retribution should he be released. We were convinced any licence would not allow him near the city but, as ever, we all hoped for the best and planned for the worst.

I retired in 2013 before any real progress was made to re-charge Bishop under the new laws but the abolition of double-jeopardy safeguards and the admissibility of bad character evidence would take on great importance in the future and create significant problems for the defence and prosecution alike.

52

When a middle-aged and slightly less mobile Barrie Fellows answered the door of his Cheshire home to a gaggle of detectives at 7.30 a.m. on 7 April 2009, he could have been forgiven for anticipating the news he had been waiting twenty-two years for. Especially when they said they were from Sussex.

Instead they delivered a thunderbolt.

All of a sudden, his house, which he shared with his new wife Karen and their family, was filled with police officers and social workers. Words like 'arrest', 'allegation' and 'abuse' echoed around as computers, videos, DVDs and mobile phones were bagged up, labelled and stacked into the waiting police cars. Little did he know that the same scene was being played out at Dougie Judd's Brighton home. He was kept in the dark about exactly what the allegation was as he was driven away in a police car. When the convoy arrived at Blakeham Police Station's custody block he was horrified.

Marion Stevenson, now thirty-nine years old, had made a statement to the police which, more or less, repeated her story paid for by the *News of the World* in 1987. This time the police were acting on it. The horror of being accused of sitting in your own home while watching a homemade video of your lodger raping your daughter can only be imagined. Barrie was furious. As far as he was concerned, all this had been dealt with, investigated and dismissed. Instead he had been dragged out in front of all his neighbours, his house searched, and social workers were crawling all over his children. All, in his view, on the word of a silly girl who had been manipulated by a monster.

The interview lasted just twenty minutes but he was held for five hours. He held nothing back, making it crystal clear that he knew no one who owned a video camera and that the geography of the room meant that Marion could not have possibly seen the television in the way she described. He was adamant that she had made the whole thing up. His revulsion towards anyone with the temerity to suggest such an evil thing of him – a grieving, loving father – was plain. His anger burned well beyond the twelve weeks it took for the police to decide that there was no evidence to take these ancient allegations further.

He was lucky to have such understanding neighbours. This was not long after a paediatrician in South Wales was driven out of her home because some idiot confused the name of her profession with the word paedophile. Barrie's employer suggested he stay away from work as customers might react violently to him. Thankfully they did not and the local and national media supported him well with appropriately outraged articles. Despite the horror Barrie felt, DCI Adam Hibbert's reasons for the arrests were valid. Marion Stevenson had come forward once more, formalizing her allegations which, by twenty-first century standards, needed a thorough investigation.

Hibbert, a Major Crime Team SIO, searched high and low for anything that suggested all this had been comprehensively investigated at the time – anything that showed Barrie and Dougie had been interviewed or any hint that their houses had been searched for the video.

He found nothing.

Then came the thorny issue that, if these allegations were true, how did that leave Barrie's new family? Were they safe? While still in the pre-Savile era, Child Protection in 2009 had moved on apace and any suggestion that a child may be vulnerable to abuse was doggedly investigated. Adam applied modern-day rigour to these mid-1980s allegations. As hard as it would have been for those on the receiving end, he took the view that to find out once and for all whether Dougie had raped Nicola, and her father had casually watched a video of it while relaxing in an armchair, arrests would have to be made.

He drew no pleasure from ordering this drastic action but this could not continue as a thorn in the side of Operation Salop. Taking the twenty-two year delay out of the equation, however, there was some good that came from the arrest. A thorough, if traumatic, police investigation found not a jot of evidence that the rape had happened or the film existed. In working with social services, the rumbling rumours were dispelled as Barrie emerged with a clean bill of health as a father.

The matter was closed down once and for all, allowing Sussex Police to focus on finding the right time to relaunch the investigation with Bishop still the one and only suspect.

Had Barrie not gone through this harrowing experience, the accusations he faced nine years later might have been far harder to refute and justice denied once more.

While Barrie was ruing his arrest, Adam Hibbert, who was never one for loose ends, felt now was the time to look once again at Bishop's acquittal.

53

Having followed the retrial of Gary Dobson and David Norris for the murder of Stephen Lawrence, and their subsequent conviction, Sussex Police commissioned an internal forensics review of the Bishop exhibits to see whether, with all the developments and renewed sensitivity of DNA profiling, there was the chance of discovering any new and compelling evidence. They remained quietly optimistic but only too aware that they had gone through the same motions over the years but to no avail.

The team responsible for the retrial of the Stephen Lawrence killers had employed LGC – now Eurofins – Forensics, the leading cold case scientists, to use their cutting-edge expertise and facilities to prove Dobson's and Norris' guilt, so Sussex Police turned to them.

DCI Adam Hibbert knew there had been some false starts around 2005 and 2006, when scientists found new fibre links between the Pinto top and Bishop's home, but this had proved insufficient to launch a double jeopardy investigation. He needed to be sure that not only was he sending the right exhibits for testing but also of the strengths and, crucially, the weaknesses of any findings.

He pulled in Principal SOCO Nick Craggs to discuss a way forward. Nick had nearly thirty years of crime scene experience and despite his placid manner was no yes-man. I had worked closely with him and he was the type to tell you if you were talking nonsense, however senior you were. Later to be supported by Senior SOCO Stuart Leonard who was cut from the same cloth, Nick audited all the exhibits that were seized during the original investigation and made attempts to locate them. The items that would be sent to LGC were prioritized, with a brief as to what needed to happen to them.

The first item was the Pinto sweatshirt.

Roy Green, LGC's senior scientific advisor who had helped solve the Lawrence case, had also worked on the death of Diana, Princess of Wales, and the mysterious death of government scientist Dr David Kelly. Coincidentally he also had a link to Moulsecoomb. He had lived there at the time of the murders while studying at the nearby University of Sussex. He also worked as an assistant to Dr David Northcutt, the forensic scientist who had helped convict Bishop for his attack on Claire.

He knew the Babes in the Woods murders to a certain degree and was only too willing to put his steely objective skills to good use, whatever the outcome.

Roy cuts the figure of a humble man, quietly confident in his own expertise. You'd pass this fifty-something, bespectacled chap with his mop of grey hair and matching suit in the street, oblivious to his razor-sharp intellect and his knack for translating his eye-wateringly complex specialism into simple layman's terms.

Having received a lengthy briefing from the review team, Roy Green invited them to his laboratory in rural Oxfordshire to mull over what could and could not be done. Drawing on his recent Stephen Lawrence experience, Roy was clear that any scientific tests must be aimed at discovering evidence that was new and compelling. It would not do to rehash the 1986 tests or to find links that could have been found back then. The bar was high and Roy was committed to seeing if he could help Sussex Police reach it.

DNA profiling was not available in 1986 but was by 1990, as Bishop found out to his peril. However, since then, the science had improved exponentially, meaning that by 2012 it was possible to extract a profile from a minute trace of even badly degraded DNA. The possibilities this opened up for reviewing historical cases were boundless. This was the most exciting development in forensics since 1892 when the first conviction using fingerprint identification was achieved.

Roy Green suggested he examine parts of the Pinto sweat-shirt not previously checked for DNA. One such area was the inside of the cuffs. Roy surmised that, as the cuff was formed of a double layer, it was hypothetically possible that traces of DNA had passed through the weave and were sitting on the inside. If that was the case, the person whose DNA it was could have worn the sweatshirt and be the killer.

The sweatshirt's history up to the point that Mr Gander picked it off the path was a mystery but, despite what Jenny Johnson had initially said, Bishop had vehemently denied own-ing or wearing it. So, if it could be linked to him through foren-sics, he would have a lot of explaining to do.

Adam knew he would have to wait for his answer, so life continued as normal but, in early 2013, things were about to change. Roy had been his usual diligent self in picking the sweat-shirt apart and, having swabbed the inside of the cuff, he sent it for DNA testing against samples retained from Bishop's 1990 conviction.

The result was everything Adam had hoped for but dared not expect.

Testing that tiny area, a part of the sweatshirt no one else would think of checking, had returned a one in a billion DNA match to Russell Bishop. This was the missing link. Generations of police officers already knew that the sweatshirt was worn by the killer at the time of the murders but, after Jenny had changed her mind, only circumstantial evidence had linked it to Bishop.

Despite probably, at the time, never having heard of DNA, Bishop had shed enough of his on that sweatshirt for it to come back to haunt him twenty-seven years later. All of a sudden, Adam's ducks were lining up.

54

When I was the duty Gold commander for Sussex Police between 2009 and 2013, I would start each shift by checking to see who I might have to work with if the wheels fell off. As Gold, it was my job to oversee all critical incidents and command any firearms and public order jobs. Some firearms Silver commanders induced tranquillity, others acute anxiety, and certain public order tactical advisors were more inclined to peaceful resolutions than others. One name, however, was always a true delight to see in the 'Senior Investigating Officer' column. Detective Chief Inspector Jeff Riley.

I was not there to take over murder investigations; that was down to the SIO. However, they needed to let me know what they were doing, whether they needed more staff and how much of the county they had locked down.

The variety in competence and composure was broad. Jeff was at the top of both scales. If any poor unfortunate was murdered on his watch, his quiet proficiency and cast-iron leadership skills would kick in, however complex or high-profile the circumstances.

I had been promoted to detective inspector at the same time as Jeff in 2000 and had remained friends with him since. His trim physique gave the lie to the myth that detectives spend all their time in the pub or curry house. He wore his fifty years well through his love of sailing and I envied his ability to keep a healthy perspective to his work. Only his salt-and-pepper close-cropped beard hinted he was close to retirement.

I remember Jeff calling me, out of courtesy, to describe the horrific torture and murder of an antique dealer whose hog-tied body was only discovered when the fire brigade doused his burning house, no doubt ignited in an attempt to destroy evidence. I could almost smell the smouldering debris as he moved around the perimeter of the scene trying to hang on to his mobile signal. His briefing was full, to the point and oozed his signature mastery. He knew what I would need to know, omitted irrelevance and was clear what logistical support he would like me to arrange. He would have known how difficult it would be to find the killers but he showed no hint of fluster. He indeed caught the four responsible, who were subsequently sentenced to a total of ninety-three years' imprisonment.

The law had changed, science had moved on and, thankfully, Bishop was still locked up. Adam Hibbert had recently been promoted to detective superintendent and was in no position to take on an enquiry of this magnitude, so in early summer 2013, Jeff was summoned to a secret briefing with the overall head of CID, Detective Chief Superintendent Nick May.

Having spelled out the ground-breaking developments, Nick revealed why he was taking Jeff into his confidence.

'Jeff, I'd like you to become the SIO and to see this through to the end, whatever that might be.'

Jeff thought for a moment then said, 'I'd be honoured to but I have some conditions. I need to be struck off all other duties to do this justice. I want to handpick my team and I want to run the enquiry from a remote police station, say Littlehampton.'

It was crucial that word of what they were doing did not leak out. If things went the way he planned, Jeff would need to convince the Court of Appeal that Bishop would get a fair trial. It would only take the media to sniff out a reinvestigation for that to become impossible. Sequestering the team in the far reaches of Sussex was one way of keeping prying eyes away.

It was Nick's turn to think before he agreed to every

condition. 'We will need to brief the Deputy, Jeff, to get his green light to the staffing and money.'

After a couple of weeks of checking facts, swotting up on the implications and rehearsing his arguments, Jeff steeled himself to persuade the deputy chief constable, Giles York, that the force should fund a full reinvestigation into the Babes in the Wood murders.

During the brisk meeting, Jeff spelled out the case so far, explaining what had happened in the meantime and, critically, Roy Green's landmark find. He described the forensic team's experience as well as the expectations of the girls' families. With all that optimism and opportunity, however, Jeff made it crystal clear that were Mr York to agree to pay for a full reinvestigation he could provide no guarantees of success or even cost. And this was a time when cash was in short supply.

I know Giles well and could have predicted his response. He was an ardent proponent of doing the right thing. How would he sleep at night knowing he had turned down a once-in-a-lifetime opportunity to get justice for the Fellows and Hadaway families?

'Jeff,' he said, 'those are things for me to worry about, not you.'

With the funding in place, Operation Yukon was born.

Everyone who worked on the case, was briefed about it or was asked to work alongside it was required to sign confidentiality agreements. That included witnesses, scientists, crown prosecutors, counsel, senior police officers and, of course, the families.

This was a tricky one for Jeff. It was unthinkable to launch an investigation without providing the bereaved parents, siblings, uncles, aunts and cousins the courtesy of telling them.

Because of their deep-rooted and completely understandable sense of injustice, the Fellows and Hadaway families had an excellent and high-profile relationship with the media. Their tireless calls for the investigation to be relaunched, new laws to be applied and emerging science to be tried never went unpublished. Neither did each anniversary of the girls' deaths. Barrie too had his own reasons to be angry. Trust and warmth towards the police did not come naturally to those who felt they had been forgotten.

In November 2013 Jeff called the families to a meeting at Littlehampton Police Station. He expected them to be emotional, some angry, some just weary of yet another decade with nothing to show for it.

They knew something was different when, before he spoke, Jeff invited them all to sign the confidentiality agreement. Then, in his trademark measured tones, he broke the news they had been waiting to hear since December 1987. Sussex Police were reopening the enquiry.

Jeff was quick to manage their expectations. This was one DNA hit which may, or may not, mean anything. The team had only just been established so what else they would find remained to be seen. He spelled out the mountainous bar to even secure the Director of Public Prosecution's authority to interview Bishop, let alone appear at the Court of Appeal, a place not in the habit of lowering its standards to quash an acquittal. So, this was the first step of the thousands that, perhaps, would lead to Bishop standing in the dock of the Old Bailey.

He urged them to be patient. This was a marathon, not a sprint.

They sat, they listened. They had a few questions but they remained calm, considered and most of all grateful that finally there might, just might, be a glimmer of hope. Jeff's pleas to not reveal anything to the media could only find favour if there was trust on both sides. If they continued to believe he would do the very best he could, then surely they would keep their side of the bargain. But only time would tell. Keeping a secret in the police is another challenge altogether. Only rogue officers leak confidential information but one of the personal specifications for becoming a cop is to be bloody nosy.

Jeff puts it well when he says if a police officer sees a closed door, he or she wants to look behind it. The other side to that coin is that they love to talk about what they are up to. Not to outsiders, but they can't resist a good natter with a pal they have worked with about their last big job.

I suppose that is why some write books when they retire.

Jeff forbade his team from even talking to their partners about what they were doing. If asked, they were told to politely, or maybe impolitely, blank the question. Something else police officers tend to be pretty good at.

His master plan was to focus on the new forensic opportunities that now existed but had not been around at the time of Bishop's original Babes in the Wood trial. The results would, hopefully, build a case strong enough for the DPP to authorize Bishop to be interviewed again and for forensic samples to be taken from him. At that stage, once Bishop knew he was under the spotlight again, no confidentiality agreement could possibly guarantee secrecy. Dim as he was, Bishop could still leak his interview to the press.

Just prior to that big day arriving, they would therefore seek an order from the Court of Appeal forbidding any publicity. Once they had that, they could approach witnesses and prepare them for the possibility of reappearing in court.

But all that was a long way off.

55

The problem with storing any evidence for any length of time is that it can get lost, moved, damaged, degraded or interfered with.

In March 2012, following a two-year wind-down, the government closed the Forensic Science Service – the FSS. This bastion of the fight against crime, serious and minor, had been the centre of excellence in the development and application of science. The private sector had muscled their way into the market and, as is the way with privatization, could provide the same service for less while carrying all the risk. That was the fate of many public-owned service providers.

As well as carrying out the bulk of the country's forensic testing, the FSS also retained material from decades ago. These could be items of clothing, tapings and blood samples. Just about anything that had been submitted to them over the years. With its closure came a problem. What would happen to all these parcels of potential evidence? The private providers would not want them. Certainly, police forces did not have the room or the right environment to store them. They could not just be destroyed though.

After much angst, the Forensic Archive was established. A government-owned facility, it was formed to retain and manage case files from all investigation work previously undertaken by the FSS. The archive now stores forensic material, some of which dates back to the 1930s, including millions of case files, frozen material (such as DNA extracts) and items including microscope slides, fibre tapings and recovered hairs.

Jeff knew that whatever was not lurking in the stores, cupboards and basements around Sussex Police buildings was likely to be at the archive. Principal SOCO Nick Craggs and Senior SOCO Stuart Leonard drew up a comprehensive list of every single item seized during the 1986 investigation and any of the subsequent reviews. That meant not just looking at exhibit lists but poring over statements and reports. Next was to locate them. That was trickier than it may seem. Some were not where they should have been. Some no longer existed – the very testing of an item can destroy it – and some were at the archive.

Once found, the challenge was to show every step of each item's life from the moment it came into the police's possession to the present day. It was vital to prove the chain of continuity, otherwise even the most definitive forensic result would be worthless. Jeff's insistence of this sparked numerous trips to the archive over many months and Nick and Stuart delivered. Anything that could be found was found and brought back to Sussex.

The marathon Jeff promised the family was proving to be just that. In practical terms, there was no rush provided he and his team worked expeditiously. Bishop remained locked up in a Category A prison and any thought he might have about coming out on licence would no doubt have been quashed after a confidential briefing to the chair of the Parole Board, as well as some lobbying by the families.

Jeff learned from the Stephen Lawrence investigation to adopt a twin-track forensic approach. On one side he would have Roy Green looking at fibres and DNA and Dr Louissa Marsh examining the paint. On the other side would be Ros Hammond, also a senior scientific advisor for LGC, who would be charged with raking over every exhibit, every scientific process and every outcome, testing whether there was any opportunity whatsoever for the results to have been compromised by poor handling, poor storage or poor science. Effectively she was being pitted against her colleagues and the investigation team to see if she could catch them out.

Like Roy Green, Ros oozed assured confidence, safe in the knowledge that her expertise would do all the posturing for her.

Dr Louissa Marsh seemed a little tenser but that belied a scientist who knew more about paint than is probably healthy for any one person.

The Lawrence team advised that it was better for the police-commissioned scientists to do this from the outset than have the defence ambush them at trial with some faux pas they had not spotted. It made total sense. Scientists are used to being peer reviewed and challenged – it is an established aspect of their work. The police are less so, but it would prove to be one of the most crucial decisions Jeff made.

Things were going well. The exhibits were coming together. The team was getting a grip of what they had, what they could use and what was lost forever. Even the science had moved on a step further. A new technique, DNA 17, came online in July 2014. It was more sensitive, meaning even smaller and older samples of DNA could be profiled and offenders identified, with the risk of erroneous matches greatly reduced. Jeff was never one to count his eggs before they hatched, which was just as well.

It was all about to come crashing down.

56

Come July 2015, two years after Bishop's DNA was found in the cuff, Jeff and the team were still waiting to find out from Ros Hammond just how safe the DNA match on the Pinto top was. The entire investigation had been triggered by that find and it still hinged on it. The eagerly awaited telephone call started with Jeff expecting validation. Only Roy Green and Ros Hammond knew they were about to rip the heart out of Operation Yukon.

The good news was that the DNA found on the cuff was, without doubt, Bishop's. That was the only good news. Ros went on to explain she had studied the file of statements the police had given her relating to the whole continuity of the sweatshirt. She had its full history, from it being found by Moulsecoomb railway station, its arrival at Brighton Police Station, to the FSS laboratory, back to Sussex Police and then to LGC. She had looked at the handling, the packaging, the continuity and the finding.

She knew the police were very excited by the result, but they had asked her to do a particular job and she could not compromise that to spare their feelings, so she broke the news. As a result of the handling and storage of the sweatshirt in the ensuing decades, she could not exclude the possibility that Bishop's DNA had been inadvertently transferred to the cuff.

After it left the lab back in the late 1980s, it had been stored in the basement of Brighton Police Station. The uncontrolled temperature and humidity, together with the time the bag had been there, meant the tape sealing it had degraded, drying out.

She could not exclude that the breaking of the seal might have allowed the Pinto sweatshirt to have become contaminated.

Only one hundred per cent certainty that the forensic results were reliable would do. Jeff knew that. They all knew that. They had lost their sole piece of new and compelling evidence. Their raison d'être.

This was the darkest of days for Jeff and the team. They were crestfallen. What would they tell the families? What would they tell Giles York, by now the chief constable, who had put so much faith in them?

Roy and Ros, however, were more upbeat. They took the view that if this one item contained Bishop's DNA, then surely others would too. Stuart and Nick had recovered a treasure trove of exhibits from the archive, many of which had not been examined before. There would have been no scientific reason to do so back then but there was now.

Collectively they took the decision that, to maximize reliability, they would examine only items that were, effectively, time capsules. Even though DNA had not been quite upon us in 1986, fibre, paint and foliage evidence were. It had been as important to guard against their contamination when looking for that evidence as it is now for DNA. The techniques and precautions were very similar, so there was a glimmer of hope.

The tapings that Dr West and Dr Peabody had lifted from skin, clothing and other surfaces in 1986 had locked in the evidence they held, immune from all contamination, whether that be in the hands of the police, the FSS or the forensic archive.

Providing Ros was satisfied that the tapings had been taken and sealed properly, then not interfered with, any secrets they held would pass her, and the court's, stringent test which might, just *might*, finally deliver justice.

Forensic science is anything but glamorous. But hours spent poring over microscopes and data-filled spreadsheets seal more cases than cops tearing around in souped-up BMWs or thumping interview tables while glaring at nonchalant suspects ever do.

Having dusted themselves down from losing that first DNA hit, the investigation team, SOCOs and scientists had renewed vigour. They were confident that using the sealed tapings taken at the post mortem examinations or during the first forensic examinations meant there could be no contamination.

Back in 1986, Dr Peabody had taped the entire surface of the clothes he was asked to examine and Dr West the bodies. These were then handled pretty much as they would be now.

Fibres trapped in the tapings are compared by placing each sample under a separate microscope before looking at them simultaneously using an optical bridge. A trained eye can determine whether the fibres are likely to be the same. Various light sources are then applied which, when read by a computer, can determine to a high degree of certainty whether or not the fibres are from the same source.

Given the millions of types and colours of fibres on the market, that is pretty convincing evidence to put to a jury.

How much of a fibre is transferred depends on the material and the nature of the contact. Two people wrestling while wearing Aran jumpers will find far more of their opponent's wool on their own jumper than if a couple of suited businessmen brushed past one another on the tube.

How many fibres remain depends both on the cloth and on the time since the contact took place – and whether the host's clothing has been agitated or remained static. There are other ways fibres can transfer. For example, if I put my coat down on a chair and then pick it up, the next person who puts their own coat on that chair will find some of the fibres from my coat on theirs. If there is two-way transfer, such that fibres from my coat are on yours and vice versa, the likelihood of that happening by any means other than our coats touching is so remote it can be disregarded.

The Pinto sweatshirt was covered in paint, as were Bishop's trousers, and there were flakes on the girls too. In 1986, Bernie

Wells had been so optimistic that it would be paint that would link Bishop to the sweatshirt but that was not to be.

Paint can be applied in three ways: brushed, rolled or sprayed. Each method leaves its own traces. Tinned paint, once dried, can last indefinitely, especially on fabric. This is also the case with sprayed paint but as it is made up of microscopic paint balls it can also sit on surfaces before being absorbed. Flakes of dried paint quickly fall off any surface they transfer to.

Therefore, if paint flakes or the microscopic balls from a spray gun are found, it's a pretty sure sign that contact has been recent and the surface they are found on has remained quite static.

Like fibres, there are millions of types and colours of paint which are all distinguishable from one another. That is not to say it is an easy task to determine that paint stain A and paint stain B definitely came from the same tin, but the science nowadays can provide much more certainty – on a batch-by-batch basis – than in 1986.

The mother of all forensics, however, is DNA profiling. Since the mid-1980s it has become the single most important forensic tool in the box. Its ability to identify individual people from invisible traces, leading to them being locked up sooner, prevents many a further murder.

During the investigation into Bishop's attack on Claire, scientists needed samples around the size of a ten pence piece to extract DNA. Nowadays, providing they have a microscopic amount of cellular material – and they don't even need to know what that material is – they can identify a person to the odds of a billion to one because DNA can be grown, or copied, to generate millions of copies of itself.

Sometimes, with these new sensitive techniques, scientists find DNA from more than one person in one sample so they have to separate out the various strands to identify whose is whose. Under the old methods, sometimes they could not separate the profiles.

The new technique of DNA 17 is even better able to evaluate more strands, so the likelihood of two people sharing exactly the same profile plummets.

Once the profile is found, it is compared with that of any suspects or against the National DNA Database which contains the profiles of five and a half million people arrested or convicted of offences in the UK. Once a person has been linked to the DNA found, it does not end there. It is up to the police to work out how the evidence got where it was found, when, and whether that was while the person was committing a crime.

Other DNA techniques, such as Y-STR profiling, which looks at the male lineage and mitochondrial DNA which is passed through the female line, became crucial in the efforts to prove Bishop's guilt but Jeff was determined to base any prosecution on DNA 17 as it was the most accurate at implicating and eliminating suspects.

He had a dilemma though. He wanted to see this new DNA 17 science prove its worth through successful prosecutions elsewhere, but he was up against the clock. Double jeopardy investigations have to be conducted expeditiously.

He needed time but he stuck to his guns. In any case, until they were permitted by the DPP to gather fresh DNA from Bishop, all the testing would be against samples taken over two decades ago following his arrest for Claire's attack. Only when they had up-to-date samples could he apply DNA 17.

This also gave him time to consider an even more convincing way to present the evidence. The CPS senior prosecutor, Libby Clark, said to me, 'Think of forensic evidence as being like strands of varying thickness of twine, each of differing strength. Now think of those strands twisted together into a length of rope. How much stronger that would be. We wanted to present the forensics, with all the strands locked together.'

Roy Green had the task of twisting the rope and providing compelling proof that Bishop was the killer.

Back in 2005 and 2006, other forensic scientists had tried to find new links to support a double jeopardy investigation into Bishop. They'd examined tapings and slides taken in 1986 and made some progress. A total of forty-five fibres matching clothes found in Bishop's house were found on the Pinto top, as were five matching his teenage girlfriend, Marion Stevenson's, skirt.

On the Pinto there were fourteen fibres that matched those from Karen's green top and one from her T-shirt. There were also eight fibres which matched Nicola's pink jumper and one which matched a snagged fibre found at the crime scene.

On Karen's T-shirt there were thirty-four fibres which matched the Pinto as well fourteen on her green top, three on her 'T-shirt/ skirt', eleven on her skirt, and five on her knickers.

Her green top also carried two fibres that matched those from Marion Stevenson's towelling skirt.

Nicola's pink jumper showed up fourteen fibres from the Pinto; four were on her skirt and one on her knickers. Like Karen's jumper, Nicola's also had three fibres matching Marion Stevenson's towelling skirt.

As well as fibres, the scientists examined hair found on the Pinto. It was possible to examine only the mitochondrial DNA but they could say there was moderate support that they came from Bishop, or someone on the same maternal line.

This was the limit of the science in 2005. The evidence was edging towards compelling but not close enough to take the one-way street to launching a double jeopardy investigation. Now, with the 2015 forensic regime under way, the results rolled in.

Roy Green was able to confirm all of the 2005 findings, except where fibres had been destroyed in the testing. He was able to put scientific interpretations to all of his findings, which would go into the mix when the prosecution bound all the forensics together. He was able to say, considering each fibre's colour, type, property and rarity, that they provided at least 'very strong support' (in some cases 'extremely strong support' – his top level of confidence) for the assertion that they arrived as a result of primary contact between the Pinto and both victims rather than through some other indirect route.

He also established that the combination of fibres linking the Pinto to 17 Stephens Road provided 'extremely strong support' for the notion that it bore fibres from that flat rather than them being chance matches. The links between the Pinto and Bishop's home were new and there was greater scientific confidence in the strength of the evidence.

The paint on the Pinto and his trousers remained as crucial now as it was in 1986. Using more sensitive techniques and drawing on decades of research, Dr Louissa Marsh found significant links between the stains on those garments and on the girls'. Paint found on the Pinto cuff and flakes on Karen's T-shirt and skirt together with those on Nicola's sweatshirt and knickers matched that on a maroon Mini that Bishop had sprayed. A maroon paint flake found on Nicola's neck also matched an identically coloured stain on the Pinto.

Dr Marsh also linked red paint stains on the Pinto sweatshirt to the paint used to daub the outhouse doors in Stephens Road. She gave these findings her second-highest level of confidence, so added to the jigsaw that was putting Bishop and the Pinto together with the girls on the night they died.

Turning to the ivy hairs, the Deputy Director of Science at Kew Gardens examined the tapings taken in 1986 and found 584 ivy hairs on those from Nicola's clothing, 452 from Karen's T-shirt and skirt, 749 from her knickers and green top and 491 from the Pinto. She was clear that the den was rich in the same type of ivy hairs and that clothing pressed against these would pick up a high number of them. The path the Pinto was recovered from was only sparsely covered in foliage so the sweatshirt would have been unlikely to have picked up that volume of ivy hairs from there.

With some variations, down to improvements in science and previous samples being destroyed in the testing process, the fibre, paint and fauna findings were, on balance, slightly more damning for Bishop than before.

The links between the Pinto and his home were new and there was greater scientific confidence in the strength of the evidence. More was said about how long fibres and paint balls would persist having been transferred, so it was possible to infer when contact took place but, on their own, these findings would not be enough.

The enormity of quashing any acquittal, especially one provided by a jury after a full and fair trial, needed the silver bullet that, until now, had been just out of reach. But there was one on the horizon.

During the post mortems on the night the girls were discovered, Dr West had diligently taped both girls' bodies, not for DNA but for any fibres, loose hair or debris. These were sealed and submitted to the forensic laboratory.

These tapings, and dozens of others, were retrieved from the forensic archive and taken to Roy Green. Given the promising but now abandoned DNA match on the cuff of the Pinto, Roy decided that anything which might have preserved cellular material, such as skin flakes or hair, should be tested for DNA.

When Karen was last seen, she was wearing her long-sleeved green sweatshirt and no one described her without it that evening. She had not seen Bishop that day and, being a clean girl, had washed that morning and the sweatshirt itself had been laundered the day before. When she was found, that sweatshirt was beside her along with her knickers and her arms were exposed.

The tapings Dr West took from Karen's arms could well be

significant, Roy realized. If any alien skin flakes were present and if he could extract DNA from them, there was a pretty good chance they would belong to the killer. After all, the only person who could have touched her on the bare arm, other than those who moved her to the mortuary and Dr West himself, was that brute.

Roy examined the taping taken from Karen's left forearm. Sure enough, he detected some skin flakes so he removed and tested them. The results surpassed those from the Pinto cuff. The analysis showed a mixture of DNA from at least two people. It was mostly that of Russell Bishop with the remaining probably Karen's and an unknown person.

There was no definitive sample of either Karen or Nicola's DNA but the gender strand, and the profiles from other items, led Roy to infer which DNA was and was not from the girls.

Through statistical evaluation, Roy could say the findings were around a billion times more likely if the DNA came from Bishop, Karen and an unknown person rather than from Karen and two unknown people. This, he said, provided extremely strong support (nigh-on certainty) that the sample contained Bishop's DNA.

He estimated the Y-STR profile he extracted would only be present in one in 29,000 men worldwide and so that was the probability it came from Bishop.

Any scientific result is only as good as the proof of how the sample ended up where it did. Roy, with all his years of expertise and access to research, said the skin flakes would not have remained on Karen's arm for more than a few hours while she was alive. The rubbing of clothing, movement and washing would soon dislodge them. Therefore the finding of Bishop's DNA on Karen's naked arm was extremely significant, probably the most important piece of evidence in the whole case.

Having found Bishop's DNA once, on the Pinto cuff, Roy was certain he would find it again, albeit this time in the tapings taken from it.

In 1986, Dr Peabody and his team had taped both the inside and outside of the sweatshirt during their forensic examinations. Despite all the unfair criticism foisted on the SOCOs and scientists over the years, this was visionary. It was probably fairly obvious to tape the outside of the sweatshirt as this was where you would expect to find fibres and ivy hairs. But who would have known in 1986 that decades later science would reveal who had worn a garment from skin flakes trapped on the inside?

DNA from both Jenny Johnson and Russell Bishop, together with at least one unknown person, was found on the tapings from inside the Pinto. The probability was not as strong as before, up to one in 140,000, but Roy was able to say that, for some of the tapings, there was 'very strong support' that Bishop's DNA was present. Tapings from the outside were even stronger. He found DNA on the front which was one in a billion times more likely to be Bishop's and an unknown person's than two unknown people.

On the back, he found DNA from Bishop and Mr Gander – the electrician who handed the sweatshirt in – together with that of two unknown people. This, again, was one in a billion times more likely to be the case than if it was Mr Gander and three unknown people.

So, with all this state-of-the-art science, the stunning results on their own now pointed towards Bishop having worn the Pinto, the Pinto being worn by the killer and, now, Bishop having touched Karen's arm around the time she died. How did that look when twisted into a rope? Roy's conclusions were irrefutable.

The matching fibres, paint and hairs, taken together with the DNA, gave extremely strong support to the notion that Bishop had worn the Pinto, that it had been in his flat and it had not been worn much since it was there. The hundreds of ivy hairs on the Pinto showed the sweatshirt had most likely been in contact with the same type of ivy as that growing at the murder scene, probably through prolonged and firm contact.

The fibre and paint findings again provided extremely strong support that the Pinto had been in recent contact with Nicola and Karen. And finally, the DNA found on Karen's forearm provided extremely strong support that Bishop had touched her.

Taken together, Roy Green was confident that all this was what he might expect to find if Bishop, while wearing the Pinto, had close contact with Karen and Nicola at or around the time of their deaths

This was what Jeff Riley had been waiting for. Surely this would get them over the line?

58

Before he triggered the process that would be the point of no return, Jeff needed Ros Hammond's assessment on the handling and integrity of the forensic exhibits. He held his breath.

Ros started from the premise of the 'worst case scenario', as she put it. She assumed, when examining the history of every significant exhibit, every handling, every movement and every scientific process that if there was a chance of inadvertent transfer of forensic material, it happened. She would then look to prove, one way or another, whether it actually had.

She looked at how the Pinto was seized, its packaging, how it was stored, when it was shown to Jenny Johnson and what happened to it at the police station and the lab. She scrutinized Dr West's 1986 procedures in taking forensic samples from the girls' bodies. She checked whether items, stored or transported together, could have rubbed up against one another. She inspected photographs, statements, packaging, case notes and the items themselves.

Crucially she showed that the girls' clothing and the Pinto were never both in unsealed packaging in the same building. It was impossible that they had ever come together, except at the murder scene.

While she could not go back in time to watch the testing take place, assuming that the scientists, pathologist and SOCOs followed the procedures of the day, Ros could tell from the records and findings whether anything had happened that should not.

One thing did bother her. Scientists' and police training teach that when opening a sealed exhibit bag, you cut the bag in a previously uncut place, do what you need to do, then reseal it with a label to show who has made the opening and when.

As she ploughed through the statements, she could not correlate the number of times the Pinto bag had been opened with the number of cuts in it. They should have matched. She went back and looked at some other items Dr Peabody had examined over the years, and there lay the answer.

Previously, scientists were taught to cut open the original seal rather than make fresh cuts. So however many times he and his colleagues opened a bag, they would break the same seal. It is easy to see why practice and training changed but old habits die hard and, once again, Ros was satisfied that there had been no malpractice at play.

After hours of checking, rechecking and peer review she was able to deliver her verdict. For each item she examined there was either no possibility of inadvertent transfer or the probability that if it had happened it was minute and could be discounted.

Finally, Jeff had the new, compelling and, crucially, reliable evidence he needed to seek the Director of Public Prosecution's consent to arrest, interview and take samples from Bishop. It was time to make their move.

59

The first half of 2016 was huge for Jeff Riley and his team.

The decision to work alongside the Crown Prosecution Service from the outset was inspired. Not only did their knowledge, expertise and inherent caution help guide the investigation, it ensured that they were preparing for the application to interview Bishop from day one.

In the end, the consent itself came quite readily on 5 April 2016. Clearly, as Jeff's investigation ran its course, the Director of Public Prosecutions, Alison Saunders, had absorbed the whole case from October 1986 to now in great detail. It was fortunate that, in her previous role as Chief Crown Prosecutor of London, she had overseen a similar application to her predecessor Sir Keir Starmer QC for the Stephen Lawrence retrial.

Now armed with the permission for the next steps, Riley and the team were faced with planning for the big day when they would arrest Bishop. He was still in prison for his attack on Claire but it was not just a case of rocking up at the prison gates, rapping on the door and demanding to interview him.

Being a double jeopardy investigation, the police needed to obtain an arrest warrant from a district judge as other powers of arrest could not be used. This meant another confidentiality agreement and going through what would have been an alien procedure for them. Then came the problem of transporting a Category A prisoner to a police station.

Those who come under Category A, the highest security regime imposed on an inmate, are defined as prisoners '*whose escape would be highly dangerous to the public, or the police or the security of the State, and for whom the aim must be to make escape impossible.'*

Around one per cent of inmates are this category, and for them, life is pretty grim. They are housed in one of the UK's highest security prisons, their movements are severely restricted and they are transferred around the prison estate in the utmost secrecy to keep them from forming dangerous liaisons. Such high-risk prisoners are rarely, if ever, transferred to police stations for interview. The logistics, the staffing and the security requirements are too eye-watering to consider. The police normally have to come to them.

Those blessed with never having seen the inside of a police cell block are fortunate in not knowing quite how variable they are. Some are in the basement of decrepit Victorian police stations while others are state-of-the-art purpose-built quasi-penitentiaries miles away from civilization. The one common denominator is that all of them are unremittingly forbidding. Only the most impregnable of police custody blocks are cleared to house Category A prisoners, with permission needed from the highest echelons of the Prison Service.

The planning was intense. Jeff and his team spent hours briefing the team at Frankland, the prison in County Durham where Bishop was currently being held, the accredited police station and senior officers in both forces. Bishop's production had to be seamless but, for security reasons, Jeff could only tell the northern police force they were to expect a Category A prisoner. Not who. Not for what.

On 10 May 2016, for the 9,592nd time, Bishop would have woken behind a locked closed door with the tedium of another day in Frankland maximum security prison lying ahead. The cycle of eat and sleep was only broken by trips to the gym and rare time mixing with other inmates. His hope of parole applications had ebbed away. While he had finally admitted to probation officers that he had attacked Claire, he still denied attempting to kill her or any sexual motive.

To reduce the chance of Category A prisoners being sprung, unless travelling to court, the first they know of being moved is when a team of prison officers fill their cell doorway barking the order: 'Pack your stuff. You're on the move.' Bishop had heard these words before as he zig-zagged his way across the country, enjoying the delights of another super-max jail. On that May morning he would have assumed this was another leg of HM Prisons' Mystery Tour.

Nothing about the yellow and green overalls he was told to slip on over his baggy blue T-shirt and beige trousers would have piqued his suspicions either. That was de rigeur for all journeys. Neither would the multiple handcuffs and guards seem out of the ordinary. He knew the score. He would have sat back as the key turned in his mobile cell, the only one occupied in the armoured prison van, switching his mind to neutral for however long he would be cooped up. One thing prisoners excel at is patience. He did not need much that day.

After just four miles, he would have been curious as he felt the driver slow and the truck manoeuvre in a tight circle. Peering out of the shatterproof polycarbonate porthole at the line of marked police cars and vans, he would have had the first inkling that after nearly thirty years his past was catching up with him.

Durham Police Station is one of the few accredited for Category A prisoners but the tiny custody reception area the five prison officers shuffled Bishop into was at odds with its fortress-like protection. At 9.37 a.m., as the entourage crammed into the small space, joining Jeff, two other Sussex detectives and two Durham custody officers, DC Allan Smith uttered the words Bishop had only heard in his darkest nightmares.

'I'm Detective Constable Smith of Sussex and Surrey Major Crime Team and I have a warrant for your arrest. The warrant has been obtained under the provisions of Section 87 of the Criminal Justice Act 2003 and is signed by a district judge. I'm arresting you on suspicion of the murders of Nicola Fellows and Karen Hadaway on or around Thursday 9 October 1986. The grounds for arresting you are that there is fresh evidence linking you to the murders of both Nicola Fellows and Karen Hadaway and it is necessary to interview you and take forensic samples from you. I've got to caution you, as I've arrested you, and that caution is, you do not have to say anything but it may harm your defence if you do not mention, when questioned, something which you later rely on in court. Anything you do say may be given in evidence. Do you understand that, Russell?'

Bishop could only manage a quivering, 'Yes, no reply though. Can I contact my lawyer please?' in response.

From that point on he was treated as any other suspect arrested for a serious offence. His solicitor was called and an appropriate adult – someone to help him understand what was happening – was summoned too.

Relief washed through Jeff. Four years of covert planning, the painstaking dedication of his team and the faith of his bosses had finally paid off.

Bishop was in *his* custody.

There had been a moment that morning, however, when he wondered whether he would be facing the long drive south with egg on his face. The prison transport was late and they had sent no words of reassurance they were on their way. He anxiously peered out of the windows, hoping to glimpse the white prison van pull up at the station gates. He knew a call to the prison would be fruitless – they were hardly likely to tell someone, who for all they knew could be some random guy on the phone, they were about to leave with a Category A prisoner.

He also grew impatient fielding calls from the CPS, understandably waiting for news. At least now he could reassure them the deed was done.

Since Bishop was last arrested, a significant addition had been made to the caution: '. . . but it may harm your defence if you do not mention, when questioned, something which you later rely on in court' was added by the 1994 Criminal Justice Act which, some say, swept away the centuries' old convention that defendants are protected from incriminating themselves.

What it actually did was inject a little common sense into the system which previously allowed defendants to keep quiet during interviews before conjuring up elaborate explanations at trial which, if they had revealed in an interview, the police would have had a chance to check. Now, in certain circumstances, a jury can draw adverse inferences should the person come up with explanations at their trial which they could have but did not raise after arrest.

This is not all one way. The police now have to provide enough information to the suspect or their solicitor for them to know the bones of an allegation and if the adverse inferences may apply. They also have to give a 'special warning' should the person not answer a question that might invoke some of those provisions.

All of this would have been new to Bishop but not his solicitor, Mr Styles. However, Bishop was not overly blessed with humility and, despite the advice Styles clearly gave him, he just could not help himself. To sidestep the 1994 provisions, most solicitors advise their clients to make a prepared statement at the outset, then say nothing. That statement is normally a deft balance between providing sufficient detail to ward off any adverse inferences but not enough to incriminate themselves. Once the statement is read, sometimes by the solicitor, the plan is for the suspect to keep quiet or, at most, answer 'no comment' on all questions.

The police will often only disclose just enough information and almost always hold back key facts. If and when those are revealed the solicitor is entitled to have another chat with their client. In fact, this chat is essential for the police as if the suspect does not have the chance to receive advice on the key questions, adverse inferences cannot be drawn.

Of course, all this only helps the suspect if he actually keeps to the script.

Thankfully Bishop had been in regular contact with a firm of solicitors over the years and it was these people he wanted by his side. That made life easier for Jeff and the interviewers. Had Bishop opted for the local duty solicitor, bringing them up to speed on a thirty-year investigation would have taken some doing.

The murders themselves were complicated enough but at least these solicitors would have considered a double jeopardy investigation at some time and prepared, at least a little, for this day.

Jeff and the team could finally crack on.

60

After a lengthy consultation the first interview started in a predictable way at 2.30 p.m. In another change for Bishop, all interviews were now videoed. Even if his words did not betray his arrogance, his body language bellowed it loud and clear. The preamble out of the way, his solicitor, Mark Styles, read a statement on Bishop's behalf.

'I, Russell Bishop, make the following statement in relation to the allegation that I was responsible for the murder of Karen Hadaway and Nicola Fellows. I completely and utterly deny any involvement in the deaths of Karen Hadaway and Nicola Fellows. I was tried for these offences in 1987 and found not guilty by a jury after only two hours' deliberation. Evidence in relation to the Pinto sweatshirt and other clothing, as well as evidence relating to a red Mini, was put to the jury at my trial in 1987. I was found not guilty.'

DCs Gary Pattison and Richard Slaughter, two mild-mannered, quietly spoken yet utterly forensic interviewers, set about slowly yet courteously turning the screw. Bishop made the mistake of falling for their gentlemanly 'good cop, good cop' routine and did not spot he was throwing away his own cell key.

The problem for suspects lies not so much in not answering questions, although on certain matters they need to come up with something, it is thinking of an excuse later at the trial. Bishop might have thought by answering 'no comment' that it would protect him. It would not.

DC Gary Pattison reeled him in.

He began: 'If you had any contact with those girls on 9 October, tell us about what happened to those girls.'

Bishop: 'I've got no comment.'

DC Pattison: 'Did you touch any of their bodies?'

Bishop: 'I've got no comment.'

DC Pattison: 'Just focusing on Nicola . . . what areas of the body did you touch on that date?'

Bishop: 'I've got no comment.'

And so, the questions went on, Gary trying to elicit any indication that Bishop had touched either Nicola or Karen, each question rebuffed with a rhythmic 'No comment'.

That first interview lasted for just half an hour. Jeff Riley should have been watching on a remote link, appraising each question and answer, working out ways forward, but infuriatingly it was broken. He had to pace the room waiting for breaks so he could be given updates then direct Gary and Richard on where he wanted them to press. He cursed his phone when, again and again, CPS solicitors called for updates. In his heart he knew this was as big a day for them as him, but he really would have preferred to just get on with his job.

After a half-hour break, Gary and Richard resumed. This time Bishop had had enough of the incessant questions and his solicitor's expectation that he remain silent. Banging the table, he ranted, 'The only evidence on that Pinto from them victims are the fibres. The Pinto and the children's clothing was examined on the same table at the same time by a police officer, who admitted it under oath, it's all on record, now go away and look at it, end of subject. This case has nothing to do with me, nothing to do with me whatsoever, I cleared my name by a jury of my peers and you come in here saying there's new evidence, there's no new evidence, it's all been before the jury, all these tapings of this that and the other, it's all been before the jury, all the hairs, been before the jury, *been before the jury*, it's not new, unless it's been planted and I hope that's not the case. But I'm telling you now, there is no case to answer, I'm sorry, I want the case solved but you're looking in the wrong place. Now I've got no comment to make, please. Please bring this to a close.'

He flounced back in his chair, hoping he'd had the final word.

Gary and Richard suspended the interview and regrouped. No doubt Mr Styles was doing his best to shut Bishop up. Just over an hour later, the third interview was under way. The two detectives knew they had their man on the ropes, but they were not going to let him know that. Gary introduced the DNA evidence and gently probed for an explanation.

DC Pattison: 'If you go back to the start here, so we're talking about a mixed DNA profile that has been obtained from a taping taken from the left forearm of Karen during the post mortem examination on 10 October 1986.'

Bishop: 'Carried out by Dr West.'

DC Pattison: 'That's correct.'

Bishop went to carry on but his solicitor reminded him of the rules.

Bishop: 'I'm sorry, I've got no more comment.'

DC Pattison: 'So how can you account for . . .'

Bishop: 'I've got no more comment . . . Seriously, no more comment, I know you've got to, yeah, go on . . . I know what you're gonna say.'

DC Pattison: 'So you've asked me who took the taping and I've explained to you that it was taken at the post mortem examination, which is in the disclosure document on 10 October '86 . . . and you said no more comment. What's the reason for that?'

Bishop: 'I have no more comment.'

Bishop reverted back to his no comment mantra but Gary had to put the questions to him.

DC Pattison: 'What would you like to say about this disclosure that you've gone through?'

Bishop: 'I've got no comment at this stage.'

DC Pattison: 'In relation to this new evidence IEW/10?' (This was the swab from Karen's forearm.)

Bishop: 'I've got no comment whatsoever at this stage.'

DC Pattison: 'Have you got any reasonable explanation as to why your DNA could be found on Karen's left arm?'

Bishop: 'As I say, I've got no comment at this stage . . . I totally understand, but I have no comment at this stage and I can assure you now I'm totally innocent of this offence and, but I've got no comment.'

DC Pattison: 'But you keep saying you're innocent . . . so help us establish that you're innocent.'

Bishop: 'I wish I could, but I can't so . . . I can't give that information at this moment in time, I apologize for that, but I've got no comment.'

DC Pattison: 'At this moment in time?'

Mr Styles could see his client was struggling, so tried to come to his aid, give him some breathing space and relieve the pressure.

Mr Styles: 'He's being asked to comment at the moment, he's had questions put to him this afternoon and this evening particularly in relation to quite advanced DNA analysis techniques, at the moment that is what the question surrounds a DNA sample upon Karen Hadaway. He's only able to provide an expert answer to that.'

As any good detective would do, Gary ignored the interjection and homed in on Bishop.

DC Pattison: 'If there's any innocent explanation as to why your DNA is found on Karen's left forearm, then we're interested in listening to you.'

Bishop: 'I've got no comment whatsoever.'

He was back into no comment mode. Gary came at the question in different ways but they all boiled down to the same simple thing. Was there any explanation for Bishop's DNA being on Karen's arm? Each time he refused to answer, although he did hint that he might have an explanation 'at some time in the future'. He could have got away with that in the 1980s, but this was 2016 and that would not wash.

Later, Richard took over. Perhaps a different voice might lever some answers. At first, his questions were blanked like Gary's, but he did not have to wait long for another outburst.

Bishop: 'I've got nothing to say, I'm not responsible for this, I had nothing to do with it, I'm innocent, I've been tried and now I've got no comment to make whatsoever, there are some fucking stuff genied up thirty years later, I'm sorry but I've got no comment whatsoever.'

Richard's passive reply must have riled him: 'But, I understand what you're saying there Russell . . . As I said, on putting the technical side of this to one side and you've told us to refer back to what was said before, but we're asking you now. That's not clear to us where your position stands on touching Karen's forearm.'

With finality Bishop barked: 'I didn't touch no one, so I'm innocent and as I said I've got no comment to make.'

There it was. Job done. *'It may harm your defence if you do not mention, when questioned, something which you later rely on in court.'* Any variation in the witness box from *'I didn't touch no one'* would be suicide for Bishop, so he would have to think long and hard about why Roy Green found his DNA. Through his arrogance and stupidity, he had boxed himself into a corner and there seemed no way out.

All that needed to be done now was for a mouth swab to be taken for that important DNA sample the DPP had authorized. Jeff ordered it be driven straight down to the lab to ensure it contained a usable profile.

Satisfied it was viable, Bishop was not charged but technically bailed from custody. Normally bail involves restoring a detainee's freedom but he was going nowhere other than the short drive back to HMP Frankland and a long wait to hear his fate.

61

While Bishop was being interviewed, a reporting restriction order granted on 12 April 2016 was circulated to the media. To the world at large this ensured that there could be no coverage of the ongoing enquiry – an enquiry those on the outside were oblivious to up until that point.

For Jeff and the team, however, it provided them with a freedom they struggled to come to terms with; they had been so used to working away under a veil of secrecy. Now, with the safety net of the media blackout, they could start approaching witnesses.

The first to know were the families. Their patience had been extraordinary. Even during their annual visits to Wild Park, they kept their part of the bargain. It would have looked odd if they had clammed up completely but, in hindsight, their calls for justice were subtly muted while the enquiry had been going on. The family liaison officers, who had been alongside them throughout the reinvestigation, were delighted to break the news that finally Bishop had been arrested. This was what the Fellowses, Hadaways and Heffrons had campaigned so hard for, but they saw the bigger picture. Any elation, or otherwise, would have to wait. Let the police do their job. Let justice prevail.

As word trickled out more widely, Jeff instructed his intelligence cell to monitor any online mention of Bishop or the case. Occasional blogs would crop up and some social media posts, but swift visits to the unwitting offenders damped down any breaches and soon silence was restored.

Up until this point Operation Yukon had been identifying

and locating witnesses who might be called in any subsequent trial, but the team had been unable to approach them. This was a task in itself as many had moved, some had died and some just seemed to have disappeared off the face of the earth. Regardless, the time the team had spent beavering away, using state-of-the-art analytical tools, meant they tracked down all of those still alive, one way or another.

It must have felt odd finally knocking on strangers' doors and breaking the news that the Babes in the Wood enquiry was again up and running. The overwhelmingly positive reaction the officers received emboldened them. In hindsight it was probably not surprising that each witness, whether civilian or ex-police, had lived with this case since the day Bishop walked free from Lewes Crown Court. Few had truly moved on and once they were reassured that, in the event of them being called to give evidence, it would not be a memory test all were keen to play their part – even those who knew they would be in for a hard time.

As with the families, however, it was crucial to prepare witnesses for the long haul. Nothing was certain. The DNA tests were being rerun with DNA 17 against the excellent profile from the sample obtained from Bishop at Durham Police Station. Counsel were considering all the evidence, including the new interviews, and the Court of Appeal had yet to rule on the 'safety of the acquittal.'

Once all the witnesses had been warned, the team began working frantically to pull together the submission for the DPP to authorize the next stage. While the police had a dedicated team who were well versed in the case, others were continuing with with their day jobs. Scientists, CPS solicitors and counsel were all juggling other cases, and this created a frustrating delay for Jeff Riley.

The forensic results seemed to take forever. Conferences with counsel and the CPS were a nightmare to co-ordinate. Everything seemed so sluggish. Despite working on this for four years, Jeff was more used to the cut and thrust of fast-time live investigations: a body found, witnesses to interview, suspects to arrest, evidence to secure. He did not do slow time.

A constant fear also nagged away at him. The Court of Appeal might think there was an acceptable case for the acquittals to be quashed but may also feel it had taken too long to bring the case. As an experienced SIO, Jeff had ensured that there were no unnecessary delays in any aspect of this huge, unprecedented case that were within his control. He reluctantly had to respect that others were not in the same position but at least he did all he could possibly do.

In March 2017, having considered all the evidence, with the relevant legal and public-interest tests applied and after a final verbal briefing from CPS lawyer, Libby Clark, and her boss, Nigel Pilkington, DPP Alison Saunders signed the authority which paved the way to the Court of Appeal. Now there was no turning back. The families were cautiously ecstatic. Another hurdle cleared, but many more on the horizon.

In August that year, the CPS hosted a meeting with the families where they set out the next steps, providing them with the reassurances that everyone was on their side.

Finally, the day came. On 6 December 2017, the families, police and CPS met at London's Royal Courts of Justice for the long-awaited Court of Appeal hearing. Brian Altman QC, over the course of three hours, set out the Crown's argument that there was new, compelling and reliable evidence to justify quashing Bishop's acquittal. He covered the science and what it all meant, before drawing the comparisons between the attack on Claire and the murders of Karen and Nicola. Meanwhile Joel Bennathan QC, for Bishop, raised concerns regarding the integrity of the forensic evidence and how difficult it would be for witnesses to remember exactly what they did over thirty years ago.

The following day the court heard from Ros Hammond, who sought to provide them with the reassurances they needed that the science was new and the results reliable. The court, at this stage, was only concerned with the new evidence as this was what the threshold demanded. After two long days, the judges adjourned until 12 December, offering their condolences to the families for their unimaginable loss.

Everyone gathered on that Tuesday, nerves jangling, knowing the finality of what their lordships' decision could bring. The judgement, delivered by Sir Brian Leveson, the President of the Queen's Bench Division, was brisk. He and his colleagues found that the tests set by the Criminal Justice Act 2003 had been met and thereby quashed Russell Bishop's acquittal, effectively ordering the retrial many had thought impossible.

Jeff, his team and the families allowed themselves a brief moment of elation before steeling themselves for the biggest uphill struggle of their lives.

PART THREE

62

Tuesday, 16 October 2018, thirty-two years and six days on from the murders of Karen and Nicola, the day so many had waited for finally arrived. After two trials, one civil claim and a finely judged appearance at the Court of Appeal, this was the day Russell Bishop would have to stand and reface the charges he had so very nearly escaped.

London's Central Criminal Court, or the Old Bailey as it is affectionately dubbed, stands a mere 200 yards from St Paul's Cathedral with part of the building being on the site of the long-since-demolished Newgate Prison. Its eighteen courts dispense justice not just to London's villains but to high-profile cases from across the country.

Those from outside the capital who have made the one-way trip to 'the Bailey' include Soham child killer Ian Huntley, the Yorkshire Ripper Peter Sutcliffe and Brighton Bomber Patrick Magee. Although Magee's was not quite a one-way trip as, despite blowing up five people while trying to assassinate the entire UK government, he was released under the Good Friday Agreement, having served a mere fourteen years.

Bishop's name still struck fear in Brighton and few who knew the case did not harbour a theory as to his guilt or otherwise. A trial anywhere in or near Sussex was out of the question and this was the oldest double jeopardy case so far to be brought back to the courts. It was an intriguing juxtaposition of old and new legislation, policing and science. Never before had two legal timeframes been brought together so skilfully. Only the top court in the land would do.

The reporting restriction imposed back in 2016 had been modified to allow reporting of the case up to the limits that would be permitted for any other murder trial. Bishop's identity, the offences he was charged with, his plea and the trial date were now public.

Day one was a bit of an anti-climax. As with most high-profile and long-running trials, this one took a little while to get up a head of steam. A good deal of the logistics had been thrashed out at Plea and Case Management Hearings beforehand. It had come as no surprise to anyone that Bishop was pleading not guilty to both charges on the indictment. Given the fusion of new and old legislation, what counsel were and were not allowed to present as evidence or argue in cross-examination was anything but straightforward. The trial judge, the Honourable Mr Justice Sweeney QC, had already ruled on most aspects with the theory being that both sides would just get on with presenting their cases and calling witnesses. It never quite works like that, as anyone who has served on a jury will tell you – jurors seem to spend as much time in the waiting room as they do in court, while the intricacies of the law are thrashed out in their absence.

Therefore, the only progress made on that first day was to select a shortlist for the jury panel. Unlike in other countries, there is little horse trading over jury members. It is quite a swift affair, where counsel have just a moment to object to any prospective juror being one of the twelve before they are sworn in and the trial gets underway.

At 10.30 a.m., the trial started properly.

Over forty journalists representing newspapers, television and radio from across the country packed out Court Sixteen. The usual press benches were set aside for the two reserve jurors the judge would select, so the hacks lined the walls opposite.

This court was not one of the statelier rooms but it still effused pomp and formality. The judge sat alone, high above those he would guide and advise, with his neat red robe and ruffled horsehair wig symbolizing both order and experience.

Bobbing up and down on the rows of benches beneath him were his clerk, counsel for the prosecution and defence, their juniors, the CPS lawyers and Bishop's solicitor. Finally, tapping away at their laptops in the rear seats, sat Jeff and his team.

Sitting almost unnoticed between the dock and exit was Michelle Hadaway, now Johnson, her daughters and family liaison officers. She would sit there throughout the whole trial, dignified and stoic, while listening once again to the horrors that would be methodically and clinically exposed.

Russell Bishop entered the Perspex-encased dock to a rattle of chains, surrounded by three prison officers, their tattoos and skin-tight white shirts rippling with their every move. Two flanked him while the third wedged himself in front of the small door that led to where the rest of us sat. His security category meant that even here, in one of the most secure courts in the country, HMP Belmarsh, his home for the duration of the trial, were taking no chances.

Bishop had aged beyond recognition. His bald head and craggy face were a stark contrast to his boyish flop of hair and the bum-fluff moustache we had last seen in the 1990s. Dressed scruffily in a grey open-necked shirt and wearing rimmed glasses, he looked a good decade older than his fifty-two years.

The jury candidates came forward one by one. Some had already provided reasons why a two-month trial would present them problems and the judge readily released them to other courts, for shorter commitments. The rest, seven men and five women, took the oath and settled in their benches which would be home until nigh-on Christmas. The diversity of those chosen – young, old, black, white, Hindu, Muslim, Christian, no faith at all – was refreshing.

For completeness, the indictments were once again put to Bishop and his clipped 'Not guilty' set the trial in motion.

63

After the judge spelled out to the jury, in necessarily painstaking terms, their role and his, what they must and must not do and what would be expected of them, he handed over to the lead prosecuting counsel, Brian Altman QC. The barrister, robed in his Queen's Counsel gown and wig, carried an air of command that told of the many victories he had scored in this very building. The most notable example being his successful prosecution of Levi Bellfield for a total of three murders (including that of Surrey schoolgirl Milly Dowler) and an attempted murder. He was ably supported by his junior, Alison Morgan (now a QC herself), who had performed the same role in the Stephen Lawrence retrial. This was the same team that had so successfully argued the quashing of the acquittal in the Court of Appeal ten months previously.

Altman's supreme confidence and magisterial bearing, accentuated by his quiet, measured yet rapier-sharp oratory, exemplified advocacy at its very best. Mr Altman warned the jury that he would take the rest of the week to deliver his opening statement. Luckily for the journalists, copies were handed out before he started and for those with particularly pressing deadlines, emailed too. The rules on publication had changed once more so anything said in open court, with the jury present, could now be reported.

Courts rarely produce the drama newcomers expect. Barristers remain fixed behind their benches; approaching the jury or witnesses is strictly forbidden. The detail is everything and it is the evidence, not the counsels' opinions, that matter.

These opening statements and the closing address are the only times when counsel can make overt efforts to sway the jury and, through Altman's seventy-five-page speech, that was what he intended. The trick with advocacy, or indeed evidence-giving, is reducing complexity to everyday language. Taking it slowly, methodically and making simple points backed up by coherent argument is the only way to help twelve ordinary members of the public, who had probably never heard of Russell Bishop and the Babes in the Wood, do their job.

Over the next four days Altman took them step by step through the highlights of his case. Every so often he paused, asking them to familiarize themselves with locations from the albums of photos and maps they shared.

The uninitiated might have been tempted to urge him to 'get on with it', but impregnable fortresses rely on solid foundations and this was what he was building, layer by layer.

Relief, for some, came on the third day of Altman's speech. Following planning which would have put the military to shame, the judge, jury, counsel and court clerks boarded a coach outside the Old Bailey and headed for Brighton. Like the visit during the 1987 trial, this was effectively a mobile court in session. The precautions to keep the jury separated from others were in place, with the public kept at bay and a record made of everything that was said and done. The only difference was that those who normally sported them spurned their wigs and gowns for the day. Bishop was entitled to go but chose not to, much to the relief of the police and prison officers.

When the dark blue Readybus coach, escorted by police outriders, swung off the A27 into Wild Park the jurors were met with the poignant sight of a hawthorn tree decked in pink flowers, beads and crystals. This memorial, just yards from where the girls died, has served as an enduring shrine to Karen and Nicola. Large pink balloons picked out the number '32' as they fluttered in the breeze, a reminder of the anniversary which had just passed. Two small teddy bears sat next to the plaque dedicated to the young victims.

Judge Sweeney had warned the jurors they would pass this place but told them they would not dwell there, not out of disrespect but because it was not relevant to the case. They gathered by the pavilion that PC Pete Coll had searched around when hunting for the girls. Once an elderly rambler was swiftly diverted away by a police officer, Mr Altman pointed out the area where the girls' bodies were found. 'This is the pavilion which was here, as you saw, in 1986. Behind the pavilion is the grass bank, now overgrown, and the steep slope leading into the woods. And it was above this spot that the girls were found dead on Friday 10 October 1986 up there in that sort of area,' he said, the poignancy no doubt sinking in.

From there they were shown a large red-berried bush. 'This is the tree where the girls were seen playing,' Altman said. He then pointed across Lewes Road, drawing their attention to the chip shop the girls were outside just before they were last seen. Then they took in the subway and Newick Road – where the girls both lived – before taking the short walk to the litter-strewn footpath next to Moulsecoomb Station where the Pinto was found.

No map in the world could do better than this excursion in drumming home to the jury exactly how close all these important landmarks were and how utterly possible it was for Bishop to have done what the prosecution alleged.

64

In a criminal court, while the judge has the best seat and we all stand and sit at his or her command, seasoned barristers know it's only the jury that matter. Every witness chosen, each argument made and every syllable of their rhetoric has just one purpose: to persuade every juror that their version of events is the correct one. Underpinning all of that, however, are tactics.

Brian Altman had spent nearly a week embedding his case in the jury's minds and now he would move straight into calling his witnesses who, with their sworn testimony, would bolster his side of the story.

Despite it being nearly a year since the Court of Appeal quashed Bishop's 1987 acquittals, and there had been the Plea and Case Management Hearings intended to sort out all the legal argument in the meantime, Joel Bennathan QC, who had remained Bishop's counsel since the Court of Appeal hearing, needed to create some time for the ferocity of the prosecution's opening statement to fade in the jurors' minds.

An appeal specialist, Mr Bennathan has an unrivalled reputation in overturning wrongful convictions and miscarriages of justice. His dexterity in arguing the nether reaches of law, procedure and convention make him a formidable opponent, even for the likes of Altman. Knowing he risked the judge's wrath, he asked permission to take the unusual step of addressing the jury prior to Altman calling his witnesses. This, he said, would involve discussing a point of law. He would have known that, despite the fact he'd had months to argue the points he was now raising, no judge would deny a previously acquitted defendant the opportunity of a fair trial. Certainly not on procedural grounds alone.

A full eight days later, the jury were finally back in court. None will have known what the gap week was all about but they would soon find out. Crucially for the defence though, the jurors may have forgotten the strength of Altman's arguments.

With the legal argument won and his opening statement green-lit, Bennathan took to his feet. In a thinly disguised jibe, he assured the jurors he would not keep them a week, far from it. He made four simple points.

For the first time in public, Bishop – or in this case his barrister – effectively admitted the attack on Claire. Under the bad character rules, this had been ruled in as evidence but Bennathan had a different take. Awful as this was, he urged the jurors not to be fooled into deciding Bishop's 1986 guilt on that attack alone. He cautioned them against being seduced by the science. It was complex and far-reaching but just because certain results emerged, did it necessarily mean Bishop was guilty? He reminded them of the 'mind-boggling' sensitivity of DNA which made it hugely prone to contamination.

He then moved on to the fact that Bishop had changed his story time and again and said this was being held against him. Why? So many others had done this too. Why was it damming for one person to be unreliable, but for others their explanation was accepted?

Finally – and this was his trump card and the basis for the week's legal jousting – what if there was another suspect they should keep an eye on? Despite there being only one person on trial, he said, Bishop could point to facts that indicated another person might have committed the offences. Someone close to the girls who had no alibi. Who made comments after the killings which were far more incriminating than anything the defendant had ever said. Someone who might have been able to order Nicola to go to the park. Someone with a guilty secret regarding the sexual abuse of the little girl.

What if the police and CPS had been looking at the wrong man for thirty-two years? What if, instead of Bishop, they should have been looking at someone else? What if that someone else was Barrie Fellows?

65

The press seats cleared almost immediately. Within minutes headlines such as '*Alleged killer's lawyer accuses father of dead schoolgirl*', '*Russell Bishop accuses Barrie Fellows of killing daughter Nicola*', and '*Murder accused points finger at girl's dad*' flashed across screens up and down the country, together with photos, old and new, of the man who had yet to put his side of the story.

The decision to allow this alleged bad character evidence of Barrie Fellows based on the Marion Stevenson allegations was lawful but the media explosion devastated both Jeff and Barrie. The jury had been told to ignore any media coverage of the trial but how could you ignore this? It changed the whole focus of the coverage. For several days it was nothing to do with the forensics, Bishop's selective memory or his strikingly similar attack on Claire. It was all about Barrie Fellows. Bennathan had played a blinder.

As any good fighter will tell you, the best thing to do once knocked down is to get back up again. That was exactly what Brian Altman did in calling his first witness.

By now, one male juror had been replaced by a woman, making an equal gender split and the remaining back-up jury member had been stood down. To protect her dignity, the court was cleared as Michelle was helped into the witness box. Her disabilities, leaving her wheelchair-bound, had not weakened her resolve however, and once she was seated the court filled once more and she gave her dignified evidence.

Dressed all in black, her tattoos in homage to her family worn proudly on her arms, Michelle looked ready for this. She was clear and confident as, like in 1987, she affectionately described for the jury Karen's playful loving ways, her homely and sweet nature and her love of life. She said how she had regarded Bishop and Stevenson to be a bad influence so she forbade Karen from seeing them. She took the jury through the events of 9 October 1986. How she last saw Karen when she ran out to play and the horror of searching for the girls throughout the night. She described her awful realization that the girls' bodies had been found when she saw the intense activity beneath Jacob's Ladder the following day.

Wisely, Bennathan was gentle with Michelle. He tried to persuade her Karen had been closer to Bishop than she had maintained, but Michelle remained resolute. In a brief lighter moment, she called the barrister out for referring to his client as Russell Brand, instead of Bishop.

He then started to introduce the idea that Barrie might be the killer to Michelle. Nothing too damning, just asking her to reflect on what he saw as odd behaviour: not going straight out to search, mentioning when he came back from the mortuary that Karen had not been beaten. All very gentle but paving the way for the onslaught to come.

Next came Susan Fellows – now Eismann. Smartly dressed in a mustard top, she was clearly nervous but projected her heart-breaking evidence lucidly to the jurors opposite. Altman's questions took the same form as those he had asked Michelle; helping the court get to know Nicola, describing that awful last day and covering how well she knew Bishop.

Her pain when she had to confirm to the court that her and Barrie's son, Jonathan, had died just weeks before the trial was palpable. Throughout her evidence, however, she remained breath-takingly composed until she had to describe what Nicola had been wearing. Weeping quietly, she quickly collected herself and continued.

Bennathan's cross-examination was more pointed. Predictably he homed in on Barrie's use of corporal punishment, how he once broke his grandmother-in-law's nose and how he would tell Nicola off if she overstepped the line or used bad language. Susan countered by emphatically describing how Nicola was dotty about her father and how much of a daddy's girl she was. She denied Barrie meant to hurt her grandmother and, despite them being divorced for decades, Susan's defence of him was genuine.

66

The following day, to save overwhelming the trial with multiple unnecessary witnesses, the prosecution's junior counsel, Alison Morgan, read out a series of statements and facts that had been agreed between the prosecution and defence. There would be a series of these throughout the trial but to keep the chronology clear in the jury's mind, this batch just covered the girls' last movements and some uncontentious meetings they had on the way.

The prosecution had long ago rejected the notion that the girls were dead by 6.30 p.m. and so called Mrs 'White', who in 1987 had been a defence witness. This time there was no suggestion she wanted anonymity so, when she answered the first question of 'Can you tell the court your name?' with 'I don't want to say,' eyebrows were raised.

In the interests of expediency and in the absence of any objections from either side, she was allowed to continue in this vein. However, she was to prove more troublesome to the prosecution.

Throughout the investigation and the first trial, she had been crystal clear that she had seen the girls across Lewes Road waving in her direction at 6.30 p.m.

However, the day before giving evidence this time – thirty-two years later – she suddenly remembered that it was more like 8.20 p.m. She put this down to the fact that she was waving her dad off as he left her house for his own to watch a film – *The Runaway Train* – that started at 9 p.m.

Why she changed her mind, why she remembered the film

and why so much later, neither prosecution nor defence could fathom. She did say she had been harassed after giving evidence at the last trial, but her new timings stretched all credibility and other than bemusing the court and angering the judge, her impact on the trial was negligible.

However, after a few more agreed facts, this time regarding sightings of Bishop, the real drama was waiting in the wings. Whichever version of events Bishop was opting for this time, he needed to explain his DNA on Karen's arm. Despite 'failing to mention when questioned . . .' there were two witnesses his barrister needed to destroy.

And they knew it.

67

With the trial now a couple of weeks old and in full swing, strangely most of the press seats now lay vacant. The prosecution case had been laid out in fine detail and even the defence had shown their hand, so many of the journalists could pick and choose the witnesses they wanted to hear.

Crown Court trials, even the double jeopardy double murder variety, would not make good television. The drama is sporadic, the legalese turgid and the pace interminable. Meanwhile, in the background the police and prosecution teams, and probably the defence too, work tirelessly to make sure the right witnesses appear, giving the right evidence at the right time.

When one side drops a stone in the water, like the defence's intention to name Barrie Fellows as the killer, the ripples are tidal and efforts to rebut or challenge are frenetic. Brian Altman QC was the most seasoned of advocates. His questioning and cross-examinations were finely tuned and his vision was breath-taking. He never lost his temper, raised his voice or was wrong-footed.

His skill in wooing witnesses into a false sense of security was only matched by his genial way with the jury. But, to all intents and purposes, he was a hard taskmaster. He needed to be. To appear so deft while on his feet, his team needed to have done their homework for him.

At each adjournment – and they became frequent and often lengthy – his junior and the police team would huddle around him then starburst to do his bidding. From my career I knew all the officers in court and some were there all day, every day, and had been living this enquiry for six years.

Pressure affects different people in different ways and this was evident as the trial progressed. Everyone had worked like troupers to bring this quite unique case back to court and anything other than a swift conviction and lengthy prison sentence was unthinkable.

That said, most carried the pressure well – happy to pass the time of day, to explain how they had coped and mull over old times. Some, on the other hand, were less able to kick back and were unrecognizable compared to their former selves. The relentless toing and froing, the demands of the court and counsel had ground certain individuals down to the degree that their upbeat personas I had known for years had been replaced by a dismissive surliness.

I do not hold this against them but just hope that they are now able to reflect on the fruits of their graft and are proud that they have been central to bringing such an intractable case to its conclusion.

Jeff Riley had a completely different approach. He wore his burden lightly, and made it clear to journalists and writers alike that he wanted to work with them to help get the right story to the public and not let mischief-making headlines fill a vacuum. He would often be seen chatting to national and local reporters – gauging for them when key witnesses would appear and offering them opportunities to interview him at the right time.

With this mature, modern stance he rightly won the media's hearts and, as shown by the post-trial reporting, presented himself as a breath of fresh air set apart from some 'cardboard cut-out cops' they might have met in the past.

He remained open and candid with the families – who after all had grown suspicious of so many here-today-gone-tomorrow senior police officers. His personal chats with them in the corridors seemed tender yet honest, explaining the vagaries of an archaic system which can sometimes seem to forget the human beings who should be at its centre.

68

The defining quality of folk born and bred in Moulsecoomb is their low tolerance of pretension or condescension. They know what they know and believe what they believe. Period. We had already seen that shine through in Michelle's and Susan's courageous and dignified testimonies and we were about to witness it again.

Kevin Rowland and Matthew Marchant knew what they were in for. Like so many others, they had not forgotten their ordeal in the witness box over thirty years previously. Their evidence had not changed, its pitfalls were the same but their certainty remained unshaken.

Kevin cut a very different figure from his teenage days. Now bald with a closely cropped beard, he was smartly turned out in a beige suit and stood erect while facing the jury, projecting each crystal-clear answer across the void towards them. The apprehension he no doubt felt gave his replies a clipped edge as he waited for his Achilles-heel topic to be raised. Did he see one or both of the girls in the clearing? He dealt with Mr Altman's questions deftly, answering fully and surely.

When Mr Bennathan rose to his feet, Kevin tensed ever so slightly, girding himself for an onslaught. Unlike Altman's style, Bennathan came straight out with it. 'I suggest you did not see just one girl, you saw two.' There it was. The nub of the dispute.

If Bennathan could persuade Kevin to admit to seeing both girls, then Bishop could have seen them too, hence his vivid description of how they lay. If, as a bonus, Bennathan could get Kevin to say Bishop had approached the bodies then that would explain how his DNA appeared on Karen's arm despite him denying it in interview. To do this he tried to play tricks with Kevin's memory, suggesting that his evidence now conflicted with what he said at the time. He failed. Kevin rebuffed him by referring to the statement he made at the time – when his memory was fresh.

Still Bennathan found holes to pick. At the time, Kevin had first said he had seen two girls, then one. He later told the *Evening Argus* he had seen two and said to Barrie he had seen the two 'as if they were asleep'.

Kevin remained firm. There was only one. He might have been misquoted in the *Argus* or might have assumed there were two. He stuck by his first statement. He had told Barrie he had seen both girls out of compassion. He and the prosecution were vulnerable on these conflicting accounts but he stood firm.

One girl.

From a distance.

Bishop went nowhere near.

End of story.

Kevin's pal, Matthew, endured the same treatment. Mr Bennathan suggested his story was unreliable, that he saw two girls and his only mention that Bishop tried to get to the girls was three weeks after finding them – the day Bishop was arrested.

It was a good try. Kevin and Matthew's accounts had indeed fluctuated – as had Bishop's – but after the initial confusion they stuck to their guns.

69

Next, the post mortem evidence was reviewed and presented by Dr Nat Carey as Dr West had since died. He confirmed all of his late colleague's findings and added one crucial point of clarification. There was absolutely no evidence of Nicola having been sexually assaulted in the months prior to her death. Certainly nothing that would support Marion Stevenson's allegation against Barrie and Dougie.

One of the many striking aspects of this trial was that none of the officers involved in the reinvestigation were ever called to give live evidence. Courts discourage calling witnesses just to make a point. It makes a ponderous process even slower, confuses juries and inconveniences the witnesses themselves. Where evidence can be produced in other ways – say through agreed facts, reading statements or showing video footage – then that is what happens.

In 1986 there was no technology to record interviews and it was only at the beginning of that year that contemporaneous notes were required when interviewing anyone under caution. This normally involved one officer posing questions while the other scribbled furiously, trying to capture every reply, every nuance, and every silence. It left little room for any spontaneity or tactical switching from one interviewer to another. Once over, all present, including the suspect, had the opportunity to read and sign the notes. But some suspects, including Bishop, preferred not to. This could present problems down the line if the accuracy was questioned, but at least they had the chance.

Witness interviews had even fewer safeguards. Often officers would scribble brief notes in their pocket book then translate them into a statement which would normally consist of just the highlights. Nowadays, interviews with suspects are video-recorded as are those involving significant witnesses. Bishop would have fallen into both categories at various times had the 1986 murders happened today.

This leaves no doubt as to the questions asked, the way in which they are put and any verbal or non-verbal aggression that might take place. There is no point in calling interviewers to jus-tify whether or not they had questioned a suspect, or witness, fairly. You just play the tape.

Given the lack of technology during the original investiga-tion, on the Monday of the fourth week of the trial, the first of a line of former officers called out of retirement appeared to answer for his actions thirty-two years previously.

Former DC Barry Evans has the striking look of a friendly grandfather more at home spoiling his grandkids on a day out to the zoo than browbeating young men in sweaty interview rooms. His mop of grey hair and piercing blue eyes set off his cheerfully chubby face which is seldom without his trademark smile.

When I first met Barry, he was a fraud squad officer, never happier than when poring over ledgers and spreadsheets in his quest to catch out some corrupt company director. So, when he was accused in this trial of bullying and cajoling Bishop into changing his story during his pre-arrest interviews, using his senior years to strong-arm him into telling the story the police wanted, I could not reconcile this with the Barry I knew.

He was probably chosen to speak to Bishop because of his gentle ways, not because he would push him back in a chair or seek to shock him with photos of the girls as was suggested. Barry also rebuffed the suggestion that when he asked Jenny Johnson to identify the Pinto sweatshirt, which she did, he removed it from the packaging. This was important to the defence in terms of cross-contamination as any suggestion that it could have picked up traces of Bishop from 17 Stephens Road during that visit would blow all the subsequent DNA findings out of the water.

Like other witnesses before and after, Barry stood up to the interrogation and stuck by his recollections of interviews undertaken properly and his fastidious handling of exhibits.

DC Dave Wilkinson was next up. I worked with him in Brighton CID in the early 1990s when he returned from his stint in the Regional Crime Squad. Unlike the stereotype of 'squad types', Dave was a calm grafter who very generously taught me and my fellow rookie detectives a lot about investigating top-tier villains. He shared his intimate knowledge of Brighton crime families thus lifting the veil from those who, until then, I assumed to be untouchable.

In October 1986, Dave arrested Bishop then, with DS Phil Swan, interviewed him over the days that followed. Having explained for the court the ancient art of contemporaneous note-taking, he became somewhat vulnerable under cross-examination.

Even the most adept secretary or journalist would struggle to swear that every word written over three days of interview was exactly as it had been spoken. It was generally accepted that the notes were, by and large, accurate.

The problem came when Dave was asked about the three hours of interview prior to the arrest. Seemingly no notes were made during this time even when they took Bishop out in the car to find where he had fallen in the dog faeces.

Dave Wilkinson's statement of 20 November 1986 was the first time those conversations, covering the anomalies in the statements Bishop had provided to Barry Evans, were written down. Given these notes included direct quotes, Dave left himself vulnerable to challenge by not having anything more immediate to refer to.

Despite some uncomfortable moments though, Dave's evidence survived intact and the case could move on.

70

Defence counsel would very much have liked to haul SOCO Eddie Redman into the witness box for a grilling. Since the acquittals, quite unfairly in my view, Eddie had evolved into a convenient Aunt Sally for Operation Salop. The allegations that he was less than fastidious in handling exhibits – including Bishop's malicious assertion he examined the Pinto and the girls' clothes on the same bench – became received wisdom when quite the opposite was true. Other than some mud thrown around during the first trial, there is no basis for the claim that any item was carelessly left vulnerable to cross-contamination. Ros Hammond verified that through her meticulous tests. Her only reservation was how the Pinto was stored in the decades since that first trial, not beforehand.

It is highly unlikely the first jury, given the short time they debated their verdicts, even considered forensic handling; to do so would have taken much longer. That being the case, their acquittal was probably not down to them thinking that there had been a conspiracy or cock-up in the labs. Let's not forget that it was Eddie's sharp eye that spotted the relevance of the Pinto in the first place.

Had his health allowed it, I am sure he would have relished the opportunity to forcefully spell all of that out to the new jury. His powerful Scottish brogue projected from his paradoxically diminutive frame would have left them in no doubt about his competence and, hopefully, silenced his critics once and for all. But neither he nor Mr Bennathan had the opportunity for that duel, so his statements had to do.

Next up was Dr Anthony Peabody. He looked every inch the retired forensic scientist. White-haired, bearded and wearing a dapper bow tie, his clipped tones and received pronunciation completed his professorial air.

Despite their depleting numbers, several reporters returned for this. Notwithstanding being told he was not there as an expert – science had moved on too far since he had retired – many expected similar spectacles to the 1987 trial where he whipped out his notebook to record his indignation in response to what he felt were suggestions he had fiddled with the forensics.

Dr Peabody confidently went through how he received, logged and examined the exhibits delivered to him at the Forensic Science Laboratory. He recounted his visit to the scene to harvest samples of foliage. He gave his findings as they were at the time. However, the press led on the salacious snippet that a police officer had pinned him to the wall after he gave evidence at the 1987 trial, a fact Dr Peabody graciously acknowledged as true. The more serious cross-examination was around his certainty that minute traces of DNA could not have passed from one item to another. Mr Bennathan explored whether the edges of tape might have been vulnerable to contamination. Dr Peabody referred him to his own research paper on cross-contamination and reassured the court that, for that very reason, he ignored any material found on the edge of the tapings when he concluded his evidence. The back and forth produced none of the theatrics the press was hoping for and finished with the prosecution case firmly intact.

The court was eerily sparse when the most important evidence was called. The headlines, showing the forensic links between Bishop, the Pinto and the girls, had already been spelled out in Brian Altman's opening statement. But the jury needed to hear the ins and outs of every mark, every fibre and every DNA profile. There was no way to dress that up. Roy Green, Dr Louissa

Marsh and Ros Hammond spent days in the witness box, pains-takingly explaining their qualifications, experience, methodolo-gies and, finally, their findings. Each started with an overview of their specialism, cleverly explained in layman's terms so the jury were not bewildered from the outset. Then they trudged through the detail.

It was hard to pull these brilliant scientists' evidence apart. The strategy to use Ros Hammond to do that from the outset paid off. Mr Bennathan tried several tacks. Were they cognitively – or inadvertently – biased in wanting to prove their results implicated, rather than eliminated, Bishop? No, they could show that this would have been picked up through peer review.

How sure were they that the fibres found were not subject to secondary, or even tertiary, contact? Very. The volume they had retained made that virtually impossible. Could Barrie's DNA be one of those noted as from an unknown person? No. They were not common across the examinations and his DNA had been eliminated from all but one sample.

'How usual was it for people in low-income areas to respray cars in the 1980s?' Bennathan asked Dr Marsh. The judge was having none of that, making the point that she was a paint ex-pert and not one on the second-hand car market of the last millennium.

Could the paint flakes have been transferred by chance or from some time ago? It would be too coincidental for that to be realistic.

Had Ros Hammond considered whether anyone had been wilfully negligent in her 'worst case scenario'? There was no evi-dence to suggest that had happened.

It was no surprise that the science survived unscathed. What was a surprise, though, was the absence of any defence scientists being called.

It is inconceivable that, at some time over the previous two and a half years since Bishop's arrest, the defence had not sought a second opinion on each of the disciplines so eloquently presented by Green, Marsh and Hammond. Given they called no one to rebut the findings, nor did they examine any of the items in question at the lab, their conclusions on reviewing the prosecution forensic statements must have been bad news for Bishop.

It was worth the defence prodding these seasoned experts but more in hope than expectation. In any case, Mr Bennathan was sharpening his knives for who he really felt was the prosecution's weak link. There was standing room only when Barrie Fellows limped into the court.

I knew what I was about to witness would be uncomfortable but I was not prepared for its brutality. In British law, as in most free countries, the accused is entitled to a full and robust defence team. Defence barristers are there to put their client's case forward in the most effective way possible and the judge ensures fair play.

Fair play are not bywords for courtesy though; in a court of law, the gloves come off. I had been on the receiving end of those punches many times over the years.

In this case, at least we had been given fair warning that Barrie Fellows was going to be in for a rough ride. Bishop, not Mr Bennathan, had decided that. As he pulled himself into the witness box, Barrie cut a very different figure from the ruggedly handsome, yet broken, man of the 1980s. His health was failing, he struggled to walk and his stricken face told of the recent tragic deaths of his son and second wife. Despite that, he looked up for the fight that was to come. The two other bereaved parents were treated with respect but he knew Bishop had lined him up as his 'get-out-of-jail-free card.'

He made himself as comfortable as possible in the tiny witness box then, in clear and concise terms, explained to the prosecution and the jury his precise movements on the day Nicola went missing. The only confusion came when he assumed the judge and jury had more knowledge of the number 49a bus route than they actually did, but he got there in the end.

There were no deviations from what we already knew. Hardly surprising, given Barrie would have lived that day and the next over and over ever since. He choked up as he recalled having to identify the bruised and battered body of his little girl. He described his shock when, out of the blue, Bishop turned up while on bail to deny any involvement in the killings.

The prosecution's questioning was always going to be heart-wrenching but compared with what was to come it was plain sailing. As Altman sat down, Bennathan rose to his feet. The expectant hush was only broken by the scratching of industrious journalists hard at work. The defence barrister's first attack was on Barrie's timeline, from leaving work to arriving at Theresa Judd's house. It was fairly easy pickings in front of a jury unfamiliar with the geography and who could not picture the walk from Woodruff Avenue to Church Road in Hove. A lesser man would have been confounded by the alternative theories Bennathan suggested – that the gap in times gave him opportunity to kill his daughter and her friend – but Barrie stuck to his guns because it was the truth. At one point he looked the QC in the eye and said, 'You are trying to mislead me, sir. It's not happening.'

Every minute of that evening was accounted for and any suggestion – obscene as it was – that he had diverted to Wild Park to sexually assault and murder Nicola and Karen was quashed by his quiet but certain consistency.

Bennathan tried a different tack and put to Barrie that he was prone to violence. He brought up a visit he made to see Nicola's headmaster where he was said to have threatened to cut Nicola's fingers off if she stole from the school again. He then asked about the injury to his grandmother-in-law and his use of corporal punishment. It would have been easy to deny all of those but Barrie Fellows had waited for his day in court and he was not going to perjure himself. Why would he? He had nothing to hide. Rumours and innuendo had rumbled on since the girls died. Many still thought he was the killer and this was his chance to silence the ignorant once and for all. Barrie was a loving parent but, as mine and many others did, enforced boundaries.

Bennathan asked, 'On Monday of the week she died, did you smack Nicola for not doing homework?'

'No,' replied Barrie.

'Did you ever smack Nicola about the head?'

'I used to give her what they call a thick ear.'

'Did you strike your grandmother-in-law on the nose then throw an ashtray which smashed a window?'

'I broke her nose by accident. We stood up at the same time and I accidently hit her. That's how her nose was broken.'

'That's not true, Mr Fellows, is it?'

'It is.'

'Do you remember an incident in school in September that year? You and she went to see the headmaster as it was suspected Nicola had stuff that wasn't hers. You took hold of her hand and put it on the headmaster's desk. You made a chopping motion with your hand and said, "If she does it again she'll know what will happen." You threatened to cut her fingers off.'

'I would never have done it,' Barrie insisted.

Really, those questions were just designed to soften him up, before Bennathan launched into his real attack.

Barrie could easily have been forgiven had he lost his rag when Bennathan set about him. 'Were you party to Nicola being filmed in a pornographic video, Mr Fellows?'

'No, sir.'

'Were you and another man watching a homemade pornographic film of your own infant daughter?'

'No, sir.'

'Were you anything to do with her death?'

'No, sir.'

The QC then tried to eke out a different story by suggesting that Barrie himself owned a video camera – very uncommon in those days – and that he had taken Nicola to a secret place in Wild Park.

In his denials, Fellows repeated that the girls should never have been at the park, that it was dark and unsafe. Despite him trying every which way, Bennathan could not shift the little girl's father on a single detail and Barrie was unfazed by the onslaught. If anything, the battering he gave Barrie weakened Bishop's case, possibly fatally so.

Brian Altman, for the prosecution, could have left it there. Barrie had done well and there was no reason to believe the jury doubted him but, in some ways, he had stood up too well. Barrie had been strong but sometimes juries need to see emotion come through. Brian felt the court needed reminding of what had just happened. The barrister started his re-examination by asking about how it felt to have to identify Nicola.

'It's not nice going into a clinically white room. It's difficult talking about it anyway. I walked in there and there was a sheet over my little girl up to the neck. I asked if I could give her her pocket money and they let me put 50p in her hand.' He shook as he sobbed.

Altman paused as Barrie wiped away his tears and collected himself. Then he quietly told him, 'What is being suggested is, you are being accused of having killed Nicola. You are being accused of having killed Karen. You are also being accused of having sexually abused your own daughter and Karen in that den, and having punched Nicola in the face, do you understand that?'

Barrie wailed. He heaved, his head in his hands, unable to answer. It was probably the most distressing scene I have witnessed in a courtroom in many years. I could not have been alone in wanting to dash up to him and put my arms around him. People shuffled, waiting for what seemed an age for him to be ready to answer.

'I understand. None of it's true.'

'You've been campaigning for the police to re-examine the exhibits, for the police to publicly say you are not guilty and for the killer to be brought to justice. Is that what you wanted?'

'I want that now,' replied Barrie.

To everyone's relief, the judge told Barrie his evidence was at an end and he was free to leave. He stepped out of the witness box and walked, dignified and purposeful, past the dock, making no attempt to look at Bishop, and left the court. None of us there will ever forget what the man surrounded by prison officers had just put that grieving father through.

72

Dougie Judd, the supposed rapist, got off lighter than Barrie. His account of 9 October 1986 matched Barrie's and, despite some probing here and there from Mr Bennathan, he emerged from that part of his evidence relatively unscathed.

The real focus was always going to be whether or not he raped Nicola on camera, or indeed at all. He accepted that there were fictitious rumours of him having an affair with Marion Stevenson. He knew her for sure, and accepted that he smoked cannabis with her and Russell Bishop from time to time, but that was as far as it went. He remembered exactly what he was doing when he heard that he was supposed to have been filmed abusing Nicola.

On Sunday 13 December 1987, three days after Bishop's acquittal, he was working in a cafe on Lewes Road when a friend phoned to quiz him about that morning's *News of the World* article. It did not take a lot of working out that the lodger referred to in the column was him and Dougie remembered being both shocked and bewildered. Later, Marion Stevenson and Russell's brother David came into the cafe. David glared at him as they took a seat. Dougie sat down with them and demanded to know if the person Marion was talking about in the newspaper was, indeed, him.

Dougie repeated the conversation for the jury. ' "Yes, I thought you knew. I was a hundred per cent sure," she said. I told her, "You've made a big mistake. You want to get your bloody eyes tested." I would be straight down to the police if I knew anything about a video and the kids.'

Brian Altman asked: 'Did David Bishop say, "If it's not you in the video I feel very sorry for you"?'

'Correct,' replied Dougie.

'Did you ever watch any videos while at Barrie Fellows' house?'

'No.'

Bennathan focused on the discussion in the cafe more than the footage itself. He was curious why Dougie only told Marion she needed her eyes tested rather than denying it outright. Dougie maintained this was his way of denying what he regarded as an outrageous allegation. The defence barrister said, 'Did you get mixed up with Barrie Fellows in a bad way? Did you get mixed up with Barrie Fellows and paedophilia?'

'No.'

'Did you ever have an improper relationship with Nicola?'

'No. The first time I heard the story I thought it was a wind-up.'

He described to the court how he had been arrested and interviewed about this back in 2009, as had Barrie, and that the police had found absolutely no evidence to back up the claims. As he had with Barrie, in re-examination, Altman wanted to leave clarity ringing in the jurors' ears. 'It is not just you getting mixed up with Barrie Fellows in a bad way and paedophilia. It's not just an allegation of improper relations with Nicola. The allegation is you were in a video with Nicola either completely naked or semi-naked having sex with Nicola. Is there any truth in it?'

'There is no truth in it whatsoever. Total lies,' replied Dougie with a steely gaze and cast-iron certainty.

73

As Alison Morgan, Altman's junior, described Bishop's arrest and read out edited highlights of his interview, many of us thought that this was the prosecution case coming to an end. After all, we had heard from all the witnesses, the science had been explained in simple terms and we'd watched the dignity and fortitude of the parents as we heard Bishop's pathetic attempts to wriggle free once more. But the cunning prosecutor had one more arrow in his quiver.

'Finally, it's been agreed that I read some letters that the defendant sent while on remand in prison in 1987,' Brian Altman said.

These letters emerged, not by accident, but through the diligence and painstaking attention to detail of the police and CPS. For years they had been sifting through every piece of paper they held on the case in order to gauge its relevance to either side. The letters were found languishing in an archived box, but would prove dynamite.

For the first time in five weeks, Bishop reacted.

'It's not agreed evidence. Stop it right now. I'm not having this shit or I'm having a retrial,' he called from the dock.

For a moment the court was in confusion. Clearly this had all been discussed, it was just that Bishop knew what was coming. Many newspapers reported that the court had to be cleared because Bishop had kicked off and was being restrained. The truth, as ever, was far more mundane. The judge wanted to give Mr Bennathan the chance to speak with Bishop but the geography of the Old Bailey would mean that it would take an age for the accused to be escorted back to the consultation rooms in the cells to have what was hoped to be a brief chat and then to trudge back up again. The judge cleared the court only as a pragmatic alternative so counsel and client could talk there, saving probably an hour or so of precious court time and a good deal of momentum. As Libby Clark of the CPS said to me outside while we waited, 'I don't know why he's asking for a retrial. Doesn't he realize that this *is* his retrial?'

Those of us not in the know were intrigued. What could possibly be in these letters that would have any bearing on the case? Surely they were just tying up some loose ends, but if so, why the reaction? We soon found out.

The girl, who I will not name, was just thirteen in 1987. She came to know Bishop, and Jenny, when she was living with her mum in the same temporary accommodation as them in Kemp Town, Brighton. Bishop used to babysit for her. The letters started in the March of that year.

Dear **** how are you my love . . . I cannot do no dirty rhymes as this letter will go to the police before you get it . . . I can't do them to Jenny neither . . . Be good for me now won't you. Love from Russell xxxx

As the weeks went on he became bolder.

Love you must not tell Jenny a thing what I put in my letters to you. She thinks something is going on. Sorry you did not get to see me I put you on the list will do it again.

Last time you see me at the bus stop about 20 weeks ago can't say what it was but you know. You know that I love you and you love me. Mustn't tell Jenny about it. When we get out I think you know what we'll end up doing.

Don't give the letter to no one not your mum not to Jenny not to no one. If you love me you won't . . . If you show them to Jenny she won't let me see my kids no more.

*I can get a way out of it. You'll have to go on the pill if that's
what you want. Have to get rid of this page. There is just one
thing what you can tell me are you a – or not. If you know
what I mean. If not I've put the letter at the end.*

At the foot of the page was the letter V.

Later that month his letters continued, his intentions becoming crystal clear.

*How old are you now? You must be getting on for 16 so that
parts ok. I must stop doing letters like this or someone will
get the wrong idea. There's just one thing I just find a way
out of marrying her. I don't want to marry no one. It's been
115 days and I've had nothing. You can help me out if you
know what I mean. Why do you think Jenny won't let me go?*

Bishop continued suggesting they spend some time in a bed
and breakfast on his release. Then, on 28 March, he wrote:

*Don't worry I'm not going down for this. No way I'm going
down for this. I'd put you on the list so you can come and see
me but police won't let me. I know how old you are baby
hehe. Don't matter though. No worry about that anyway.
16–17 weeks and I'll be out and up to no good. Hope you can
handle it cos I'm a man not a boy. All I need to do is get out
of here so it can happen rather than on paper. I don't know
if you will tell me about that. When was the first time, how
many times, you don't have to tell me if you don't want to.
Don't tell me too much or you will get a name. It's the one
thing I miss in here. In B & B was the first time. You were
11 years old then who knows could marry one day but that's
a long way off.*

Clearly his letters were not being monitored as this blatant
attempt to groom a thirteen-year-old-girl went unchecked. He
maintained he thought she was approaching sixteen but by referencing them staying in the same B & B, he would have known

she was much younger. The final letters left even less to the imagination.

> *Thanks for the photos of you. Jenny won't see the photos. You*
> *won't handle 12 inches nor could Jenny. I can't wait to get*
> *out and you will know all about it. I think your mum knows*
> *something is up but I don't think she will say anything to*
> *you or me . . . I can talk her (Jenny) into doing what I like.*
> *We can have some fun. When we were in B & B some girls*
> *came up for a bit of fun. Jenny said if you go with girls as*
> *long as they aren't dogs that's ok just don't do it behind my*
> *back. When I saw you today you didn't seem to love me. If*
> *you want to just be friends that's ok I'll come and see you . . .*
> *I want to know where I stand.*

It seemed she had, after all, been granted a visiting order which, given she was thirteen and he was charged with the sexually motivated murders of two nine-year-olds, appears negligent to the point of outrageous.

His final letter, in September 1987 – two months before his original trial – once again suggested that she go on the pill. It would not be a huge leap to infer that might just be in preparation for him abusing her in the event of an acquittal.

After those shocking letters, at 4.23 p.m. on Wednesday 21 November, five and a half weeks into the trial, Mr Brian Altman QC closed the case for the prosecution.

74

Now it was the turn of the defence and the big question. Would Bishop finally take the stand and face the grilling he shirked in 1987?

The court did not sit the following day. There are always reasons, usually very good ones, for delays and adjournments and it suited both counsels to take stock and prepare for round two of this epic trial.

On the Friday, word soon got out that Bishop would be giving evidence. Getting him to and from the witness box would take some choreography however. As a Category A prisoner, there was no way he would be allowed to move around the insecure areas of the court untethered but the judge was also reluctant for the jury to see him in cuffs and chains. Neither did he want the families put through that.

Much to the disgust of some of the journalists, the judge also ruled that during the time Bishop was out of the dock, no one could enter or leave the court, save the jury and families. Members of the press were speculating on what would happen were there to be a breaking news story elsewhere that they might be expected to react to. That cut no ice. The doors would be locked. If you were in, you were in. If you were out, you stayed out.

Just as we all settled in to finally hear what Bishop had to say, Mr Bennathan afforded himself the luxury of a second opening speech. A second bite of the cherry. It was a good tactic. The prosecution had been setting its stall out for well over a month and his little interlude after the legal argument might have faded in the jurors' memories. The slant he took on some of the headlines made me wonder whether I had been sitting in the same trial. He sensibly warned the jury that they might feel battered by the volume and depth of the scientific evidence and that they might think the findings were proof in themselves that Bishop was guilty. He reminded them that no one had seen Bishop wearing the Pinto on the day and it was true that it had not been sealed the moment it was handed in. Who was to say it was Bishop's? Who was to say his DNA did not arrive on it some other way – through fair means or foul? He mentioned that some forensic interpretations might have been made to fit the prosecution's preferred narrative rather than being completely objective.

He asked the jury to give Bishop the same courtesy afforded to others regarding the effect thirty-two years can have on the memory. If others can err over that period, why not the defendant? He made no mention that Russell Bishop's version of events flipped several times within the same interview just days after the attack.

On Bishop's behalf, he accepted that he had committed 'awful, shameful offences' in 1990, but he had been tried and convicted for those. He urged the jury not to be swamped by the depravity of those offences as he was not on trial for them.

Next, he turned to Barrie Fellows. Mr Bennathan suggested that some of the prosecution case made no sense at all if Bishop was the killer but fell into place if it was Barrie. He mentioned the video, the secret den, the assertions that Barrie had a violent streak and the supposed gap in his movements after work on the 9 October.

Finally, he addressed those letters from prison. Yes, Bishop wrote them. Yes, he sent them. That was all agreed. What was not agreed, and what led to Bishop's outburst, was that he knew the girl's age. He assumed her to be nearly sixteen, and given that he was not long out of his teens himself at the time, Bennathan suggested that was not paedophilia. He made no mention of him babysitting her, when she was eleven, a few years previously. Speech over, the jury were asked to leave, the family were escorted to the lobby by their family liaison officers and Bishop was taken to the witness box. He shuffled down from the dock, the three prison officers huddled around him. The clank of chains echoed around the hushed courtroom. Once ensconced in the box, his cuffs and chains were removed and a burly prison officer sat guard by its door. Others positioned themselves at the exits and, unbeknown to most, Jeff Riley placed detectives in the judge's corridor and at other escape routes.

75

With Bishop securely in place, the jury and family returned and the door locks clicked shut. The court clerk handed the card for Bishop to read the affirmation from – he had clearly not found God in prison – then Bennathan launched into the standard questions for Bishop to swear his innocence by.

'Did you kill Karen Hadaway?'

'No, I didn't.'

'Did you kill Nicola Fellows?'

'No, I didn't.'

'Do you know who did?'

'No.'

He missed this opportunity to point the finger back at Barrie.

Next Bennathan wanted to dispense with the thorny issue of him strangling, sexually assaulting and leaving a seven-year-old girl for dead in 1990. Of course, Bishop's answers turned out to be all about himself with no remorse or pity for Claire. He bleated on about how depressed he had been since his arrest for the Wild Park murders. He said that day, for the eighth or ninth time, he'd discovered that his brake pipes had been cut. I don't recall any of these crimes ever having been reported to the police at the time.

Once he'd fixed the pipes he said he drove over to his brother's house in Whitehawk to fit a satellite dish but his brother was not in. He must have been having a terrible day as when he returned to his red Ford Cortina, he found he had a flat tyre. Of course this made him cross, but things were going to get a lot worse as, while he was repairing it, he hurt his hand, which threw him into a rage. At that moment, Claire skated past and he found himself grabbing her and throwing her into the car boot. He said all this in quiet, measured tones, as if reacting that way was the most natural thing to do in the world. Predictably, Bennathan did not want to dwell on the horror of what happened next and allowed Bishop to gloss over it by benignly admitting he had 'done those things I was convicted of in court. I accept everything that has been said about that and I am deeply ashamed.'

This was a landmark moment. Not once, in the previous twenty-eight years, had he even come close to publicly admitting what happened on 4 February 1990.

The horror of poor Claire having to brave Lewes Crown Court to recount things no seven-year-old should even know about, let alone experience, the smearing of honest, hardworking police officers and the pathetic attempts at appeals, all happened because this coward, now holding court, could not face up to his depravity.

When asked whether he gave evidence at his 1990 trial he replied, 'Yes, I did.'

'Did you tell the truth or did you lie?'

'I did not tell the truth in any shape or form.' Had he forgotten that one of the questions he answered no to back then was: 'Did you kill Nicola Fellows and Karen Hadaway?'

Moving on swiftly, Bennathan took Bishop back to his childhood, racing through time to the state of his relationship with Jenny back in 1986. There were affairs on both sides, pregnancy and financial worries. We even heard about a shoulder injury he sustained playing football.

Bishop talked about his previous convictions, how he met the young Marion Stevenson and his recreational use of cannabis. He did not sound that bothered when he recalled how Jenny found out about his affair with Marion, despite the fact he'd had to move out of Stephens Road. Having tried living with Marion in a bed and breakfast for a couple of weeks he went back, tail between his legs, to Jenny but carried on with the affair nonetheless.

Finally, Bennathan asked about Nicola and Karen. Bishop remembered telling the girls off a few times for following him and Marion. He may have taken them on trips out too – but only with permission and only in a crowd. He made it sound as if he hardly knew them. Occasionally his voice dropped and when it did Mr Bennathan would chide him as if a naughty schoolboy. There was a clear tension between advocate and client and it was strange to see it spill over.

Bishop's movements on 9 October 1986 were pretty much as the prosecution had already set out. He did reveal that once his car had broken down, he went to the University of Sussex car park to steal another. Even the most cynical detective could forgive him from missing that little detail from his first accounts. He described what he was wearing – not a Pinto sweatshirt obviously – and his plans to see Marion at 6 p.m. – a plan he never kept.

It was obvious he had committed every word of his evidence to memory – when referring to his conversation with the park constable, he casually called him 'Roy Victor Dadswell. I've known him for years.' You would only normally trot out some-one's middle name if you had seen it written down, on a witness statement for example. It is not the way you would refer to some-one you call a life-long acquaintance, as Bishop did.

He stuck to his story about buying the cannabis that the drug dealer Angie Cutting said she never sold him, getting home at 6.30 p.m. and speaking to an insurance salesman who called at the door shortly afterwards. In his blind arrogance – or dumb stupidity – he did not even acknowledge that the police had long since shown he received no such caller.

He then alibied himself by giving a bland account of doing the washing, reading the classified ads for a new car and describing what he watched on the television before Jenny came home at 8.40 p.m. It was strange that he now included *The Runaway*

Train in his supposed TV viewing, echoing Mrs 'White's' reason for her time changes earlier in the trial. Now Bishop suddenly remembered it too. Moving to the next day, he confirmed being in and around Wild Park, both with and without his dog Misty. He was on fairly safe ground so far; no point in lying yet. There were too many witnesses and, other than his odd comment to PC Chris Markham, nothing he did or said so far that day had been suspicious. That was until he met Smudge, with whom he rushed to the bodies.

He realized he had made some silly remarks about the girls going up north and that he might be suspected if he found them. He wandered off at a tangent, saying he had briefly been arrested for the IRA bombing of the Grand Hotel and that his father Roy had been detained, then exonerated, for the 1978 Margaret Frame murder, across the road from his house in Stanmer Park. This seemed to justify his certainty that he would be blamed for anything that might have happened to the girls. These snippets, again, had not come out before but twenty-eight years in prison is a very long time to conjure up stories.

Then came the moment we were all waiting for. Which of his stories would he opt for today? In his reinterview he said, eventually, that he 'touched no one', so how would he explain his DNA?

76

Bishop began slowly: 'I heard two young boys come out of the woods saying they'd found the girls. They were a couple of hundred yards away so I walked closer to hear. The police officer told me to go to where the victims were and get everyone away. I ran up to where the boys were and I saw I knew them by face. There was a lad sitting down who said he didn't know whether they were alive or dead. I went straight to the victims and felt for the pulse. I felt the neck on Nicola and Karen's right arm.'

'How did you know about taking pulses?' asked Bennathan.

'There was a lad from school who died suddenly. They told us about taking pulses after that.'

Another detail that was new to me.

'Once I'd taken their pulse,' he continued, 'I realized they were dead. I backed off, went back to the path and sat down next to the lads. It was another five, six or seven minutes before the police arrived. I remember Smudge shouting from the undergrowth so I went down to help him up to where the girls were. After more police arrived, about five minutes later, I was told to leave the area which I did before the police took me home.'

So he was now 'relying on something in court which he failed to mention when questioned'. He now wanted us to believe he *had* approached the girls and touched them. Nicola's neck – where the paint flakes were – and Karen's arm – where the DNA was found. But why did he say right not left?

He then tried to account for the differences between his statements. How the police had confused him. How, over the various interviews, they had brow-beaten him hour after hour and called him a liar which made him change his story time and again. He said they had come up with the term 'blood-flecked foam', but he had seen that. He insisted before he signed them that they read the statements to him rather than reading them himself, maintaining he could not read very well. That was true, yet he had managed to trawl through the classified ads for a replacement car.

His arrest and the interviews on 31 October 1986 came as a surprise to him. He was put out that, for the first of four interviews, he did not have a solicitor, although he would have been entitled to one. Eventually, Mr Oxford, the solicitors' clerk, was called but Bishop thought he was a fully qualified lawyer. That should not have made a difference – many solicitors send accredited representatives to advise and sit with clients in police stations – but it seems peculiar that, given the gravity of the allegations, they did not send the real McCoy. Once bailed, he was advised to move away, which he did from time to time. He spent a short while in Wales and some time in Nottingham. He eventually came back as he wanted to clear his name, which led him to visiting Barrie to protest his innocence. While back in Brighton he also met up with Marion. He was devastated when he was recalled early but, in the meantime, his original firm of solicitors had withdrawn their services and Ralph Haeems took over.

Once charged, Bishop knew his remand in custody was inevitable but that did not make his incarceration any easier. He said the time was made a little better when Jenny told him a girl wanted to write. He was adamant her name meant nothing to him – she was one of a few who wrote – but he still sent letters most days. Despite the letters' content he continued to try to persuade the court to believe he thought she was nearly sixteen.

His first trial was an ordeal for him even though he gave no evidence. Now he trotted out the version of events no one else recalled. SOCO Eddie Redman, he insisted, admitted examining the Pinto and the girls' clothing on the same bench. That could not have happened, as Ros Hammond had shown, but Bishop still clutched at this straw.

He thought things would calm down after his acquittal but was angry when the police told the press they were not looking for anyone else in connection with the murders. He felt this was a slight on him and the jury and it plunged him into a depression. This was not helped when he and his home were targeted by bricks and firebombs, leading to the family having to move. Despite Jenny saying in his 1990 trial that Bishop was his 'usual happy-go-lucky self' he said he had driven with his children to a local notorious suicide spot – Beachy Head – intending to drive off. He broke down in tears at this point and it was hard to tell whether or not they were genuine.

Moving on to his arrest and the interviews in 2016, he tried to justify his silence and denials by blaming them again on confusion and having no opportunity to go through the statements. It was a poor explanation, as lame as his reasons for bottling out of his evidence during his lawsuit against Sussex Police at the High Court. He had been caught out and that was that.

His evidence ended on a fair point.

'Mr Bishop, did you wear anything under the sweatshirt you had on the day the girls went missing?' asked Mr Bennathan.

'No.'

'So, did you discard a sweatshirt where the Pinto was found?'

'No, cos if I did I would be running through the estate to my flat half naked and I'm hardly likely to do that.'

He probably would not have by choice, but if the option had been that he took the evidence-encrusted garment home, not knowing if and when the police would come knocking, who knows what really happened?

With his evidence-in-chief finished, timing had worked in Brian Altman's favour. Being Friday afternoon, there was no point in starting what would be a long and detailed cross-examination now. Best wait until Monday, he suggested to the judge. Luckily he agreed, which gave the prosecution QC two days to perfect his attack.

77

Over the weekend, those close to the case and those, like me, who were looking on, mulled over Bishop's evidence. The words self-pitying, dissembling and evasive sprung to mind. He had clearly spent the first weeks of the trial absorbing witness testimony and shaping his pitiful answers accordingly. I mentioned to a few friends that I wondered how long Bishop would last under Altman's scrutiny. I gave him an hour, tops. Others thought he would go the distance, burying himself in the process.

Once again, for this act, the court was rammed. With Bishop safely back in the witness box and the jury and families settled in their places, Brian Altman slowly got to his feet. 'Mr Bishop, you've had all weekend to think about what you told the court on Friday.'

'I haven't given it a thought,' he replied.

'Is there anything you would like to change in your evidence?'

'No.'

'Did you tell the jury any lies?' Altman asked.

'No, I don't believe so.'

'What you said on Friday was you were in a bad state when you committed the offences in 1990.'

'Yes.'

'There was a hate campaign against you? You contemplated suicide and killing your children. Ending their lives.'

'Yes.'

'Things had got to such a state you were mentally ill.'

'I was mentally unstable and deeply ashamed,' Bishop expanded.

'Your brake pipes had been cut on your car and not for the first time.'

'Yes.'

'Why did you not mention brake pipes to the police at the time?'

'I didn't answer any questions.'

'Yes, you went "No comment" because you knew you were guilty, didn't you?'

'Yes, I was guilty of the charges and convicted.'

'You were given a discretionary life sentence and you are still serving it.'

'It's turning into a whole life sentence.'

This was a virtuoso cross-examination. Altman knew the answers to all of his questions and Bishop was too dense to realize he was being led down the garden path. He may have believed this was just fact-filling for the jury but for those of us who had seen this before, we knew he was being taken by the hand to a cliff edge.

Mr Altman fast-forwarded to Bishop's efforts to secure parole and his excuse that it was the years of victimization that led him to attack Claire. For the first time, the public heard that Bishop had in fact admitted the facts of the 1990 offence earlier, but only when he believed his release on licence hinged on a confession. It seemed, as with everything, his sole motivation for doing anything was whether it would benefit him.

'You said you agreed with what this court has been told about that case and what happened next. They are in the agreed facts,' Altman reminded him.

'I've always been deeply ashamed of what I done so I always try to cover things up. By denial.'

'Is that why you appealed the convictions and sentence?'

'It was more to do with sentence,' insisted Bishop.

'No, you have a choice. You can appeal against conviction, sentence or both. You appealed against both.'

'Yes.'

'Did you remember denying the attempted murder of Claire?'

'I do deny the attempted murder, but by my actions she could have died.'

Bishop then went into a rant about the incompetence of the police surgeons and pathologist who gave evidence in his 1990 trial. He tried to argue that, by putting his hands around Claire's neck, thumbs to the front, and squeezing, he did not try to kill her.

Altman said that in 2006 Bishop had pressed his solicitor to revisit Claire in an attempt to elicit a statement saying he did not strangle her. She would have been in her early twenties by then, but even the thought of approaching her in this way could only come from a man with no comprehension or empathy for anyone but himself.

Despite him admitting the attack on Claire, while denying any intention to kill, he now denied a sexual motive. It emerged that his appeal was turned down at the first hurdle and the Criminal Cases Review Commission – the organization set up to investigate suspected miscarriages of justice – refused to take his case on.

'You said you had no sexual interest in children?' Altman asked.

'I don't have a sexual interest in children,' Bishop confirmed.

'Was your attack on Claire sexually motivated?'

'No.'

Altman then showed Bishop the agreed facts document relating to the 1990 offence.

'Your semen was found on Claire's vest.'

'The semen came from my tracksuit bottoms,' replied Bishop.

Altman questioned whether semen on his tracksuit could be wet enough to transfer to Claire's vest, then continued. 'This was all about sexual motivation, Mr Bishop. You are a predatory paedophile. That's why you stripped her naked, wasn't it?'

Rather than deny it, Bishop made the mistake of attempting an intellectual joust with the eminent QC on the definition of a paedophile, spectacularly losing when his Parole Board notes were read back to him.

Brian Altman reminded the jury that in all three trials, 1987, 1990 and now, Bishop blamed police misconduct for putting him in the dock. Bishop was now admitting that was nonsense in 1990 and he was in fact guilty. Having made that point Altman returned to why Bishop chose Claire.

'The victim on the fourth of February could have been anyone,' Bishop claimed.

'So why did you sexually assault her?'

'That's how the trauma came out.'

Altman then described the attack, step by disgusting step, emphasizing that it finished with Bishop inserting his finger in Claire's vagina. 'Why did you attack her in that way?'

'To belittle and to shame her. It could have been anyone because of what happened to me,' Bishop said.

I turned to the journalist on my right to check I had heard him correctly. None of us could believe what he was saying.

'Why not a man?' Altman asked.

'Because there wasn't anyone there,' replied Bishop, as if that were obvious.

'Why did you dump her in the bushes?' Altman asked, drawing a parallel to how Nicky and Karen were left.

'I left her on the pathway,' he replied, making no attempt to explain why she was discovered with such livid fresh gorse scratches.

Suddenly, the cracks in his defence were beginning to show.

Bishop turned and glared at the judge. 'What am I on trial for? Your honour, is this legal?'

'Yes, and if it isn't I'll stop it,' snapped Mr Justice Sweeney.

Altman continued. 'You didn't give evidence in 1987, did you?'

'There was no need to.'

'You did in 1990 and that was a load of lies, wasn't it?'

'Yes.'

'Your case in 1990 was based on alibi. You couldn't have committed it because you were elsewhere. You were saying you couldn't have been at Devil's Dyke because you were elsewhere. That was lies, wasn't it?'

'I just said I lied. Are you deaf?' Bishop barked.

I checked my watch. We were coming up to the hour mark. Maybe my prediction would be right.

'You told that jury lies to get them to acquit you of an offence you did commit. Don't you agree that what you did in 1990 was very similar to what the killer did in 1986? The killer of the two girls was the same person as committed the offences in 1990.'

'No.'

Not for the first time, Altman spelled out each and every similarity between the attacks, including the sexual assaults. The more he could remind the jury of these, the more likely they would be to convict, especially on the back of Bishop's momentous admissions.

'Why did you take Claire to Devil's Dyke?'

'I didn't have a plan,' Bishop admitted.

'You didn't have a car in 1986, did you? It had broken down that morning. In 1990 you realized you made a mistake in 1986 by being on foot. That's why you took your car and drove fourteen miles, wasn't it?'

'No.'

Some might have been surprised that Brian Altman had yet to even touch on the murders. There were so many targets to aim for in the current case – the DNA, the fibres, did he or didn't he touch the girls and all those lies. Why did he not go straight for the jugular? He intended to come to that.

This provided the jury with something more. Throughout the trial, with one exception, Bishop had sat quietly, listened and not reacted. This entrée was a chance to showcase the man for what he was. A self-centred, arrogant, murderous paedophile. No amount of 'Yes you did', 'No I didn't' would illustrate that as strongly.

Altman turned next to those letters from prison. We already

knew Bishop had written the letters, because Bennathan had said as much. So, what about the girl's age?

'She was thirteen or fourteen in 1987,' said Altman.

'I believed she was close to sixteen,' Bishop replied.

Altman spelled it out. When Bishop and Jenny moved into the bed and breakfast where the girl and her mum also lived it was 1984. She was born in August 1973. When Bishop used to babysit for her she was eleven. Therefore, how old was she in March 1987 when he was writing to her? Thirteen. Despite referring to the babysitting in the letters, Bishop maintained that when he wrote them he did not know her, so felt it reasonable to believe she was nearly sixteen. He agreed if she was thirteen it would have been wrong to sign his letters, 'Lots of love and kisses xxx'.

'Jenny must have told me she was fifteen,' Bishop said.

'She couldn't have done as she wasn't fifteen,' argued Altman before continuing. 'You wrote, "the last time you see me was at the bus stop about twenty weeks ago you did something." What was that?'

'Ain't got a clue.'

'"The times when Jenny and I come up to see you." Is that in the bed and breakfast?'

'Ain't got a clue.'

'"You know what we'll end up doing",' Altman said, staring at Bishop. 'Is that sex?'

'I don't know. I wouldn't tell you.'

This was getting too personal for Bishop's comfort now. Altman read on.

'"You will have to go on the pill. You know what I'm on about. You'll have to get rid of this page."' Again, he looked at Bishop. 'Why did you suggest she go on pill?'

'Because after sixteen I wouldn't want her to have a child.'

'What was the reference to "are you a . . ." with the letter V at the end of the page? Are you asking if she is a virgin?'

'Probably.'

'Were you suggesting you would take her to a bed and breakfast for sex?'

'If she was of age, yes.'

'"I know how old you are hehe." What's that about?'

'Fifteen or sixteen?'

'Thirteen?'

'No, I'd have stopped writing.'

This was certainly ticking all of Altman's boxes, and rightly so, but Karen Hadaway's mother and sister, Michelle and Lindsay, were becoming upset. It was hardly surprising, given what these revelations were saying about his designs on young children.

'"You won't handle twelve inches. Jenny couldn't." What's twelve inches?'

'It's obvious.'

'Your penis?'

This was the final straw for Bishop. He refused to answer any more questions and talked over Mr Altman when he tried to put them. Mr Justice Sweeney felt compelled to intervene, chiding both for not listening to each other. He decided the court would take its customary mid-morning break and resume when everyone had cooled off. After the jury were escorted away to allow Bishop to be cuffed and taken to the cells, my prediction came to pass.

'That's it, I've finished giving my evidence,' Bishop pronounced.

78

Keyboards tapped and pencils raced across notepads. Lawyers whispered as we all tried to work out what would happen next. I have known plenty of defendants decline to give evidence – that is their right – but I have never seen one throw in the towel part way through.

Things had become heated. The questioning would have made anyone uncomfortable, but the implications for Bishop were huge. It was a mark of the judge's experience and skill that he effectively put his foot on the ball. He ruled that, after a fifteen-minute cooling-off period, Bishop would be invited back into the witness box to continue his evidence. If he declined to do so he would allow Mr Bennathan to speak with Bishop to set out the consequences of his refusal to be cross-examined. Normally, counsel cannot speak with defendants midway through their evidence, but this was exceptional. Before he rose to allow Bishop to reconsider, he reminded the court that the conduct of cross-examination was for him to adjudicate and, so far, Mr Altman had come nowhere near crossing the line which would trigger his intervention.

We all cleared the court and, as I stood in the lobby, Mr Bennathan and his junior rushed past, no doubt to plan their next move. They might not have expected this but it was always a possibility, so no doubt they had some contingency. I chatted with the seasoned court reporters to hear if any of them had more experience of this than me. None had. Police, CPS and counsel huddled together, probably weighing up what had just happened. I would imagine the pros outweighed the cons. The jury would be instructed that they could now draw inferences from Bishop's decision, and those were unlikely to support the defence.

Half an hour later we were called back in. It came as no surprise that Bishop had not changed his mind. Why would he? Altman held all the cards and this was exactly as Bishop had behaved during the civil suit in 1994. The court adjourned until after lunch, giving Bennathan ample time to explain exactly how much indelible ink Bishop was putting on his death warrant.

No one actually believed he would listen. His arrogance would not allow it and his hair-trigger temper would not last. Sure enough, the last business of the day was at five past two when the judge revealed to the jury why their fifteen-minute break had turned into nearly two and a half hours. Having explained that Bishop had refused to continue and did not wish to be cross-examined further – he would direct them on that later – he sent them home as other defence witnesses could not be present at such short notice.

The next witness, however, would be every bit as dramatic as Bishop himself.

79

Only judge, jury and counsel actually saw Marion Stevenson as she sat in the witness box. For legal reasons she was allowed to give her evidence from behind a screen. The nonsense was that, despite this being the new wing of the Central Criminal Court, nobody had thought that some witnesses may need to enter and leave court unobserved. So, every time Marion entered and left the court, we were all cleared out and had to trudge to the far end of the building so we could not see her. I have no issue with protecting her identity but the inefficiency of how that was achieved is typical of our criminal justice system.

Her initial evidence consisted of her reluctance to be there. Now she did not care whether Bishop lived or died but, as a sixteen-year-old, she had been besotted by him. She described visiting the Fellows house shortly before the girls were killed, primarily with Bishop, to see Dougie Judd and smoke weed. She explained walking into the lounge on the way to the kitchen one day and seeing Barrie Fellows watching a video of Nicola being raped by Dougie.

No one saw her in the lounge. She never made it to the kitchen and, strangely, when she went back to Dougie's room, she did not mention this to Bishop when they were alone again. She said she'd told Dougie she had seen a video of 'Nicola on a bed with some bloke' – not 'I've seen a video of you raping, or having sex, with Nicola' – and Dougie told her not to worry about it. He denied ever hearing about it until after it appeared in the newspaper. She maintained that she told this to DS Phil Swan after the murders and had made statements about it since, the last being in 2007.

As far as examinations-in-chief go this seemed brief. We all knew that Altman would take her apart bit by gentle bit in cross-examination, so why Bennathan did not cut him off from the outset, only he will know. Altman was forensic.

These events took place when Marion was just sixteen years old. Naive and love-struck. Not only would the passage of time have faded her memory but her maturity now might have made her slightly embarrassed about the things she had done and said.

Given her stated hatred of Bishop, it was surprising how faithfully she stuck to her guns. This was good for the defence as, they would say, she gained nothing and stood to lose a lot by keeping to the same account. She had made a total of nine witness statements, on top of being arrested and interviewed, and in none of those did she mention the video. Altman took her through each and every one. Who was with her, what was said, what was not said. Her opportunities to tell someone were numerous. Even if she did not want to open that particular can of worms at the outset, when she was arrested, after Bishop was bailed and some time before the trial, she might have thought it relevant. She repeated that she told DS Swan about seeing Barrie watching the video but, oddly, this never appeared on paper, and she did not ask why at the time.

The cross-examination spanned two days but kept coming back to the same point. Despite Marion saying she saw a father sitting in his front room, with other people in the house, watching his own daughter being raped, no record of that exists. No one else saw it. No one else knew about the video and, other than a police officer she said she hated, she told no one but Dougie. Not until the chequebook-wielding *News of the World* arrived on the scene did she tell the story. She could not answer why, despite having a fabulous line of defence for Bishop's 1987 trial, she did not even tell him even though it was clear that it had been

Russell Bishop's mother – Sylvia – whose idea it was to go to the press.

Altman soldiered on. Marion's description of the lounge did not stack up. She could not have been standing behind the sofa, as she said, since the sofa was against the wall. She could not therefore have walked into the lounge and remained unseen by Barrie. He turned to her 2007 account in which she said she told no one about the video until then. He picked out discrepancies between that statement and the *News of the World* article and her fear of Mrs Bishop.

By the end Marion was sobbing. She had stuck to her story, even saying at one point, 'If you want me to say I'm lying I will. But I'm not.'

This was Marion's evidence, and it was for the jury to make what they would of it. But this case, even at this late stage, still had a sting in its tail.

80

After reading statements from Nicola's head teacher about the incident in the office and the great-grandmother about her broken nose – both of the actual people had sadly died – the defence closed what I regarded as a pretty flimsy case.

That was not the end of the evidence, however. A little-known stage of the court process is the prosecution's right to call witnesses to rebut the defence case.

DS Phil Swan had interviewed both Bishop and Stevenson. Shortly after the 1987 interview, he and another officer had been required to resign from the force due to a number of charges that they neglected their duty and committed 'falsehoods'. This related to their use of a police vehicle during another case and whether it was authorized. He knew, when he walked into court to refute Marion's assertion that she had told him of the video tape, his past would come back to bite him.

Prosecution junior counsel Alison Morgan covered his fall from grace before the defence could. On the point at issue he firmly dismissed any suggestion he knew of the allegations against Barrie before he read them in the *News of the World*.

Bennathan could not shake him, despite trying to link his misconduct to his reliability as a witness.

'Mr Swan. Let's be clear about why you left the police. You were found guilty of three neglects of duty and five falsehoods. You were required to resign as alternative to dismissal. That's correct, isn't it?' Bennathan asked.

'Yes, I was found guilty and required to resign,' Swan replied.

'Was a recording device put on the Stevensons' phone behind Marion's back?'

'Yes, but with her parents' permission.'

'Was Bishop's flat bugged?'

'Not that I am aware of.'

'Was he under surveillance?'

'Not that I'm aware of.'

'You had a junior officer with you when a statement was taken from Marion Stevenson, didn't you?'

'Yes, WDC King.'

'Did you suggest the defendant's flat was bugged?'

'No, she said it.'

'Is this a falsehood and you've tweaked it?'

'Absolutely not.'

'She told you about Barrie Fellows watching a video of a man having sex with Nicola, didn't she?'

'No, absolutely not.'

He delved into other parts of the investigation, expecting Swan to know details of surveillance and the rationale behind passages in some witness statements referring to pornography, but he made little headway.

The last live witness was a very impressive former family liaison officer, Sonia Clark. She came with no baggage and was resolute that, despite what had been alleged elsewhere, she knew nothing of the video so could not have told Susan Fellows as had been mooted. She was utterly convincing when she said she would have been horrified had she known and would have re-ferred the matter straight to a senior manager.

To wrap up nearly seven weeks of evidence, Morgan read statements from DS Swan's colleague, WDC King, who had sup-ported her sergeant regarding Marion never mentioning the video and Barrie's brother denying he had called a senior police officer saying Barrie owned a video camera.

With that, late in the afternoon of Wednesday 28 November,

and with legal matters to deal with in the meantime, the judge adjourned the trial until the following Monday when closing speeches would commence. We had no idea that we would never see one key person – the defendant – in court again.

81

Having already been granted a weekend to hone his cross-examination and now another to finesse his closing speech, the scheduling gods were once again on Brian Altman's side. The finale of any trial is when counsel can get to their feet to implore the jury to believe their arguments one last time. These are the words they hope will ring in the jurors' ears as they weigh up guilt and innocence. Often, it's also a time to elicit a subtle reaction from the defendant in the hope that the jury will see him wince as the pieces of the jigsaw are firmly put together.

That would not happen in this trial.

The word came through about an hour before court sat on 4 December that Bishop had refused to come out of his HMP Belmarsh cell. I had been surprised when he continued to turn up after flouncing from the witness box the previous week, but expected him to put on a last show for the jury in these closing stages. Perhaps he realized he had played all his cards and stood no chance of recovering their favour. It was disgraceful cowardice, but more than that, it would rob the families of watching him as the verdicts were delivered. But that was Bishop all over.

Once the jury were settled, the judge told them not to hold Bishop's absence against him. The elegant Brian Altman QC rose to his feet, turned to the jury and delivered his well-prepared synopsis of the devastating prosecution case. He began by putting to bed the outlandish claims that Barrie Fellows was the killer. The apparent gap in Barrie's timeline simply did not exist. People could be forgiven for not checking their watches every moment of the day, but that was not the point here. Barrie, and others, could account for every moment of that terrible last night of his daughter's and Karen's lives. The notion that Barrie had made more significant comments than Bishop and that he was the one person who could have lured Nicola to Wild Park to silence her was, Altman said, a smokescreen to ensure that Bishop would get away with the murders for a second time.

Returning to Barrie's supposed 'missing hour' – 6.25 p.m. to 7.25 p.m. – Altman referred the jury to Dr Carey, the pathologist who had revisited his deceased colleague's findings. In his view, the deaths were any time from 18.30 onwards. Dr West had said 7 p.m. to 8 p.m. at the original trial and the defence were clinging to this. That would only have left twenty-five minutes for Barrie to murder the girls and get home. 'That's just not feasible,' said Altman.

Barrie said he had purchased some ham from George Street in Hove that afternoon to have for his tea. Based on the defence's timings, he would have had to be carrying the ham under his arm when he sexually assaulted and murdered the girls. Then how would he have dumped the Pinto in the opposite direction to his house? To get home for 7.25 p.m., he would have needed to run, arriving sweating and panting. It simply did not stack up.

Altman drew attention to the fact the defence were relying on Barrie's alleged violent past, based on one occasion when, they claimed, he assaulted his grandmother-in-law. That was six years previously, never reported at the time, and both Susan and Barrie Fellows said he struck her by accident.

Altman asked the jury to consider this instead. Barrie had no history of strangulation of little girls – Bishop did. Barrie had no history of sexual assault – Bishop did.

Next, he moved to the video. Dougie Judd had told the court it was absolute rubbish. Marion Stevenson, having been paid by the *News of the World*, said she would give some of her fee to charity. Bishop said the same about his supposed press payout, when he turned up at Barrie Fellows' home while on bail. Was that a coincidence?

What about Marion saying she was put up to this by Bishop's mother? What should the jury make of that? Why had she not told the police about what must have been a very distressing video? A video she waited until the first trial was all but over to recount. A video depicting acts that expert evidence, provided by the pathologist Dr Carey, proved highly unlikely to have occurred. No one else knew about this footage – it could have provided a strong line of defence for her then-boyfriend in 1987.

He finished debunking the defence by saying Barrie had been dragged through the mud in this case, accused of all manner of things from being a paedophile to a violent man. 'It is,' Altman said, 'a defence born of desperation to deflect the case against Bishop.' He made the point that 'had Bishop not thrown in the towel halfway through his evidence he would have been asked about some of these issues'.

Turning to the scientific evidence, he told the jury, 'It's essential you are able to rely on the scrutiny of the exhibits. Ros Hammond has provided extensive evidence on the integrity of the exhibits.' He pointed out that, despite how it might seem, the defence had not sought to challenge the scientific evidence in this case. Instead they made general suggestions about the continuity and integrity of the exhibits and evidence that, over the passage of time, they had been contaminated through loss of records and the unavailability of witnesses. It was open to the defence to call their own scientist but they had not.

He reminded the jury that all the forensic items the prosecution had relied on were locked in time, preventing any suggestion of inadvertent transfer. The exhibits were never in the same place at the same time, in particular the Pinto sweatshirt. Ros Hammond did not identify any time where any of the findings could have occurred from inadvertent transfer of DNA. The sheer volume of such transfers that would have been necessary to undermine the forensics made the possibility implausible.

He concluded by saying that 'the science is so overwhelming that the Pinto was worn by the defendant, and he was wearing it when he killed the girls. If you're sure about that then you should be sure he was responsible for the killings.'

Altman then directed the jury to the fact that Russell Bishop was forensically aware, which is why he discarded his Pinto. He threw away his clothes having partly undressed as he fled from scene – just as he did in 1990.

And did he wash his clothes?

Bishop had told the police in his interview he had put the washing on 'because it needed doing and I had nothing else to do'. Five days later, he gave a different excuse for washing the clothes, claiming that he fell in dog mess and could not find any clean clothes.

Altman said, 'Why did he suddenly realize this five days later? Because he had to wash clothing that could link him to the girls. He had to dispose of any evidence linking him to them, having already discarded the jumper.'

He then listed some of the inconsistencies in Bishop's alibi.

He lied about the failed purchase of a newspaper in the shop because he had no money. He lied about buying cannabis. He lied about going to the university to steal cars. He lied to Marion about why he did not meet her at six o'clock that evening.

He then catalogued Bishop's differing accounts for his movements on the night with variations that continued right up until him giving evidence a few days previously. Bishop's timings had to change to fit in with the sightings of him. He said he became confused with road names but Altman countered that it was just that his original accounts did not hold water – because they were lies – and some witnesses were just too inconvenient. Brian Altman had been on his feet all day and, although he was close to finishing, courts run to strict schedules, so he left it at that until the morning.

The following day, we were all trying to predict the end of the trial. This is never easy. Although it was likely Mr Bennathan's speech would be much shorter – perhaps pithier – than Altman's, how long it would take the judge to sum up remained to be seen.

True to his word, Altman took just shy of an hour to wrap up. He picked up where he left off, overlaying sightings of the girls with those of Bishop's movements, proving, in his words, that he had no alibi for when Karen and Nicola were killed – because he killed them.

Next Altman suggested that the reason Bishop remained around the search area was because, in his mind, he needed to keep an eye on what was happening. The illusion of wanting to be close to friends and family was just that. And what about nestling up to the police searchers? Then there was his knowledge of how the bodies lay. Unless the jury rejected Rowland and Marchant's evidence, the only time he would have seen them lying as they were was when he killed them. That was also the only time he could have left the paint on Nicola's neck and his DNA on Karen's arm.

Maybe he was smarter than many had given him credit for as, when he said in evidence he took the pulse from Karen's right arm, he knew to say her left would have presented a further problem. Her left arm was underneath Nicola and even he knew he could not have got to it.

In his 2016 interviews, Altman reminded the jury, Bishop made no comment to most of the questions – questions that provided him ample opportunity to correct or explain the evidence. But he did say, 'I didn't touch no one. I've got no comment to make.'

Finally, he listed the striking similarities between Claire's attack and these murders, commenting that if Bishop was not the killer there must be two men in Brighton committing such specific offences. He rounded off by saying 'The killer is this defendant to the exclusion of all others. Put right an injustice of thirty-two years.' He sat down at 11.30 a.m., his job done.

82

Following a short break, it was Joel Bennathan's turn to address the jury, and his style could not have been more different. Both he and Altman are eminent Queen's Counsels who have fought their way to the top of their profession, and deservedly so. Both will have cut their teeth in lower courts working their way up to be entitled to practise in the highest courts, and highest-profile cases, in the land.

But, as with any individual, they have each found a manner which suits them. Neither is right or wrong, they just differ. I have to say that personally I found Mr Altman's methodical and thorough walk through the evidence slightly more palatable than Mr Bennathan's almost matey approach with the jury. His job was to cast doubt and he needed to be less forensic in his approach but, with the families in the courtroom, I found some of his oratory a little uncomfortable. He knew the prosecution case was powerful – the Court of Appeal would never have allowed us to be here if it was not. He also knew he had little to offer at this stage but question marks.

He highlighted some oddities about some of the witnesses. Mrs 'White' was a defence witness in 1987 and now she appeared for the prosecution – on both occasions too scared to reveal her name. Dr Peabody was pinned up against a wall by a policeman. The last thing Marion Stevenson wanted to do was to help Bishop. Kevin Rowland had changed his account.

He asked the jury why it was that prosecution witnesses were allowed to differ in timing and accounts as it was all so long ago, but when Bishop did so that made him a murderer? If Bishop was telling the truth, Bennathan reminded the jury, a big chunk of the prosecution case would fall away.

He turned to the Pinto. He said the evidence pointed to it being freshly dropped when the CB radio friends saw it at half past midnight. So, he asked, when was it dropped? Where had it been for four and a half hours? 'And who cares if there's ivy on it?' I was sure the families cared. He then highlighted what he saw as anomalies between the volume of fibre and paint on various items of clothing, maintaining that – contrary to Mr Altman's assessment – that pointed straight to inadvertent transfer.

He moved to the apparently damning DNA evidence – minute mixed profiles, only some of which would have come from Bishop. He referred to the evidence of Kit Bentham and Ros Hammond as 'bland assurances that just don't hold water'. Among all the opportunities and unanswered questions, the QC highlighted one which I thought was compelling. Given the killer wore the Pinto when he murdered the girls, why was their DNA not found on it?

As Bishop had done in his interview, Bennathan mentioned Eddie Redman's evidence in the 1987 trial that, he said, included an admission that he had examined the Pinto and the girls' clothing in such a way that they could have cross-contaminated one another.

Finally, he turned to the video. Standing by Marion Stevenson's account he reminded the jury that DS Swan, who denied being told, had lost his job for lying. He wondered aloud too why officers had asked witnesses throughout the investigation about their knowledge of pornography if no one knew about the tape. He repeated in some detail the defence's case that Barrie was violent, that he had a video camera and of his missing hour.

He ended as all defence closing statements end. 'If someone else could have committed these murders, the case ends there.

You have to look at it all together. You have to be sure. It's like crossing a bridge where the planks are mouldy and you are not sure. Don't cross the bridge unless you are sure, even if the tour guide, Mr Altman, assures you that you can ignore the faulty planks. You have to be sure.'

83

A cast-iron prosecution case leading to a swift unanimous guilty verdict can be undone in a heartbeat. The grounds for appeal are numerous and complex, with one of these categories being errors of law. This is when the judge might have wrongly directed the jury on a legal issue or may have shown bias during the summing-up, omitting potential defences or facts which could have led to a different verdict.

No judge relishes having one of their cases referred to the Court of Appeal, especially on these grounds. That is why their opening remarks to the jury, their judgements throughout the trial and, the stage we were now at, their summing-up remain as crucial as they did in 1987. They are detailed – full of hidden quotes from the law and cases that have gone wrong – and very repetitive but, to protect the innocent from being convicted and the guilty from going free, they are necessarily so.

On Thursday 6 December, Mr Justice Sweeney started by reminding the six men and six women, who must have created some bond by now, that he was the judge of the law and they were the judge of the facts. He directed on the law. They must heed that. He reminded them of the evidence, and it was for them to make what they would of that. Nothing counsel or he might say about witnesses or their testimony could trump their collective thoughts. He instructed them that they should reach a unanimous verdict and to dispel, for now, anything they might have heard about majority decisions.

Finally, he told them there was no rush to conclude. They must consider all the evidence, apply the law and discuss together what, if any, weight it all had. He said this was a case of circumstantial evidence – no one had seen Bishop, or indeed anyone, kill the girls. The prosecution said that a set of circumstances came together to prove he did. Science, sightings, his accounts – or lack of them – taken in the round, placed it beyond reasonable doubt that the defendant was the killer – so said the prosecution. Added to that was the bad character evidence. Bishop's conviction for attacking Claire and the letters were compelling but only in the context of the other evidence – he could not be convicted on those alone.

The judge then turned to the defence case. They did not have to prove an alibi. They did not have to prove anything at all. Some witnesses changed their accounts and some were not available. For those who changed their accounts, the passage of time could be an explanation – as it could for Bishop. For those who were not available, the jury needed to reflect that their evidence was never tested in cross-examination. They should consider carefully what weight they gave that.

For the rest of that Thursday, throughout the Friday and into Monday morning, the judge walked the jury through all the evidence, reminding them of its main points upon which they must judge the accused – an absent – man.

At 12.20 p.m. on Monday 10 December 2018, thirty-one years to the day after the 1987 jury left to consider their verdict, their present-day Old Bailey counterparts were instructed to do the same.

84

The luncheon adjournment, as it's formally called, is between 1 p.m. and 2.05 p.m. at the Old Bailey. No courts sit between those times, juries suspend their deliberations and many judges join their colleagues at the long table in the dining hall for the judges' lunch. No verdicts are taken during this almost sacred time. The court clock is stopped.

As soon as a jury walk out of the door and are sequestered in their room, no one can help trying to predict when they will return, what a quick verdict might signify or what days of waiting might mean. It's all completely pointless. But we do it anyway.

The preparations for verdict day had been in train for weeks. A nervous but cautiously optimistic Jeff Riley had provided a briefing to the print media; the families had their statements prepared and were ready and waiting. The scientists, who had lived with the case for years, dropped what they were doing and jumped on London-bound trains.

Fifty minutes into their discussions, the jury would have stopped, picking them back up again after lunch. When, at 3.05 p.m., the call came over the tannoy 'All parties in the case of Bishop to Court Sixteen please,' many had their hearts in their mouths. This really was it. There is no such thing as 'triple jeopardy'. If the words uttered were 'Not guilty', the families, robbed of justice, would go to their graves deprived of the one thing they craved.

I had been to countless trials over the years, questioned many verdicts, but every fibre of my being knew, on the evidence presented, Bishop was guilty. A second acquittal would be a travesty of justice but that was now in just twelve pairs of hands.

Over lunch, Jeff Riley had briefed Michelle, Susan, Barrie and all the others who had so much riding on this moment. This would be a final closure that would never bring back their beautiful girls, but would at least help them to move forward with their lives. He told them what the judge would repeat; that they must remain as dignified as they had been throughout, whatever the verdict. Nervously they took their seats in the well of the court, some of them for the first time as, due to their numbers, they had previously been confined to the public gallery.

The judge and jury filed in. Everyone was trying to read on those twelve faces whether this thirty-two-year fight had paid off. The dock was still starkly empty, as it had been for ten days. The clerk to the court stood and approached the jury. 'Would the foreman please stand.' A young man, of Middle Eastern appearance, took to his feet.

'Have you reached verdicts on which all of you are agreed?'

'Yes.'

'On count one, do you find the defendant guilty or not guilty?'

'Guilty.'

A muted gasp.

'On count two, do you find the defendant guilty or not guilty?'

'Guilty.'

The clerk stepped away and the foreman, his momentous task over, sat down. Soft sobs were all that broke the silence as the court waited for the judge to speak. Normally he would move to sentencing, or to at least tell the defendant when that might happen and whether he would be remanded in custody or on bail.

But with an empty dock, all he could do was command that Bishop attend the following day when he would pass sentence, excuse the jury from further service for the foreseeable future and praise the families for their dignity.

The court rose to return the next day for the last time but that was not the end for the families.

Few of the UK's most notable post-trial press statements are given without the famous stone-fronted Central Criminal Court facade as a backdrop. The City of London police have well-rehearsed plans to shut off Old Bailey, the road that gives its name to London's most famous court. Thankfully the crowds that gather today pale against the one hundred thousand or so who turned out to watch the country's first railway murderer, Franz Müller, being hanged there in November 1864.

The families emerged, not jubilantly, but with a look of satisfaction and relief that their fight for justice was finally over. Nicola's cousin, Dr Lorna Clary, would later say to me that they had made a pact that if they failed now, the fight would be handed down through the generations. She was relieved her children would not face the struggles that had defined her and many of her relatives' lives.

The cameras clicked, the flashes strobed but silence fell as the people these dreadful crimes had affected the most spoke.

Lorna, for the Fellows family, said: 'Nicola and Karen. Our beautiful girls. We will never forget their smiles that would light up a room. Their laughter. Their cheekiness. During the past eight weeks, we have endured reliving the horrific details of their murders and we have learned an awful lot about the true meaning of heartbreak all over again.

'We stand here as two families united in our grief. United in our fight for justice. And now united in our elation at today's guilty verdict. We are extremely relieved and grateful that our thirty-two years' hard-fought battle has been a success, finally getting the rightful long-awaited justice for both of our girls.

'We want to thank our police teams and counsel, who have been fantastic during the past couple of decades. If it wasn't for their efforts and dedication working with us, we wouldn't be stood here today. Together we have changed history with this double jeopardy ruling and we finally have the correct outcome – Russell Bishop remains behind bars where he belongs.

'The guilty verdict doesn't bring Nicola and Karen back, but we know that other children are now safe from the hands of Russell Bishop. He is a monster. A predatory paedophile. Russell Bishop truly is evil personified.'

Next came Michelle, who had endured every moment of every day of the trial. 'After thirty-two years of fighting, we finally have justice for Karen and Nicola. Time stood still for us in 1986. To us them beautiful girls will always be nine-year-olds. They will never grow up. We've been deprived of a happy life to watch them grow into adults. What people like Bishop inflict on the families of their victims is a living death. They take the lives of children but they also take the lives of the families left behind.

'Kaz and Nicky, as they were affectionately known, friends playing out together only to have their lives wiped out by a sexual deviant, a monster. What's been hard, horrendous and heart-breaking is to hear that they were murdered by a disgusting paedophile, who we actually knew and the two girls liked and trusted. He abused that trust.

'Bishop doesn't deserve to breathe the same clean air as we do. After all, he decided that day to strangle the life out of our two angels, leaving them no air to breathe. What makes a man want to squeeze the life out of two innocent children with his bare hands? Unbelievable when he had a child himself and another on the way.

'He's a coward, without a conscience. I don't believe you can rehabilitate evil. I think Bishop was just born that way. People talk to me of forgiveness but I can never forgive or forget what the evil monster did to my beautiful Kaz and Nicky. I'm trying so hard to get my head around this but I will cos I'm a fighter and I'll never stop being strong for my family.' With a steely air, she stepped aside.

There was one final chapter. It was not *whether* Bishop would be jailed, it was for how long. Would he be there to hear it?

87

During the whole trial, I had deliberately kept a low profile. I stuck to my pledge to Sussex Police that I would not speak to any witnesses or family until it was all over. The sanctity of the trial and the delivery of the right outcome was more important to me than any book or TV documentary.

Such was the media frenzy, you had to run the gauntlet of news crews, paparazzi and countless press reporters. They were so desperate for stories that they would grab almost any passer-by in the hope they had some connection to the case – even me. I politely turned them down.

I walked into court early in the afternoon on Tuesday 11 December to ensure I had a seat. By the time 2.05 p.m. arrived it was packed. The only empty chair was the one where the coward had sat until it all got too much for him.

Despite the judge's order he attend, he could hardly be dragged to court and restrained in the dock, so he exercised his last flex of muscle.

The day before, the judge had reminded the jury that they were welcome to return to court for sentencing, but there was no obligation. Their lives had been on hold for nearly nine weeks, and many would want to be at home, or to go back to work, to return to normality. Yet it was a testimony to how deeply they felt about the trial, underlined by the speed of their verdict, that they all turned up, taking their seats in the same jury benches as they had throughout.

A relatively recent, and very important, introduction to the criminal justice process is the reading of the victims' personal statements. In a murder trial it falls to the family to explain to the sentencing judge exactly how the brutal execution of their loved ones has impacted on their lives. Brian Altman took to his feet. Reading slowly, deliberately, but without feigned emphasis, he first set out Michelle's thoughts.

She described how devastated she was after the first trial, having lost her beautiful little girl Karen and her friend Nicky. She had become resigned to there never being justice although she had no doubts at all that Bishop was responsible. She described the emotional torture she had been through with this trial, the stress of travelling every day and the trauma of hearing what the little girls went through. She said it was particularly hard for Karen's sister, Lindsay, to hear of the horrors her big sister had endured. She reminded the judge that if Bishop had pleaded guilty thirty-one years ago, the healing could have started then.

Susan said in her statement that her world had been turned upside down, that no one thought this would ever happen to them, but for her it did. She said that in 1987, having given evidence, she could not bring herself to attend the trial again, relying on updates from her family liaison officer, and could not believe he was found not guilty.

This time it had taken five years to get to trial. Five years of huge worry and old wounds being opened up. In that time her husband Peter had died and very recently her son, Jonathan, had also passed away, having never got over the murder of his little sister. She had hoped to face the trial with him but instead she had to go home alone every day and deal with the horror of what she had heard. Like Michelle, she had no doubt Bishop was responsible and should have admitted his guilt years ago.

Finally came Barrie, for whom the trial was even more painful. He said that he had endured thirty-two years of being suspected of murdering his daughter. His heart sank back then when Bishop was acquitted and he described living an everlasting nightmare. He shared the tragedy of his marriage break-up, his brother and second wife dying and of course the loss of Jonathan. All the while he waited for justice. He reminded the judge of the horror of walking into a clinically white room, seeing the battered and bruised body of his darling Nicola; the worst thing a parent can imagine. His heart shattered completely.

He talked of Bishop's front in leading marches and campaigns for the case to be reopened and how he felt ridiculed by him and his family. He described the humiliation of his 2009 arrest, the search of his home and the probing of his children by social workers, eager to discover if they had been abused. The seizure of his computers meant his children had had nothing to study on for their GCSEs. All because of Bishop. He hoped that the doubters would now be hushed and that he could live from here on knowing Nicola could now rest in peace.

It now fell to the judge to reflect the mood of the families, and of a community, in handing down a sentence that mirrored Bishop's evil, but that would withstand any attempt of an appeal.

Addressing the empty dock, he gave his withering judgement.

88

'Yesterday, thirty-one years to the day after your acquittal for the same offences, you were convicted – on now overwhelming evidence – of the murders of Nicola Fellows and Karen Hadaway, both aged nine, in Wild Park, in Brighton, on Thursday 9 October 1986. You were twenty years old at the time. You are now aged fifty-two.

'I have no doubt that you were a predatory paedophile; that, having seen Nicola and Karen playing near the entrance to the park . . . you remained in the area in case a chance arose to lure them into the woods in the park; that chance did arise at around 6.30 p.m . . . You then lured them to a secluded den in the woods; that there, entirely for your own pleasure, you subdued them . . . and then, in turn, strangled and sexually assaulted each of them . . .

'The terror that each girl must have suffered in their final moments is unimaginable. You then left their bodies where they were and walked home, dumping your Pinto sweatshirt en route to avoid anything incriminating on it being linked to you . . .

'The following day you pretended to take part, as an innocent helper, in the search for the girls . . . After the discovery of the bodies you pretended that you had checked their pulses so that you would have an excuse if anything linked to you was found on them . . .

'I am fortified . . . by the similarities between the murders of Nicola and Karen and the offences that you committed . . . in 1990 . . . You have been serving a sentence of life imprisonment for that offence since your conviction for it later that year.

'During this trial you again falsely pretended that you were innocent and made the allegation . . . that Nicola's father, Barrie Fellows, could have been the murderer instead . . .

'Indeed, I observe that Barrie Fellows stood in the witness box and dealt with all the questions that were asked of him in cross-examination despite the understandable distress that it caused him whereas, after your initial cross-examination by the prosecution had exposed you as a paedophile and a liar, you refused to answer any more questions and have subsequently refused to attend court at all – or even, today, to attend by video link. Hence, I am sentencing you in your absence.

'The victim personal statements of Susan Eismann, Barrie Fellows and Michelle Johnson speak with great dignity and force of the extent of the loss suffered by each of their families and of the suffering that they have endured over so many years. The court pays humble tribute to them for their fortitude and determination to see justice done.

'The penalty for murder is fixed by law and thus I must and do impose concurrent terms of life imprisonment on each count. I must also fix the minimum term that you must serve, from today, before the Parole Board could consider your release. The minimum term is intended to reflect the seriousness of your offences.'

He then spelled out the complexities that Bishop's age at the time of the offences and the legal framework of the 1980s added to his task. It is likely that, were Bishop to have committed these offences today, he would have received a whole-life sentence and would have had no prospect of parole. That was not an option for the reasons Mr Justice Sweeney provided, so he continued.

'Against that background, and given that your offences are such serious ones of their type – involving two child murders, each of which was sexually motivated, each of which involved a degree of premeditation and each of which was substantially aggravated by your offences in relation to Claire, I have concluded, with your age in mind, that the minimum term that would have been notified by the Secretary of State in 1986 would have been one of thirty-six years.

'Accordingly, that is the minimum term that I impose on each count.'

With those concurrent sentences passed, the judge rose and left the court having handed down the heaviest sentence he could. Thirty-two years, two months and two days after the most brutal double child murder Brighton had seen, Bishop finally received his just desserts and was condemned to wallow in prison until at least the age of eighty-eight, but hopefully until his dying day.

EPILOGUE

Prior to writing this book – a peek behind the curtain of how the police approached, recovered from, and finally solved, two horrendous attacks that robbed two innocent girls of their lives and left another scarred for life – I was as tainted by decades of misinformation as most of my colleagues.

I had bought into the 'cock-up' explanation that underscored any mention of the injustice of the first trial. Indeed, some less thoughtful elements of the press perpetuate this myth to the extent that even Bernie Wells, one of the finest investigators I have had the pleasure to meet, started to doubt himself. It was only after the second trial, when I showed him the judge's summing-up from the first, did he understand what might have gone wrong.

There were mistakes back in 1986. Hindsight shows us how things could have been done differently but the overwhelming conclusion this reinvestigation and retrial has arrived at is that, as far as the forensics were concerned, there was more than enough to convict Bishop at his first trial. The problems seemed to lie elsewhere and we have set those out.

However, on another level, this case has shown the public the tenacity and professionalism of police, scientists and prosecutors to never give up. Sparked by indefatigable families, behind the scenes all those charged with keeping our communities safe worked tirelessly to bring a double child killer to justice.

Review teams, or 'Cold Case Squads', operate up and down the country striving to exploit the burgeoning scientific progress and the latest laws to bring justice to those denied it in the way the Fellowses and Hadaways were. We have yet to find a double jeopardy retrial that ended in a second acquittal. That does not happen by luck. It is a testament to those who run our ever-shrinking police forces that these crucial units survive.

Six months on, Jeff Riley has become the head of crime for Brighton and Hove and is looking forward to spending more time tending to and sailing his boat in retirement.

Sussex Police has changed beyond all recognition. The likes of Mac and Dudley Button no longer exist. They were casualties of the swingeing government cuts so much of the public sector still endures. Major Crime Teams, however, have raised the bar for professional murder investigations. The way the police handle witnesses, suspects, technology and forensics is light years ahead of the 1980s, as is the expectation and scrutiny from the courts, public and themselves. It doesn't bear thinking about that some pen-pusher would ever have these Teams in their sights.

There is a sense of closure within Brighton and Hove. Like so many, on each of the thousands of times I drove past Wild Park during the years of injustice, I ached for Nicola, Karen and their families. I still ache but now reconcile myself with the knowledge that, eventually, the right outcome was reached.

The estate itself is pretty much as it was, both physically and demographically, but its voice and influence on the city's policing and its politics is stronger than ever.

Wild Park looks exactly the same except the rundown pavilion is now home to the amazing Clare's Cafe that serves a full menu of homemade fare to shame any high street restaurant chain.

The police box is now a car wash and the A27 John Rodway delighted in log-jamming now skirts the city, only rejoining it at the very fringe of Moulsecoomb where Brighton and Hove Albion Football Club now play.

It's hard for the families to speak of closure. Barrie Fellows feels vindicated by the verdict but these murders ripped them apart and Bishop's arrogance and self-serving meant that many, including Lee Hadaway and Nicola's brother, Jonathan, never saw justice.

Each surviving parent has taken part in TV documentaries, one hosted by Sir Trevor Macdonald which was inspired by this book. These have provided them with a voice that was for decades muted but they will never get over the unimaginable loss Bishop inflicted on them and neither should anyone expect them to.

As in *Death Comes Knocking* Peter and I wanted to show the human side of policing and how ordinary men and women do extraordinary things to bring killers to justice. Sometimes they make mistakes, but they wear those heavily and never give up.

In telling this story, however, we hope we have served the memory of Nicola and Karen. At the time of writing they would have been forty-two years old and could well have had children of their own. One man, of unspeakable evil, snatched that possibility from them to satiate his own perverted desires. We will never know what they would have become but, if their families were their blueprint, they would have been forces for good.

The tenacity and determination of the Hadaways, the Fellowses and the Heffrons is, quite frankly, humbling. They knew Bishop had killed the girls and, as they said to us during the research for this book, they made plans for their fight to be passed down the generations if necessary. Thankfully it was not, as thirty-two years of lobbying the police, prosecutors and parliament finally brought them what they were denied in 1987.

Claire, at the tender age of seven, shared that gutsy resolve. How many children of that age would have had her presence of mind, recall and courage following an attack she was not supposed to survive? Her name, and that of her family, is protected by law so they have not become synonymous with these dreadful events but we should still remember that she too lives with Bishop's evil every day, and we pray she finds some peace in the likelihood he will never be free.

Finally, the case touched generations of police. Once they could, Sussex Police published as many details as possible on the force's external website. The thousands of views and hundreds of positive comments, many from serving and former officers and staff, showed just how many careers were defined by this extraordinary case. I know several who live with the demons of what happened back in the late 1980s and since. Their pain is nothing compared to that of Nicola and Karen's families and of Claire and hers but they still hurt day in day out.

Despite how it might have seemed, no one forgot those little girls and their families and no one ever will. No one should have to fear going to their own graves denied of justice. The law, science and professional expertise are now in place to ensure that need not happen, providing the police, CPS and the courts are sufficiently resourced to make sure it does not.

Finally, in the words of Jeff Riley, we sincerely hope that 'Russell Bishop never darkens the streets of Brighton again'.

Rest in peace, Nicola and Karen.

Acknowledgements

Telling the policing story of the Babes in the Woods murders and the attempted murder of Claire has been as humbling as it has been a privilege. It goes without saying that the pain and suffering all those close to Nicola, Karen and Claire have endured over the years has been unimaginable. Their dignity, therefore, in lobbying for justice was heart-rending.

We could not have told this story without the generous and fulsome support of a huge number of people and our sincere thanks go to them all. In particular we owe a huge debt of gratitude to Nicola's father Barrie Fellows, her mother Susan Eismann and, on behalf of the wider family, her cousin Lorna Clary. They have all endured so much. Hearing the pain they and all their families have gone through helped us not only get the story right, but reminded us of our duty to tell it sensitively.

This book is about policing, so tracking down ex-colleagues was crucial but no mean feat, especially as some are of the age where social media is not their thing. We learned so much from those directly involved in investigating Nicola and Karen's murders in 1986, particularly Bernie Wells, Dave Tomlinson, 'Kit' Bentham, Paul Richardson, Pete Coll (who – alongside Ian Pollard – covered the retrial on days we could not), Derek Oakenson, Ken Probert, Nigel Smith, Paul Smith, John Moreton, Kevin Moore, John Rodway and David Gaylor. Some we spoke to preferred not to be named so we have provided them with pseudonyms. Thank you anyway, one and all.

Graham worked for nearly a year investigating Claire's attack, so tracking down those who worked alongside him was slightly easier but no less a privilege. Special thanks go to Gordon Harrison, Malcolm 'Streaky' Bacon, Steve Whitton, Debbie Wood and Pete Cook for sharing their memories which plugged many a gap in Graham's.

The toil that went on behind the scenes in reinvestigating the 1986 murders involved dozens of officers and staff. Those who helped us reflect their efforts accurately and to whom we are eternally grateful include Adam Hibbert, Nick Craggs, Stuart Leonard, Libby Clark and Bill Warner. Special thanks and a huge well-done goes to Detective Superintendent Jeff Riley who not only led the successful investigation, but was a huge support in fact-checking and guiding us on what was appropriate for the public domain.

Behind the scenes, Sussex Police provided us with support and direction on our approach to this book, in light of the reinvestigation and trial. They set us helpful parameters and, once the retrial was over, gave us access and material. Specifically, we would like to thank ACC Laurence Taylor (now a Deputy Assistant Commissioner in the Metropolitan Police) and Tim Mahony, as well as Clare Shiel and Steve Fowler who investigated Katrina Taylor's savage murder.

Of course, it was more than the police whose encyclopaedic memories were mined. Huge thanks to journalists Jon Buss, Jim Hatley, Phil Mills Frank Le Duc, Adam Lusher, Malcolm Shaw, Andy Dickensen and Emily Walker who all recalled more about these cases than any database ever could. We are particularly grateful to the *Argus* editor Arron Hendy for access to their archive and photographs, which provided a real-time catalogue of the whole thirty-two years of injustice.

The ITV documentary *Babes in the Wood*, aired in March 2019, was inspired by this book and provided us with further opportunities to learn more about the case. As well as many of those mentioned above who graciously allowed us to interview them for the documentary, or be present when Sir Trevor Macdonald did, we would like to thank Roy Green and Ros Hammond of Eurofin Forensics who gave us a unique insight into their fascinating world of forensic science and the strict discipline they apply to ensure the guilty are convicted and the innocent freed. Of course, no mention of the documentary can be complete without a special thanks to all at Atticus Pictures including, but not exclusively, John Hay, Elliot Jenkins and David Ward. Oh, and all at Claire's Café in Wild Park who kept us very well fed and watered during the many hours of filming! If you visit the Hawthorne Tree memorial, you really must pop in. You won't be disappointed.

Turning to those behind our computer screens, our unending gratitude goes to our wonderful agents Isobel Dixon and Conrad Williams of Blake Friedman Literary Agency, who always go the extra mile. Also to the incredibly patient and inspirational Ingrid Connell, Charlotte Wright and Natalie Young, of our fabulous publishers Pan Macmillan, who provided such magnificent guidance throughout the writing. Much appreciation too is owed to our copy-editor Susan Opie, whose patience and eye for detail are something to behold, and to Linda Buckley, Sharon Oman, Sarah Middle, Danielle Brown, Susan Ansell and all at Team Roy Grace, including, again, Dave Gaylor, for their endless proofreading, guidance and support.

Last, but most certainly not least, for not only providing constant physical and emotional support and encouragement, but also for reading and re-reading draft after draft, huge love and thanks go to our wives Julie and Lara, and to Graham's eagle-eyed triplets, Conall, Niamh and Deaglan. Thank you all so much, as we literally could not have done this without you.

Glossary

Agreed facts document – A statement of facts or evidence which the prosecution and defence both agree on. Once agreed, these are read out in court preventing the need to call witnesses or adduce evidence to support them.

ANPR – Automatic Number Plate Recognition. A national network of fixed and mobile cameras that photograph and identify vehicles, enabling law enforcement to prevent and detect crime.

Bad character evidence – Evidence of, or a disposition towards misconduct, other than evidence of the offence being prosecuted. Also evidence of misconduct in connection with the investigation or prosecution of that offence.

CCTV – Closed Circuit Television. Can be either publicly owned and monitored (e.g. by the police), or privately installed in people's houses or businesses.

Chief Crown Prosecutor – The senior lawyer who is the head of a Crown Prosecution Service region. Reports directly to the Director of Public Prosecutions.

CID – Criminal Investigation Department. The arm of the police that investigates the most serious crimes. Commonly staffed by detectives.

Commanders: Silver and Gold – The senior officers in tactical (silver) and strategic (gold) command of firearms, public order and other major incidents.

CPS – Crown Prosecution Service. The independent body that prosecutes cases investigated by the police and other investigative bodies.

CSI – Crime Scene Investigator. See SOCO.

Divisional Commander – The senior police officer, normally a Chief Superintendent, in charge of policing a large geographical area such as a county or unitary authority. Sometimes also referred to as Basic Command Unit (BCU), Borough or District Commander.

DNA – Deoxyribonucleic Acid. The molecule that contains the genetic code of organisms. Used in crime investigations to identify or eliminate those suspected of offences where cellular material has been shed at a crime scene or on an item connected with the crime.

Double jeopardy – A procedural defence that prevents an accused person from being tried again on the same (or similar) charges following a valid acquittal or conviction.

DPP – Director of Public Prosecutions. The head of the Crown Prosecution Service who is the official charged with the prosecution of criminal offences in England and Wales.

HOLMES – Home Office Large Major Enquiry System. A national police computer system which automates the process of collecting and collating information and evidence gathered during a major crime investigation, enabling the investigation to be conducted in an organized and thorough manner.

Junior Counsel – A barrister who assists Lead Counsel in the prosecuting and defending of criminal or civil cases.

Lead Counsel – The senior barrister who leads a prosecution or defence team in a criminal or civil trial. Often a Queen's Counsel.

Police Search Advisor – A specialist officer responsible for the planning, organization, management and control of crime, missing person and counter terrorism searches. Reports to the SIO.

QC – Queen's Counsel. A senior barrister, who prosecutes and/or defends in the most serious criminal and civil cases. Changes to King's Counsel (KC) when the monarch is male.

Queen's Bench Division – One of the three Divisions of the High Court. It includes the Administrative Court, which provides it the power to oversee the quality and legality of the decision-making of the lower courts.

SIO – Senior Investigating Officer. The senior police officer in ultimate charge of a murder or other major crime investigation.

SOCO – Scenes of Crime Officer. A specialist police support staff officer who identifies, gathers and prepares forensic evidence for scientific investigation. Also can be a Specialist Forensic Photographer.

CHART OF POLICE RANKS*

Police ranks are consistent across all disciplines and the addition of prefixes such as 'detective' (e.g. detective constable) does not affect seniority relative to others of the same rank (e.g. police constable).

| Police Constable | Police Sergeant | Inspector | Chief Inspector |

| Superintendent | Chief Superintendent | Assistant Chief Constable | Deputy Chief Constable | Chief Constable |

* Note: these can vary between forces.

Picture Credits

The Detective Superintendent Roy Grace series

by
PETER JAMES

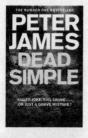
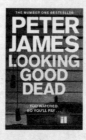

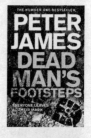

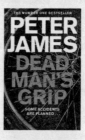
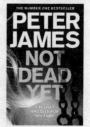

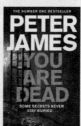
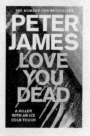

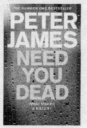
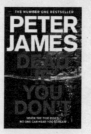
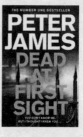